Success in Principles of Accounting: Answer Book

Success Studybooks

Biology

Book-keeping for the Small Business

British History 1760–1914

Business Calculations

Chemistry

Commerce

Economics

Geography: Human and Regional

Geography: Physical and Mapwork

Investment

Law

Mathematics

Nutrition

Principles of Accounting

Principles of Accounting: Answer Book

Twentieth Century World Affairs

Success in
PRINCIPLES
OF ACCOUNTING:
ANSWER BOOK

Geoffrey Whitehead, B.Sc. (Econ.)

John Murray

Printed in Great Britain by
Cox & Wyman Ltd
London, Fakenham and Reading

Cased 0 7195 2922 0
Paperback 0 7195 2921 2

Foreword

This is the companion volume to *Success in Principles of Accounting*, a course designed to cover syllabus material for most examinations in elementary accounting. It is especially suitable for students working for the following: O level Principles of Accounting, Scotbec Certificate of Office Studies, the Royal Society of Arts (stages 1 and 2) and CSE. Students preparing for BEC National Certificate and Diploma Courses in Numeracy and Accounting will achieve the 'learning objectives' in Accounting, while Scottish students will find the book ideal for first year Scotbec ONC/D Accounting. It is also recommended as an introductory text for students taking Accounting as part of computer-orientated courses, where a background of double entry can be invaluable, and as part of a 'General Studies' course for major disciplines such as Economics, Science, Engineering, Marketing or Personnel Management.

The answers displayed here are keyed to the questions in the course book, and page numbers in that book are also given to facilitate quick cross-reference. *Success in Principles of Accounting* is abbreviated to *SPA*, so after each answer number you will find: (*SPA page 123*).

It is particularly important that anyone preparing for an examination should be able to use the correct style of presentation in accounting work. By using the *Answer Book* in conjunction with *Success in Principles of Accounting*, students will be helped in their understanding of each topic concerned, and will gain maximum benefit from the course.

G.W.

Contents

Unit 1   Accounting to the Trial Balance
Exercises Set 1:   Accounting to the Trial Balance   1
  (1) Accounts of M. Thomas (*SPA page 15*)   1
  (2) Accounts of R. Brown (*SPA page 15*)   2
  (3) Accounts of M. Whiteside (*SPA page 15*)   2
  (4) Accounts of M. Logan (*SPA page 16*)   3
  (5) Accounts of D. Lobley (*SPA page 16*)   4
  (6) Accounts of R. Sparrow (*SPA page 16*)   5
  (7) (*SPA page 17*)   6
  (8) (*SPA page 17*)   6

Unit 2   A More Detailed Look at the Ledger
Exercises Set 2:   Debtors' Personal Accounts   7
  (1) C. Hadland's Account (*SPA page 23*)   7
  (2) G. Wakeman's Account (*SPA page 23*)   7
  (3) M. Watts' Account (*SPA page 24*)   7
  (4) R. T. Crafty's Account (*SPA page 24*)   8
  (5) M. Fisher's Account (*SPA page 24*)   8
Exercises Set 3:   Creditors' Personal Accounts   9
  (1) R. Bolton's Account (*SPA page 26*)   9
  (2) T. Robertson's Account (*SPA page 26*)   9
  (3) Universal Warehouses Ltd. (*SPA page 26*)   9
  (4) R. Jones's Account (*SPA page 27*)   10
  (5) P. B. Rowe's Account (*SPA page 27*)   11

Unit 3   More Advanced Accounting to the Trial Balance
Exercises Set 4:   More Practice in Double-entry Book-keeping to the
                   Trial-Balance Level   12
  (1) Accounts of E. Saxby (*SPA page 37*)   12
  (2) Accounts of G. Parker (*SPA page 37*)   13
  (3) Accounts of T. Lawrence (*SPA page 38*)   14
  (4) Books of M. Rowcliffe (*SPA page 38*)   16
  (5) Books of R. Turf (*SPA page 39*)   17
  (6) Books of R. Tilehurst (*SPA page 39*)   19

Unit 4   Accounting to Final-Accounts Level
      Part One: The Trial Balance
Exercises Set 5:   Drawing up Trial Balances   21
  (1)   Books of R. Fowler (*SPA page 43*)   21
  (2)   Books of A. Dealer (*SPA page 43*)   22
  (3)   Books of J. Brown (*SPA page 43*)   22
  (4)   Books of F. Fisher (*SPA page 43*)   23
  (5)   Books of I. Cooper (*SPA page 44*)   24
  (6)   Books of David Cann (*SPA page 44*)   25

Unit 5   Accounting to Final-Accounts Level
      Part Two: The Gross Profit on Trading
Exercises Set 6:   The Trading Account   26
  (1)   Books of R. Hudson (*SPA page 54*)   26
  (2)   Books of I. Brunel (*SPA page 54*)   26
  (3)   Books of T. Turner (*SPA page 55*)   27
  (4)   Books of J. Metcalfe (*SPA page 55*)   27
  (5)   Books of R. Miller (*SPA page 55*)   28
  (6)   Books of G. Poole (*SPA page 55*)   28

Unit 6   Accounting to Final-Accounts Level
      Part Three: The Net Profit of the Enterprise
Exercises Set 7:   Profit and Loss Accounts   29
  (1)   Accounts of M. Lawrence (*SPA page 59*)   29
  (2)   Accounts of W. Sandon (*SPA page 59*)   29
  (3)   Accounts of M. Chesterfield (*SPA page 59*)   29
  (4)   Accounts of R. Burton (*SPA page 60*)   30
  (5)   Books of L. Lucerne (*SPA page 60*)   30
  (6)   Books of B. Grant (*SPA page 60*)   31

Unit 7   Accounting to Final-Accounts Level
      Part Four: The Balance Sheet of the Business
Exercises Set 8:   The Balance Sheet of a Business   32
  (1)   Books of R. Long (*SPA page 70*)   32
  (2)   Books of J. Triton (*SPA page 71*)   32
  (3)   Books of T. North (*SPA page 71*)   33
  (4)   Books of M. Twain (*SPA page 72*)   33

Unit 8   Accounting to Final-Accounts Level
      Part Five: Exercises to Final-Accounts Level
Exercises Set 9:   Accounting to Final-Accounts Level—Part One   34
  (1)   Books of R. Todd (*SPA page 79*)   34
  (2)   Books of E. Carr (*SPA page 79*)   36
  (3)   Books of M. Tapley (*SPA page 79*)   38
  (4)   Books of R. Quilp (*SPA page 80*)   41

(5) Books of R. Bingham (*SPA page 81*)   44
(6) Books of M. Day (*SPA page 81*)   47
Exercises Set 10: Accounting to Final-Accounts Level—Part Two   50
(1) Books of M. Davies (*SPA page 83*)   50
(2) Books of P. Robinson (*SPA page 84*)   51
(3) Books of T. Ford (*SPA page 85*)   52
(4) Books of R. Maycock (*SPA page 86*)   53
(5) Books of A. Brewis (*SPA page 87*)   54
(6) Books of E. London (*SPA page 88*)   55

Unit 9   Books of Original Entry
          Part One: The Journal

Exercises Set 11:   Opening Journal Entries   56
(1)   Books of R. Marshall (*SPA page 94*)   56
(2)   Books of M. Leghorn (*SPA page 94*)   56
(3)   Books of M. Tyler (*SPA page 94*)   56
(4)   Books of R. Lucas (*SPA page 94*)   57
(5)   Books of G. Porter (*SPA page 94*)   57
(6)   Books of M. Larkin (*SPA page 94*)   57
(7)   Books of M. Lawson (*SPA page 94*)   58
(8)   Books of S. Thompson (*SPA page 94*)   59
(9)   Books of Peter Martin (*SPA page 94*)   59
(10) Books of Steptoe and Son (*SPA page 95*)   60

Unit 10   Books of Original Entry
           Part Two: The Purchases and Sales Day Books

Exercises Set 12:   The Purchases Day Book   61
(1) Books of M. Sibthorpe (*SPA page 101*)   61
(2) Books of R. Beech (*SPA page 102*)   62
(3) Books of M. Lawson (*SPA page 102*)   62
(4) Books of R. J. Upfold (*SPA page 102*)   63
(5) Books of R. Davison (*SPA page 103*)   64
Exercises Set 13:   The Sales Day Book   65
(1) Books of R. Hall (*SPA page 105*)   65
(2) Books of M. Thomas (*SPA page 106*)   65
(3) Books of R. Larch (*SPA page 106*)   66
(4) Books of M. Paterson (*SPA page 106*)   67
(5) Books of R. Lawes (*SPA page 107*)   67

Unit 11   Books of Original Entry
           Part Three: The Purchases and Sales Returns Books

Exercises Set 14:   The Purchases Returns Book   68
(1) Books of R. Lutterworth (*SPA page 110*)   68
(2) Books of E. S. Oliver (*SPA page 111*)   68
(3) Books of C. Hosking (*SPA page 111*)   69
(4) Books of R. Robertson (*SPA page 111*)   69

(5) Books of T. New and Son (*SPA page 111*)   70

Exercises Set 15:   The Sales Returns Book   70
(1) Books of T. Cratchett (*SPA page 113*)   70
(2) Books of Paul Luscombe (*SPA page 114*)   71
(3) Books of A. Robens (*SPA page 114*)   71
(4) Books of A. W. Manser (*SPA page 114*)   72
(5) Books of M. Lancaster (*SPA page 114*)   72

Unit 12   Books of Original Entry
Part Four: More Journal Proper Entries—Assets and Depreciation

Exercises Set 16:   The Purchase of Assets   74
(1) Books of R. Lever (*SPA page 117*)   74
(2) Books of M. Robertson (*SPA page 117*)   74
(3) Books of A. Printz (*SPA page 117*)   74
(4) Books of S. Debbotista (*SPA page 117*)   75
(5) Books of J. Scaggs (*SPA page 117*)   75
(6) Books of M. Lucien (*SPA page 118*)   75
Exercises Set 17:   Simple Depreciation Exercises   75
(1) Books of A. Reeve (*SPA page 119*)   75
(2) Books of P. Senior (*SPA page 119*)   76
(3) Books of C. Blythe (*SPA page 119*)   76
(4) Books of M. Larkins (*SPA page 119*)   76
(5) Books of Howden Ironware Co. (*SPA page 120*)   77
(6) Books of M. Burns (*SPA page 120*)   77
Exercises Set 18: The Disposal of Assets   77
(1) Books of John Kelleher (*SPA page 122*)   77
(2) Books of A. Hancock (*SPA page 122*)   77
(3) Books of D. Heywood (*SPA page 122*)   77
(4) Books of J. Scaggs (*SPA page 122*)   78
(5) Books of Allen Motors Ltd. (*SPA page 122*)   78
(6) Books of John Briggs (*SPA page 122*)   78
(7) Books of Paul Watts (*SPA page 123*)   78
(8) Books of F. Azouqua (*SPA page 123*)   79

Unit 13   Books of Original Entry
Part Five: More Journal Proper Entries—Bad Debts

Exercises Set 19:   Bad Debts   80
(1) (*SPA page 128*)   80
(2) (*SPA page 128*)   80
(3) (*SPA page 128*)   80
(4) (*SPA page 128*)   81
(5) (*SPA page 128*)   81
(6) (*SPA page 128*)   81
(7) (*SPA page 128*)   82
(8) (*SPA page 128*)   82

(9) (*SPA page 129*)   83
(10) (*SPA page 129*)   83

Unit 14   Books of Original Entry
        Part Six: The Three-Column Cash Book
Exercises Set 20:   The Three-column Cash Book   85
 (1) Books of D. Swann (*SPA page 140*)   85
 (2) Books of D. Hunter (*SPA page 140*)   85
 (3) Books of B. Gale (*SPA page 140*)   86
 (4) Books of E. Stapleton (*SPA page 141*)   87
 (5) Books of W. Allen (*SPA page 141*)   88
 (6) Books of Joseph Cotton (*SPA page 142*)   90

Unit 15   Books of Original Entry
        Part Seven: The Petty-Cash Book
Exercises Set 21:   The Petty-cash Book   91
 (1) (*SPA page 149*)   91
 (2) (*SPA page 149*)   91
 (3) Books of D. Benson (*SPA page 149*)   92
 (4) Books of R. Norris (*SPA page 150*)   93
 (5) Books of M. Jobling (*SPA page 150*)   94
 (6) Books of M. Clarke (*SPA page 150*)   96
 (7) (*SPA page 151*)   97
 (8) (*SPA page 151*)   98
 (9) Books of R. Duncan (*SPA page 151*)   99
(10) Books of R. Lyons (*SPA page 152*)   100

Unit 16   More Journal Proper Entries—Unusual Bank Transactions
Exercises Set 22:   Bank Loans, Interest and Charges   102
 (1) Books of R. Piggott (*SPA page 157*)   102
 (2) Books of M. Smith (*SPA page 157*)   102
 (3) Books of Loamshire Quarry Co. (*SPA page 157*)   103
 (4) Books of M. Dawson (*SPA page 157*)   103
 (5) Books of B. Barnard (*SPA page 158*)   103
 (6) Books of M. Kelley (*SPA page 158*)   104
 (7) Books of R. Hope (*SPA page 158*)   104
 (8) Books of M. Hall (*SPA page 158*)   104
 (9) Books of R. Homberger (*SPA page 158*)   104
(10) Books of B. Charles (*SPA page 158*)   105

Unit 17   A Full Set of Accounts
Exercises Set 23:   Accounting with a Full Set of Books to Final-Accounts
                Level   106
 (1) Books of Paul Brickhill (*SPA page 169*)   106
 (2) Books of Martin Lawrence (*SPA page 169*)   112
 (3) Books of Martin Candler (*SPA page 170*)   116
 (4) Books of John Walker (*SPA page 171*)   121

(5)   Books of Paul Dombey (*SPA page 172*)   125
(6)   Books of Gerard Eliasson (*SPA page 172*)   131

Unit 18   Limitations of the Trial Balance
Exercises Set 24:   Limitations of the Trial Balance   136
(1)   (*SPA page 182*)   136
(2)   (*SPA page 183*)   136
(3)   (*SPA page 183*)   136
(4)   (*SPA page 183*)   137
(5)   Books of R. Taylor (*SPA page 183*)   138
(6)   Books of A. Trader (*SPA page 183*)   138
(7)   Books of M. Bines (*SPA page 183*)   139
(8)   (*SPA page 183*)   140
(9)   Books of R. Whistler (*SPA page 184*)   140
(10) Books of R. Hull (*SPA page 184*)   141
(11) Books of R. T. Crafty (*SPA page 184*)   141
(12) Books of R. Lyons (*SPA page 184*)   142

Unit 19   Simultaneous Records
Exercises Set 25:   Simultaneous Records   143
(1)   (*SPA page 193*)   143
(2)   (*SPA page 193*)   143
(3)   (*SPA page 193*)   143

Unit 20   Bank Reconciliation Statements
Exercises Set 26:   Bank Reconciliation Statements   145
(1)   Books of R. Lawrence (*SPA page 199*)   145
(2)   Books of B. Grant (*SPA page 199*)   145
(3)   Books of C. Roper (*SPA page 199*)   146
(4)   Books of L. Roberts (*SPA page 200*)   146
(5)   Books of A. Reader (*SPA page 200*)   146
(6)   Books of D. Stevenson (*SPA page 201*)   147
(7)   Books of A. Trader (*SPA page 201*)   147
(8)   Books of R. Green (*SPA page 202*)   148
(9)   Books of E. Hemingway (*SPA page 202*)   148
(10) Books of M. Lowe (*SPA page 203*)   149

Unit 21   Capital and Revenue Expenditure and Receipts
Exercises Set 27:   Capital and Revenue Expenditure   150
(1)   (*SPA page 211*)   150
(2)   (*SPA page 211*)   150
(3)   (*SPA page 212*)   150
(4)   (*SPA page 212*)   151
(5)   (*SPA page 212*)   151
(6)   (*SPA page 212*)   151
(7)   (*SPA page 213*)   151

 (8) Books of Linden Manufacturing Organization (*SPA page 213*)   152
 (9) Books of A. Decorator (*SPA page 213*)   152
(10) Books of A. Motor Manufacturer (*SPA page 213*)   152
(11) Books of Plastics Ltd. (*SPA page 214*)   152
(12) (*SPA page 214*)   152

Unit 22   More about Depreciation
Exercises Set 28:   More about Depreciation   153
 (1) Books of Mills Ltd. (*SPA page 222*)   153
 (2) Books of Thompson Ltd. (*SPA page 223*)   153
 (3) Books of T. Brown (*SPA page 223*)   154
 (4) Books of Marshall Bros. (*SPA page 223*)   154
 (5) Books of Peter Walker (*SPA page 223*)   155
 (6) Books of John Mainway (*SPA page 223*)   155
 (7) Books of Tom Smith (*SPA page 223*)   156
 (8) Books of A. Trader (*SPA page 224*)   157
 (9) Books of Marketing Ltd. (*SPA page 224*)   157
(10) Books of A. Manufacturer (*SPA page 224*)   158

Unit 23   Columnar Books
Exercises Set 29:   Columnar Books   159
 (1) (*SPA page 228*)   159
 (2) (*SPA page 228*)   159
 (3) (*SPA page 230*)   160
 (4) Books of G. Jenkins (*SPA page 230*)   160
 (5) Books of Pop Musical Co. (*SPA page 230*)   161

Unit 24   The Bank Cash Book
Exercises Set 30:   The Bank Cash Book   163
 (1) Books of A. Trader (*SPA page 233*)   163
 (2) Books of George Vyner (*SPA page 233*)   163
 (3) Books of D. Lobley (*SPA page 234*)   164
 (4) Books of A. Heathcliff (*SPA page 234*)   164
 (5) Books of M. Tyler (*SPA page 235*)   165

Unit 25   Stock Valuation
Exercises Set 31:   The Valuation of Closing Stock   166
 (1) (*SPA page 239*)   166
 (2) Books of Badbuyers Ltd. (*SPA page 239*)   166
 (3) Books of Peter Lawson (*SPA page 239*)   166
 (4) Books of John Richards (*SPA page 239*)   167
 (5) (*SPA page 240*)   167
 (6) (*SPA page 240*)   168
Exercises Set 32: Stock-taking Problems   169
 (1) Books of R. and T. Traders (*SPA page 242*)   169

(2) Books of A. Trader (*SPA page 242*)   170
(3) Books of R. Marshall (*SPA page 243*)   170
(4) Books of J. Cook and Son (*SPA page 243*)   171
(5) Books of R. Green (*SPA page 243*)   171
(6) Books of R. Butler (*SPA page 243*)   172
(7) Books of A. Draper (*SPA page 244*)   172
(8) Books of R. Mortimer (*SPA page 244*)   173
(9) Books of P. Larkins (*SPA page 244*)   173

Unit 26 Adjustments in Final Accounts
Exercises Set 33: Payments in Advance and Accrued Expenses   174
(1) Books of J. Cakebread (*SPA page 251*)   174
(2) Books of Goodsell (*SPA page 251*)   174
(3) Books of P. Mugleston (*SPA page 251*)   175
(4) Books of D. Bird (*SPA page 252*)   175
(5) Books of A. Retailer (*SPA page 252*)   175
(6) Books of Unworthy Wholesaling Co. Ltd. (*SPA page 252*)   175
(7) Books of H. Hollow (*SPA page 252*)   176
(8) Books of R. Green (*SPA page 253*)   177
(9) Books of P. Green (*SPA page 253*)   177
(10) Books of F. Grosvenor (*SPA page 254*)   177
Exercises Set 34: Bad Debts and Provision for Bad Debts   178
(1) (*SPA page 258*)   178
(2) (*SPA page 258*)   179
(3) (*SPA page 259*)   179
(4) Books of N. Thorn (*SPA page 259*)   180
(5) Books of J. Wilson (*SPA page 259*)   180
(6) Books of Roberts and Brown Ltd. (*SPA page 259*)   180
(7) Books of C. Bolton (*SPA page 260*)   181
(8) Books of M. Rooselar (*SPA page 260*)   181
(9) Books of Gerard Eliasson (*SPA page 261*)   182
Exercises Set 35: Difficult Final-Accounts Exercises   183
(1) Books of J. March (*SPA page 266*)   183
(2) Books of R. Smart (*SPA page 266*)   184
(3) Books of Saul, a trader (*SPA page 267*)   185
(4) Books of S. Smith (*SPA page 268*)   186
(5) Books of Wormley, a trader (*SPA page 269*)   187
(6) Books of M. Smith (*SPA page 270*)   189
(7) Books of C. Violet (*SPA page 271*)   190

Unit 27 Partnership Accounts
Exercises Set 36: Partnership Appropriation Accounts   192
(1) Books of Sybrandt and Cornelis (*SPA page 278*)   192
(2) Books of Wheel and Barrow (*SPA page 278*)   192
(3) Books of Able, Baker and Charles (*SPA page 279*)   193

(4) Books of Hawtrey and Grigg (*SPA page 279*) 193
(5) Books of Melville and Ahab (*SPA page 279*) 193
Exercises Set 37: Current Accounts of Partners 194
(1) Books of Salt and Pepper (*SPA page 282*) 194
(2) Books of Jackson (*SPA page 282*) 194
(3) Books of Wilson and Brown (*SPA page 282*) 195
(4) (*SPA page 283*) 195
(5) Books of Smith and Edwards (*SPA page 283*) 196
Exercises Set 38: Final Accounts of Partnerships 197
(1) Books of Lester and Payne (*SPA page 284*) 197
(2) (*SPA page 285*) 198
(3) Books of Baker and Grocer (*SPA page 285*) 198
(4) Books of G. Wilson and W. Gibbs (*SPA page 286*) 199
(5) Books of Ross and Glass (*SPA page 287*) 200
(6) Books of Brown and Marshall (*SPA page 288*) 201
(7) Books of Bennett and Clark (*SPA page 289*) 202
(8) (*SPA page 290*) 203
(9) Books of Knowle and Sentry (*SPA page 290*) 204
(10) Books of Richard and Stanley Bridges (*SPA page 291*) 206
(11) Books of Rathlin and Lambay (*SPA page 292*) 206
(12) Books of Bristol and Avon (*SPA page 293*) 208
(13) Books of Bush and Mill (*SPA page 294*) 210
(14) Books of Ross and Cromarty (*SPA page 295*) 212
(15) Books of Copeland and Bangor (*SPA page* 296) 214

Unit 28 Non-profit-making Organizations
Exercises Set 39: Simple Receipts and Payments Accounts 216
(1) Newtown Football Club (*SPA page 301*) 216
(2) Jolly Wanderers Rambling Club (*SPA page 301*) 216
(3) Roman Camp Archaeological Society (*SPA page 302*) 217
(4) Robert Burns Society (*SPA page 302*) 217
(5) Kingswood Community Association (*SPA page 302*) 217
Exercises Set 40: Final Accounts of Non-profit-making Organizations 218
(1) Books of the Snowdonia Young Climbers' Club (*SPA page 309*) 218
(2) Books of the Forsyth Tennis Club (*SPA page 309*) 218
(3) Books of the Brownridge Town Band (*SPA page 310*) 219
(4) Books of the Good Companions Sports Club (*SPA page 311*) 219
(5) Books of the Mid-Sussex Gun-dog Society (*SPA page 311*) 220
(6) Tennis Club Accounts (*SPA page 312*) 220
(7) Accounts of a Social Club (*SPA page 312*) 221
(8) Accounts of the Daleshire Social Club (*SPA page 313*) 221
(9) Accounts of the New Social Club (*SPA page 313*) 222
(10) Books of the Greensward Cricket and Social Club (*SPA page 314*) 222
(11) Books of the Herring Bone Club (*SPA page 315*) 223
(12) Books of the XYZ Recreation Club (*SPA page 315*) 225

Unit 29   Manufacturing Accounts
Exercises Set 41:   Manufacturing Accounts   227
  (1)   Books of R. Rayner (*SPA page 323*)   227
  (2)   Books of M. Lockhart Ltd. (*SPA page 324*)   228
  (3)   Books of Robespierre Ltd. (*SPA page 324*)   229
  (4)   Books of Sudbury Ltd. (*SPA page 325*)   230
  (5)   Books of Rymer and Ross Ltd. (*SPA page 326*)   231
  (6)   Books of Tradescantia Ltd. (*SPA page 326*)   232
  (7)   Books of Suffolk Ltd. (*SPA page 327*)   233

Unit 30   Incomplete Records
Exercises Set 42:   Simple Incomplete Records   235
  (1)   Books of John Brown (*SPA page 331*)   235
  (2)   Books of H. Cook (*SPA page 331*)   235
  (3)   Books of John Smith (*SPA page 331*)   236
  (4)   Books of M. Law (*SPA page 332*)   237
  (5)   Books of C. Cropper (*SPA page 332*)   238
  (6)   Books of T. Newman (*SPA page 332*)   239
  (7)   Books of I. Gamble (*SPA page 332*)   239
Exercises Set 43:   Building up a Set of Final Accounts from Incomplete
                         Records   240
  (1)   Books of C. Monger (*SPA page 337*)   240
  (2)   Books of F. K. (*SPA page 337*)   241
  (3)   Books of F. L. Winter (*SPA page 338*)   242
  (4)   Books of G. Smith (*SPA page 339*)   244
  (5)   Books of W. Davis (*SPA page 339*)   245
  (6)   Books of R. T. (*SPA page 340*)   246

Unit 31   The Accounts of Companies
Exercises Set 44:   Company Final Accounts   248
  (1)   Books of Shubunkin Ltd. (*SPA page 356*)   248
  (2)   Books of Rostrevor Ltd. (*SPA page 357*)   249
  (3)   Books of Andrew Ltd. (*SPA page 358*)   250
  (4)   Books of Toleymore Ltd. (*SPA page 359*)   251
  (5)   Books of Box Ltd. (*SPA page 360*)   252
  (6)   Books of Green and Brown Ltd. (*SPA page 361*)   254
  (7)   Books of Ham Ltd. (*SPA page 361*)   255
  (8)   Books of Excel Traders Ltd. (*SPA page 362*)   256
  (9)   Books of Solarheaters Ltd. (*SPA page 363*)   257
 (10)   Books of Turnip Tops Ltd. (*SPA page 364*)   258
 (11)   Books of Dark Shadows Ltd. (*SPA page 365*)   260
 (12)   Books of Green Swan Ltd. (*SPA page 366*)   262

Unit 32   Interpreting Final Accounts: the Control of a Business
Exercises Set 45:   Gross-Profit Percentage   264
  (1)   Books of Mr. A. (*SPA page 373*)   264

(2) Books of R Dawson (*SPA page 373*)   264
(3) Books of R. Marshall (*SPA page 373*)   265
(4) Books of K. Newing (*SPA page 374*)   265
(5) Books of E. Randall (*SPA page 374*)   266
Exercises Set 46:   The Rate of Stock Turnover   267
(1) Books of L. Perry (*SPA page 375*)   267
(2) Books of A. Reddington (*SPA page 375*)   267
(3) Books of A. Trader (*SPA page 375*)   267
(4) Books of M. Lewis (*SPA page 376*)   268
(5) Books of D. Hancock (*SPA page 376*)   268
(6) Books of Downtown Do-It-Yourself Stores (*SPA page 377*)   268
(7) Books of J. F. Roe (*SPA page 377*)   269
(8) Books of M. Regent (*SPA page 378*)   269
Exercises Set 47:   Net-Profit Percentage   270
(1) Books of F. Azouqua (*SPA page 380*)   270
(2) Books of K. Penn (*SPA page 380*)   271
(3) Books of R. Spurling (a manufacturer) (*SPA page 380*)   271
(4) Books of R. James (*SPA page 381*)   271
(5) Books of M. Trueman (*SPA page 381*)   272
(6) Books of F. Fraser (*SPA page 381*)   272
(7) Books of M. Tyler (*SPA page 382*)   273
(8) Books of J. R. Tee (*SPA page 382*)   274
(9) Books of T. Lumley (*SPA page 383*)   275
Exercises Set 48:   The Appraisal of Balance Sheets   276
(1) Books of A. Brewis (*SPA page 390*)   276
(2) Books of R. Hemingway (*SPA page 391*)   277
(3) Books of Fides Ltd. (*SPA page 391*)   277
(4) Books of Coolbawn Ltd. (*SPA page 391*)   278
(5) Books of Holder Ltd. (*SPA page 392*)   278
(6) (*SPA page 392*)   279
(7) Books of R. T. (*SPA page 393*)   279
(8) Books of J. Kay (*SPA page 393*)   279
(9) Books of M. Peters (*SPA page 395*)   280
(10) Books of J. Wooding (*SPA page 396*)   281

Unit 33   Departmental Accounts

Exercises Set 49:   Departmental Accounts   283
(1) Books of R. Rogers (*SPA page 399*)   283
(2) Books of V. Bartlett (*SPA page 400*)   284
(3) Books of Carlingford Ltd. (*SPA page 400*)   285
(4) Books of Slumbersweet Ltd. (*SPA page 401*)   286
(5) Books of R. Winter (*SPA page 401*)   287

Unit 34   Control Accounts

Exercises Set 50:   Control Accounts   288
(1) R. Martin's Accounts (*SPA page 408*)   288

(2)   Sheering Ltd.'s Accounts (*SPA page 409*)   288
(3)   L. Renton's Accounts (*SPA page 409*)   288
(4)   M. Lucas's Accounts (*SPA page 409*)   289
(5)   Books of S. Hardy (*SPA page 410*)   289
(6)   L. Martin's Accounts (*SPA page 411*)   290
(7)   Bartlow's Books (*SPA page 411*)   291
(8)   Clover Ltd. Total Accounts (*SPA page 411*)   291
(9)   Accounts of Colvin and Hodge (*SPA page 412*)   292

Unit 35   Amalgamations
Exercises Set 51:   Amalgamations   293
(1)   Amalgamation of A. Young and B. Old (*SPA page 416*)   293
(2)   Amalgamation of Maker and Seller (*SPA page 416*)   293
(3)   Amalgamation of W. Sandon and M. Sandon (*SPA page 417*)   294
(4)   Amalgamation of A and B (*SPA page 417*)   294
(5)   Amalgamation of X and Y (*SPA page 418*)   295

Unit 36   Purchase of a Business
Exercises Set 52:   Purchase of a Business   296
(1)   A. Robertson's Accounts (*SPA page 425*)   296
(2)   R. Killinchy's Purchase of P. Fitzpatrick's Business (*SPA page 425*) 297
(3)   M. Phillips' Purchase of R. Morgan's Business (*SPA page 426*)   298
(4)   R. Lyons' Purchase of J. Kelleher's Business (*SPA page 426*)   299
(5)   White, Rock and Sandy's Purchase of Ardmillan's Business
      (*SPA page 427*)   300

Unit 37   Covering the Syllabus
Exercises Set 53:   Specimen Examination Papers   301
(A1) Books of M. Lucas (*SPA page 431*)   301
(A2) Books of Pop Musical Co. (*SPA page 431*)   301
(A3) Books of R. Smart (*SPA page 432*)   302
(B4) (*SPA page 432*)   302
(B5) Books of M. Rooselar (*SPA page 433*)   303

(1)   Books of R. Peters (*SPA page 434*)   304
(2)   Books of F. Jones (*SPA page 434*)   304
(3)   Books of J. Brown (*SPA page 435*)   305
(4)   Books of A. Farmer (*SPA page 435*)   305
(5)   Books of A. Firm (*SPA page 436*)   305

(A1) (*SPA page 436*)   305
(A2) Books of D. Cann (*SPA page 436*)   306
(A3) Books of M. Luckhurst (*SPA page 437*)   307
(B4) Books of A. Long (*SPA page 437*)   307
(B5) Books of B. Burley (*SPA page 438*)   307

(1) Books of Keats and Shelley (*SPA page 438*)   309
(2) Books of Happy Roadsters' Club (*SPA page 439*)   309
(3) Books of R. Lewis (*SPA page 439*)   310
(4) Books of R. Joy (*SPA page 440*)   310
(5) Books of R. Taylor (*SPA page 440*)   310

(1) Books of C. R. Wood (*SPA page 442*)   311
(2) Books of A. Trader (*SPA page 442*)   311
(3) Books of A. Fitners (*SPA page 443*)   312
(4) Books of L. Parkinson (*SPA page 444*)   314
(5A) Books of A. Wheeler Ltd. (*SPA page 444*)   314
(5B) (i) Books of Stevens and Platt (*SPA page 445*)   315
     (ii) Books of Wide and Broad (*SPA page 445*)   316
(6A) Books of a Trader (*SPA page 446*)   317
(6B) (i) Books of A. Vickers (*SPA page 447*)   318
     (ii) (*SPA page 447*)   318

(1) Books of R. Hargreaves (*SPA page 447*)   319
(2) Books of E. Taylor (*SPA page 448*)   320
(3) Books of L. Stoke (*SPA page 448*)   321
(4) (*SPA page 449*)   322
(5A) Books of Anglo Engineering Co. (*SPA page 449*)   322
(5B) Books of the South West Town Football Club (*SPA page 450*)   323
(6A) Books of R. Lucas (*SPA page 451*)   324
(6B) (*SPA page 451*)   324

Unit 38 Appendix on Value Added Tax
Exercises Set 54: Value Added Tax   325
(1) (*SPA page 459*)   325
(2) (*SPA page 459*)   325
(3) Books of R. Jones (*SPA page 459*)   325
(4) Books of N. Bennett (*SPA page 460*)   326

A Note on Answers to Questions   326

Unit One

Accounting to the Trial Balance

Exercises Set 1: Accounting to the Trial Balance

(1) Accounts of M. Thomas (*SPA page 15*)

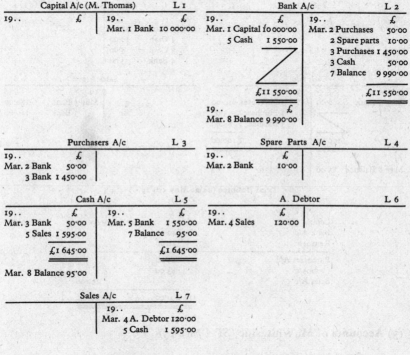

Capital A/c (M. Thomas)	L 1		
19..	£	19..	£
		Mar. 1 Bank	10 000·00

Bank A/c		L 2	
19..	£	19..	£
Mar. 1 Capital	10 000·00	Mar. 2 Purchases	50·00
5 Cash	1 550·00	2 Spare parts	10·00
		3 Purchases	1 450·00
		3 Cash	50·00
		7 Balance	9 990·00
	£11 550·00		£11 550·00
19..	£		
Mar. 8 Balance	9 990·00		

Purchasers A/c		L 3	
19..	£		
Mar. 2 Bank	50·00		
3 Bank	1 450·00		

Spare Parts A/c		L 4	
19..	£		
Mar. 2 Bank	10·00		

Cash A/c		L 5	
19..	£	19..	£
Mar. 3 Bank	50·00	Mar. 5 Bank	1 550·00
5 Sales	1 595·00	7 Balance	95·00
	£1 645·00		£1 645·00
Mar. 8 Balance	95·00		

A. Debtor		L 6	
19..	£		
Mar. 4 Sales	120·00		

Sales A/c		L 7	
		19..	£
		Mar. 4 A. Debtor	120·00
		5 Cash	1 595·00

Trial Balance (as at March 31st 19..)

	Dr.	Cr.
	£	£
Capital A/c		10 000·00
Bank A/c	9 990·00	
Purchases A/c	1 500·00	
Spare Parts A/c	10·00	
Cash A/c	95·00	
A. Debtor A/c	120·00	
Sales A/c		1 715·00
	£11 715·00	11 715·00

(*See* **A Note on Answers,** *page 326.*)

(2) Accounts of R. Brown (*SPA page 15*)

Capital A/c (R. Brown)		L 1
	19..	£
	May 1 Bank	1 000·00

Bank A/c				L 2
19..	£	19..		£
May 1 Capital	1 000·00	May 1 Rent	20·00
5 Sales	180·00	2 Purchases	55·00
5 Sales	110·00	3 Cash	100·00
		4 Purchases	75·00
		5 Balance	1 040·00
	£1 290·00		£1 290·00
19..	£		
May 6 Balance	1 040·00		

Rent A/c		L 3
19..	£	
May 1	20·00	

Purchases A/c		L 4
19..	£	
May 2 Bank	55·00	
3 Cash	10·00	
3 Cash	5·00	
4 Bank	75·00	

Cash A/c				L 5
19..	£	19..		£
May 3 Bank	100·00	May 3 Purchases	10·00
		3 Purchases	5·00
		5 Balance	85·00
	£100·00		£100·00
19..	£		
May 6 Balance	85·00		

Sales A/c				L 6
		19..		£
		May 5 Bank	180·00
		5 Bank	110·00

Trial Balance (as at May 5th 19..)

	Dr.	Cr.
	£	£
Capital A/c		1 000·00
Bank A/c	1 040·00	
Rent A/c	20·00	
Purchases A/c	145·00	
Cash A/c	85·00	
Sales A/c		290·00
	£1 290·00	1 290·00

(3) Accounts of M. Whiteside (*SPA page 15*)

Capital A/c (M. Whiteside)		L 1
	19..	£
	Mar. 20 Cash	200·00

Cash A/c				L 2
19..	£	19..		£
Mar. 20 Capital	200·00	Mar. 20 Purchases	85·00
21 Sales	46·00	21 Purchases	22·50
23 Sales	86·00	22 Rent	10·00
25 Sales	58·00	22 Electricity	5·00
		22 Purchases	10·00
		24 Bank	100·00
		24 Purchases	16·00
		26 Balance	141·50
	£390·00		£390·00
19..	£		
Mar. 27 Balance	141·50		

Sales A/c		L 3		Purchases A/c		L 4
	19..	£	19..		£	
	Mar. 21 Cash	46·00	Mar. 20 Cash	85·00		
	23 Cash	86·00	21 Cash	22·50		
	25 Cash	58·00	22 Cash	10·00		
			24 Cash	16·00		

Rent A/c		L 5		Light and Heat A/c		L 6
19..	£		19..	£		
Mar. 22 Cash	10·00		Mar. 22 Cash	5·00		

Bank A/c		L 7
19..	£	
Mar. 24 Cash	100·00	

Trial Balance (as at March 26th 19..)

	Dr.	Cr.
	£	£
Capital A/c		200·00
Cash A/c	141·50	
Sales A/c		190·00
Purchases A/c	133·50	
Rent A/c	10·00	
Light and Heat A/c	5·00	
Bank A/c	100·00	
	£390·00	390·00

(4) Accounts of M. Logan (*SPA page 16*)

Cash A/c				L 1		Capital A/c		L 2
19..	£	19..		£			19..	£
Apr. 1 Capital	100·00	Apr. 1 Equipment	35·00				Apr. 1 Cash	100·00
2 Fees		1 Purchases	23·00					
Received	6·00	3 Purchases	6·40					
2 Sales	4·50	Equipment						
5 Fees		Hire	3·00			Bank A/c		L 7
Received	3·50	7 Stationery	1·25			19..	£	
6 Sales	4·40	7 Balance	49·75			Apr. 4 Fees		
	£118·40		£118·40			Received	9·50	
						4 Sales	11·20	
19..	£					7 Fees		
Apr. 8 Balance	49·75					Received	8·00	

Equipment A/c		L 3		Purchases A/c		L 4
19..	£		19..	£		
Apr. 1 Cash	35·00		Apr. 1 Cash	23·00		
			3 Cash	6·40		

Fees Received A/c		L 5		Sales A/c		L 6
	19..	£			19..	£
	Apr. 2 Cash	6·00			Apr. 2 Cash	4·50
	4 Bank	9·50			4 Bank	11·20
	5 Cash	3·50			6 Cash	4·40
	7 Bank	8·00				

Equipment Hired A/c		L 8		Stationery A/c		L 9
19..	£		19..	£		
Apr. 6 Cash	3·00		Apr. 7 Cash	1·25		

Trial Balance (as at April 7th 19..)

	Dr.	Cr.
	£	£
Cash A/c	49·75	
Capital A/c		100·00
Equipment A/c	35·00	
Purchases A/c	29·40	
Fees Received A/c		27·00
Sales A/c		20·10
Bank A/c	28·70	
Equipment Hired A/c	3·00	
Stationery A/c	1·25	
	£147·10	147·10

(5) Accounts of D. Lobley (*SPA page 16*)

Bank A/c   L 1

19..		£	19..		£
Jan. 1	Capital	1 000·00	Jan 1	Machinery	185·00
4	Fees		1	Tools	35·00
	Received	6·50	1	Purchases	120·00
			2	Cash	50·00
			6	Rent	10·00
			6	Balance	606·50
		£1 006·50			£1 006·50
19..		£			
Jan. 7	Balance	606·50			

Capital A/c   L 2

19..		£
Jan. 1	Bank	1 000·00

Machinery A/c   L 3

19..		£
Jan. 1	Bank	185·00

Tools A/c   L 4

19..		£
Jan. 1	Bank	35·00

Purchases A/c   L 5

19..		£
Jan. 1	Bank	120·00

Cash A/c   L 6

19..		£	19..		£
Jan. 2	Bank	50·00	Jan. 2	General	
3	Sales	4·25		Expenses	5·50
5	Sales	3·30	6	Balance	79·10
5	Sales	4·50			
6	Sales	22·55			
		£84·60			£84·60
19..		£			
Jan. 7	Balance	79·10			

General Expenses A/c   L 7

19..		£
Jan. 2	Cash	5·50

Sales A/c   L 8

19..		£
Jan. 3	Cash	4·25
5	Cash	3·30
5	Cash	4·50
6	Cash	22·55

Fees Received A/c   L 9

19..		£
Jan. 4	Bank	6·50

Rent A/c   L 10

19..		£
Jan. 6	Bank	10·00

Trial Balance (as at January 6th 19..)

	Dr.	Cr.
	£	£
Capital A/c		1 000·00
Bank A/c	606·50	
Machinery A/c	185·00	
Tools A/c	35·00	
Purchases A/c	120·00	
Cash A/c	79·10	
General Expenses A/c	5·50	
Sales A/c		34·60
Fees Received A/c		6·50
Rent A/c	10·00	
	£1 041·10	1 041·10

(6) Accounts of R. Sparrow (*SPA page 16*)

Cash A/c   L 1

19..		£	19..		£
Apr. 1	Capital	50·00	Apr. 5	Purchases	8·50
21	Sales	4·25	5	Purchases	1·50
28	Sales	8·30	13	Tools and Equipment	2·40
			30	Wages	3·45
			30	Balance	46·70
		£62·55			£62·55
19..		£			
May 1	Balance	46·70			

Land and Buildings A/c   L 2

19..		£
Apr. 1	Capital	1 500·00

Tools and Equipment A/c   L 3

19..		£
Apr. 1	Capital	240·00
13	Cash	2·40

Delivery Van A/c   L 4

19..		£
Apr. 1	Capital	85·00

Capital A/c   L 5

19..		£
Apr. 1	Sundry Assets	1 875·00

Purchases A/c   L 6

19..		£
Apr. 5	Cash	8·50
5	Cash	1·50

Sales A/c   L 7

19..		£
Apr. 21	Cash	4·25
28	Cash	8·30

Wages A/c   L 8

19..		£
Apr. 30	Cash	3·45

Trial Balance (as at April 30th 19..)

	Dr.	Cr.
	£	£
Cash A/c	46·70	
Land and Buildings A/c	1 500·00	
Tools and Equipment A/c	242·40	
Delivery Van A/c	85·00	
Capital A/c		1 875·00
Purchases A/c	10·00	
Sales A/c		12·55
Wages A/c	3·45	
	£1 887·55	1 887·55

(7) (*SPA page 17*)

    (*a*) Accounting is the art of controlling a business by keeping accurate book-keeping records, etc. (*See SPA page 1*)

    (*b*) Profit.

(8) (*SPA page 17*)

    (*a*) Taxation.
    (*b*) Income.
    (*c*) Corporation Tax.
    (*d*) Double-entry.
    (*e*) Ledger.
    (*f*) Debtor.
    (*g*) Creditor.
    (*h*) Folio.
    (*i*) Personal, nominal, real.
    (*j*) Transaction.

Unit Two
A More Detailed Look at the Ledger

Exercises Set 2: Debtors' Personal Accounts

(1) C. Hadland's Account (*SPA page 23*)

C. Hadland   DL 17

19..			£	19..			£
Jan. 1	Balance	B/d	402·97	Jan. 2	Bank		382·82
3	Sales		47·50	2	Discount Allowed		20·15
14	Sales		72·50	16	Bank		100·00
14	Carriage		4·25	27	Sales Returns		4·50
16	Sales		285·00	31	Balance	c/d	304·75
			£812·22				£812·22
19..			£				
Feb. 1	Balance	B/d	304·75				

(2) G. Wakeman's Account (*SPA page 23*)

G. Wakeman   DL 32

19..			£	19..			£
May 1	Balance	B/d	5·25	May 2	Bank		5·12
5	Sales		27·55	2	Discount Allowed		0·13
7	Sales		62·50	18	Sales Returns		8·50
7	Insurance		1·50	31	Balance	c/d	95·30
29	Sales		12·25				
			£109·05				£109·05
19..			£				
June 1	Balance	B/d	95·30				

(3) M. Watts' Account (*SPA page 24*)

(*a*)

M. Watts   DL 194

19..			£	19..			£
July 1	Balance	B/d	720·50	July 3	Bank		702·49
4	Sales		41·25	3	Discount Allowed		18·01
15	Sales		142·50	5	Sales Returns		7·77
15	Carriage		1·25	29	Machinery		650·00
15	Insurance		0·75				
30	Sales		380·50				
31	Balance	c/d	91·52				
			£1 378·27				£1 378·27
				19..			£
				Aug. 1	Balance	B/d	91·52

(*b*) This balance is unusual because it is a credit balance. This means that temporarily Watts is a creditor, not a debtor, and we owe him money.

(4) R. T. Crafty's Account (*SPA page 24*)

(*a*)

			R. T. Crafty					DL 31
19..			£	19..				£
Mar. 1	Balance	B/d	405·75	Mar. 3	Bank			395·61
11	Sales		274·50	3	Discount			10·14
19	Sales		100·00	27	Returns			12·50
20	Carriage		5·50	28	Motor Vans			150·00
				31	Balance		c/d	217·50
			£785·75					£785·75
19..			£					
Apr. 1	Balance	B/d	217·50					

Answers to supplementary questions:
(*b*) Crafty was a debtor.
(*c*) On March 27th Crafty returned goods to Lee.
(*d*) On March 28th Crafty sold Lee a surplus second-hand motor vehicle.
(*e*) Crafty was a debtor.

(5) M. Fisher's Account (*SPA page 24*)

(*a*)

			M. Fisher					DL 72
19..			£	19..				£
May 1	Balance	B/d	15·25	May 2	Bank			14·49
14	Sales		10·50	2	Discount Allowed			0·76
29	Sales		12·25	30	Sewing Machines			68·50
29	Carriage		0·55					
31	Balance	c/d	45·20					
			£83·75					£83·75
				19..				£
				June 1	Balance		B/d	45·20

(*b*) Fisher was a debtor.
(*c*) Fisher settled his account less 5 per cent discount.
(*d*) Fisher sold Sandon sewing machines valued at £68.50.
(*e*) It is a credit balance; Fisher is temporarily a creditor instead of a debtor.

Exercises Set 3: Creditors' Personal Accounts

(1) R. Bolton's Account (*SPA page 26*)

R. Bolton   CL 21

19..			£	19..			£
Aug.	2	Bank	38·71	Aug.	1	Balance B/d	40·75
	2	Discount Received	2·04		13	Purchases	85·00
	18	Purchases Returns	5·75		17	Purchases	16·50
	19	Purchases Returns			27	Purchases	132·50
		(Allowance)	8·40		27	Insurance	1·50
	31	Balance c/d	221·35				
			£276·25				£276·25
				19..			£
				Sept.	1	Balance	221·35

(2) T. Robertson's Account (*SPA page 26*)

T. Robertson   CL 47

19..			£	19..			£
Jan.	12	Bank	475·00	Jan.	1	Balance B/d	500·00
	12	Discount Received	25·00		10	Purchases	2 850·00
	16	Purchases Returns	475·00		14	Purchases	388·00
	16	Carriage	12·50		29	Purchases	42·00
	27	Plant and					
		Machinery	880·00				
	31	Balance c/d	1 912·50				
			£3 780·00				£3 780·00
				19..			£
				Feb.	1	Balance B/d	1 912·50

(3) Universal Warehouses Ltd. (*SPA page 26*)

Universal Warehouses Ltd.   CL 94

19..			£	19..			£
Jan.	2	Bank	729·54	Jan.	1	Balance B/d	729·54
	11	Purchases Returns	4·55		4	Purchases	248·50
	18	Purchases Returns	16·75		11	Purchases	320·75
	18	Purchases Returns	4·05		18	Purchases	452·65
	25	Purchases Returns	15·25		19	Furniture and	
	31	Balance c/d	1 381·35			Fittings	215·50
					25	Purchases	184·55
			£2 151·49				£2 151·49
				19..			£
				Feb.	1	Balance B/d	1 381·35

(4) R. Jones's Account (*SPA page 27*)

R. Jones   CL 55

19..			£	19..				£
Jan.	2	Purchases Returns		7·70	Jan.	1	Balance	B/d	234·70
	3	Bank		221·32		14	Purchases		48·60
	3	Discount		5·68		15	Carriage		4·40
	23	Purchases Returns		4·12		17	Purchases		133·10
	30	Motor Lorry				18	Insurance and		
		(Exchange)		150·00			Carriage		7·12
	31	Balance	c/d	39·10					
				£427·92					£427·92
					19..				£
					Feb.	1	Balance	B/d	39·10

(a)

Jan.   1   This is the opening balance which Lee Bros. owe to R. Jones.

2   Lee Bros. returned some goods purchased in December, or perhaps returned empty containers, valued at £7·70.

3   Lee Bros. settled their account, less 2½ per cent discount.

14   Jones supplied goods value £48·60.

15   Jones charged for carriage on goods supplied the previous day.

17   Jones supplied further goods value £133·10.

18   Jones charged for insurance and carriage on goods supplied the previous day.

23   Lee Bros. returned goods, or containers.

30   Lee Bros. must have sold R. Jones a second-hand motor vehicle.

31   The balance on the account is carried down.

Feb.   1   This is the balance now owing by Lee Bros. to R. Jones.

(b)   Since the balance is a credit balance R. Jones is a creditor, and this means that Lee Bros. owe the £39·10 to R. Jones.

(5) P. B. Rowe's Account (*SPA page 27*)

P. B. Rowe   CL 39

19..				£	19..				£
Feb.	2	Bank		702·39	Feb.	1	Balance	B/d	720·40
	2	Discount		18·01		11	Purchases		425·50
	14	Returns		25·50		19	Purchases		285·50
	18	Motor Vehicles		1 650·00		20	Carriage		12·50
						28	Balance	c/d	952·00
				£2 395·90					£2 395·90
19..				£					
Mar.	1	Balance	B/d	952·00					

(a) On February 1st Rowe was a creditor.

(b) On February 14th M. Bright returned goods to P. B. Rowe, whose account was accordingly debited. (Debit the receiver of goods.)

(c) On February 18th M. Bright sold a motor vehicle to P. B. Rowe, whose account was accordingly debited.

(d) On February 28th Rowe was a debtor, the motor vehicle he purchased having completely outweighed in value the goods and services he supplied.

More Advanced Accounting to the Trial Balance

Exercises Set 4: More Practice in Double-entry Book-keeping to the Trial-Balance Level

(1) Accounts of E. Saxby (*SPA page 37*)

Capital A/c		L 1
	19..	£
	June 1 Sundry	
	Assets 3	500·00

Land and Buildings A/c		L 2
19..	£	
June 1 Capital 2	000·00	

Furniture and Fittings A/c		L 3
19..	£	
June 1 Capital	300·00	

Bank A/c			L 4
19..	£	19..	£
June 1 Capital 1	150·00	June 2 Rates	15·50
		2 Light and	
		Heat	5·00
		2 Telephone	3·50
		6 Balance 1	126·00
	£1 150·00		£1 150·00
19..	£		
June 7 Balance			
1 126·00			

Cash A/c			L 5
19..	£	19..	£
June 1 Capital	50·00	June 3 Purchases	35·00
4 Sales	65·00	5 Postage	2·25
		5 Purchases	7·50
		5 Purchases	15·00
		7 Balance	55·25
	£115·00		£115·00
19..	£		
June 7 Balance	55·25		

R. Marsh A/c		L 6
	19..	£
	June 1 Balance	280·00

Rates A/c		L 7
19..	£	
June 2 Bank	15·50	

Light and Heat A/c		L 8
19..	£	
June 2 Bank	5·00	

Telephone A/c		L 9
19..	£	
June 2 Bank	3·50	

Purchases A/c		L 10
19..	£	
June 1 R. Marsh	280·00	
3 Cash	35·00	
5 Cash	7·50	
5 Cash	15·00	
6 M. Walker	42·00	

Sales A/c		L 11
	19..	£
	June 4 Cash	65·00
	4 R. Lebon	68·50
	6 R. Johnson	27·50

R. Lebon A/c		L 12
19..	£	
June 4 Sales	68·50	

Postage A/c		L 13
19..	£	
June 5 Cash	2·25	

R. Johnson A/c		L 14
19..	£	
June 6 Sales	27·50	

M. Walker A/c		L 15
	19..	£
	June 6 Purchases	42·00

Trial Balance (as at June 6th 19..)

	Dr.	Cr.
	£	£
Capital		3 500·00
Land and Buildings	2 000·00	
Furniture and Fittings	300·00	
Bank	1 126·00	
Cash	55·25	
R. Marsh		280·00
Rates	15·50	
Light and Heat	5·00	
Telephone	3·50	
Purchases	379·50	
Sales		161·00
R. Lebon	68·50	
Postage	2·25	
R. Johnson	27·50	
M. Walker		42·00
	£3 983·00	3 983·00

(2) Accounts of G. Parker (*SPA page 37*)

Capital A/c		L 1
	19..	£
	July 1 Sundry	
	Assets	4 800·00

Furniture and Fittings A/c		L 2
19..	£	
July 1 Capital 1 000·00		

Stock A/c		L 3
19..	£	
July 1 Capital 2 000·00		

Bank A/c		L 4
19..	£	
July 1 Capital 1 000·00		

Cash A/c			L 5
19..	£	19..	£
July 1 Capital	800·00	July 1 Rent	30·00
2 Sales	18·55	1 Hire of Shop	
3 Sales	42·65	Fittings	27·50
6 Sales	84·75	3 Postage	4·50
		3 Travelling	
		Expenses	3·65
		3 Salaries	5·00
		6 Purchases	3·75
		6 Balance	871·55
	£945·95		£945·95
19..	£		
July 7 Balance	871·55		

Purchases A/c		L 6
19..	£	
July 1 H. Roach	285·50	
5 T. Law	120·00	
6 Cash	3·75	
6 T. Yates	75·50	

Rent A/c		L 7
19..	£	
July 1 Cash	30·00	

H. Roach A/c		L 8
	19..	£
	July 1 Purchases	285·50

Hire of Shop Fittings A/c		L 9
19..	£	
July 1 Cash	27·50	

Sales A/c		L 10
	19..	£
	July 2 Cash	18·55
	2 Rose and	
	Frank Ltd	37·50
	3 Cash	42·65
	6 Cash	84·75

Rose and Frank Ltd. A/c		L 11
19..	£	
July 2 Sales	37·50	

Postage A/c		L 12
19..	£	
July 3 Cash	4·50	

Travelling Expenses A/c		L 13
19..	£	
July 3 Cash	3·65	

Salaries A/c		L 14
19..	£	
July 3 Cash	5·00	

T. Law A/c		L 15
	19..	£
	July 5 Purchases	120·00

T. Yates A/c		L 16
	19..	£
	July 6 Purchases	75·50

Trial Balance (as at July 6th 19..)

	Dr.	Cr.
	£	£
Capital		4 800·00
Furniture and Fittings	1 000·00	
Stock	2 000·00	
Bank	1 000·00	
Cash	871·55	
Rent	30·00	
Purchases	484·75	
H. Roach		285·50
Hire of Shop Fittings	27·50	
Sales		183·45
Rose and Frank Ltd.	37·50	
Postage	4·50	
Travelling Expenses	3·65	
Salaries	5·00	
T. Law		120·00
T. Yates		75·50
	£5 464·45	5 464·45

(3) Accounts of T. Lawrence (*SPA page 38*)

Capital A/c		L 1
	19..	£
	Apr. 1 Sundry	
	Assets	1 500·00

Land and Buildings A/c		L 2
19..	£	
Apr. 1 Capital	1 000·00	

Furniture and Fittings A/c		L 3
19..	£	
Apr. 1 Capital	200·00	

Bank A/c				
19..	£	19..		£
Apr. 1 Capital	275·00	Apr. 2 Rates		15·00
		2 Light and		
		Heat		5·50
		2 Telephone		3·50
		3 Purchases		125·00
		6 Balance		126·00
	£275·00			£275·00
19..	£			
Apr. 7 Balance	126·00			

Cash A/c			L 5
19..	£	19..	£
Apr. 1 Capital	25·00	Apr. 5 Postage	5·50
4 Sales	48·00	5 Travelling	
		Expenses	4·20
		6 Balance	63·30
	£73·00		£73·00
19..	£		
Apr. 7 Balance	63·30		

Purchases A/c		L 6
19..	£	
Apr. 1 E. Sims	56·50	
3 Bank	125·00	
5 R. Large	275·00	
6 M. Rowe	45·00	

R. Sims A/c		L 7
	19..	£
	Apr. 1 Purchases	56·50

Rates A/c		L 8
19..	£	
Apr. 2 Bank	15·00	

Light and Heat A/c		L 9
19..	£	
Apr. 2 Bank	5·50	

Telephone A/c		L 10
19..	£	
Apr. 2 Bank	3·50	

Sales A/c		L 11
	19..	£
	Apr. 4 Cash	48·00
	4 R. Morton	15·00
	6 R. J. Moss	50·00

R. Morton A/c		L 12
19..	£	
Apr. 4 Sales	15·00	

Postage A/c		L 13
19..	£	
Apr. 5 Cash	5·50	

Travelling Expenses A/c		L 14
19..	£	
Apr. 5 Cash	4·20	

R. Large A/c		L 15
	19..	£
	Apr. 5 Purchases	275·00

R. J. Moss A/c		L 16
19..	£	
Apr. 6 Sales	50·00	

M. Rowe A/c		L 17
	19..	£
	Apr. 6 Purchases	45·00

Trial Balance (as at April 6th 19..)

	Dr. £	Cr. £
Capital		1 500·00
Land and Buildings	1 000·00	
Furniture and Fittings	200·00	
Bank	126·00	
Cash	63·30	
Purchases	501·50	
R. Sims		56·50
Rates	15·00	
Light and Heat	5·50	
Telephone Expenses	3·50	
Sales		113·00
R. Morton	15·00	
Postage	5·50	
Travelling Expenses	4·20	
R. Large		275·00
R. J. Moss	50·00	
M. Rowe		45·00
	£1 989·50	1 989·50

(4) Books of M. Rowcliffe (*SPA page 38*)

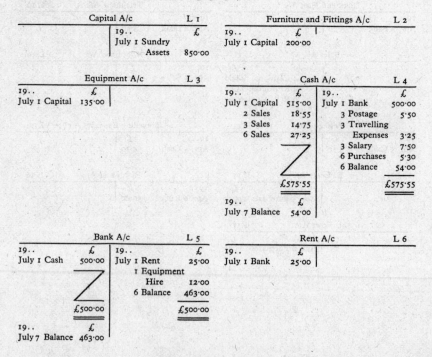

Capital A/c		L 1
	19.. July 1 Sundry Assets	£ 850·00

Furniture and Fittings A/c		L 2
19.. July 1 Capital	£ 200·00	

Equipment A/c		L 3
19.. July 1 Capital	£ 135·00	

Cash A/c   L 4

19..	£	19..	£
July 1 Capital	515·00	July 1 Bank	500·00
2 Sales	18·55	3 Postage	5·50
3 Sales	14·75	3 Travelling	
6 Sales	27·25	Expenses	3·25
		3 Salary	7·50
		6 Purchases	5·30
		6 Balance	54·00
	£575·55		£575·55
19..	£		
July 7 Balance	54·00		

Bank A/c   L 5

19..	£	19..	£
July 1 Cash	500·00	July 1 Rent	25·00
		1 Equipment	
		Hire	12·00
		6 Balance	463·00
	£500·00		£500·00
19..	£		
July 7 Balance	463·00		

Rent A/c		L 6
19.. July 1 Bank	£ 25·00	

Purchases A/c	L 7		H. Rogerson A/c	L 8
19..	£		19..	£
July 1 H. Rogerson			July 1 Purchases 142·00	
142·00				
5 R. Lyons 50·00				
6 Cash 5·30				
6 M. Loman				
47·50				

Equipment Hire A/c	L 9		Sales A/c	L 10
19..	£		19..	£
July 1 Bank 12·00			July 2 Cash 18·55	
			2 Roach and	
			Lane Ltd. 48·50	
			3 Cash 14·75	
			6 Cash 27·25	

Roach and Lane Ltd. A/c	L 11		Postage A/c	L 12
19..	£		19..	£
July 2 Sales 48·50			July 3 Cash 5·50	

Travelling Expenses A/c	L 13		Salaries A/c	L 14
19..	£		19..	£
July 3 Cash 3·25			July 3 Cash 7·50	

R. Lyons A/c	L 15		M. Loman A/c	L 16
	19..	£		19..	£
	July 5 Purchases 50·00			July 6 Purchases 47·50	

Trial Balance (as at July 6th 19..)

	Dr.	Cr.
	£	£
Capital		850·00
Furniture and Fittings	200·00	
Equipment	135·00	
Cash	54·00	
Bank	463·00	
Rent	25·00	
Purchases	244·80	
H. Rogerson		142·00
Equipment Hire	12·00	
Sales		109·05
Roach and Lane Ltd.	48·50	
Postage	5·50	
Travelling Expenses	3·25	
Salaries	7·50	
R. Lyons		50·00
M. Loman		47·50
	£1 198·55	1 198·55

(5) Books of R. Turf (*SPA page 39*)

Capital A/c	L 1		Tools and Equipment A/c	L 2
	19..	£	19..	£
	Nov. 1 Sundry		Nov. 1 Capital 320·00	
	Assets 1 042·00			

Stock A/c		L 3
19..	£	
Nov. 1 Capital	172·00	

Cash A/c			L 4
19..	£	19..	£
Nov. 1 Capital	50·00	Nov. 13 Wages	6·00
13 Sales	25·50	20 Bank	50·00
20 Fees Received	80·00	27 Wages	10·00
		27 Transport Expenses	4·50
		30 Balance	85·00
	£155·50		£155·50
19..	£		
Dec. 1 Balance	85·00		

Bank A/c			L 5
19..	£	19..	£
Nov. 1 Capital	500·00	Nov. 6 Purchases	42·00
20 Cash	50·00	13 Purchases	30·00
		20 Purchases	84·00
		27 Purchases	35·00
		30 Balance	359·00
	£550·00		£550·00
19..	£		
Dec 1 Balance	359·00		

Purchases A/c		L 6
19..	£	
Nov. 6 Bank	42·00	
13 Bank	30·00	
20 Bank	84·00	
27 Bank	35·00	

R. Coombe's A/c		L 7
19..	£	
Nov. 6 Fees	50·00	

Fees Received A/c		L 8
	19..	£
	Nov. 6 R. Coombes	50·00
	20 Cash	80·00

Sales A/c		L 9
	19..	£
	Nov. 13 Cash	25·50

Wages A/c		L 10
19..	£	
Nov. 13 Cash	6·00	
27 Cash	10·00	

Transport Expenses A/c		L 11
19..	£	
Nov. 27 Cash	4·50	

Trial Balance (as at November 30th 19..)

	Dr.	Cr.
	£	£
Capital		1 042·00
Tools and Equipment	320·00	
Stock	172·00	
Cash	85·00	
Bank	359·00	
Purchases	191·00	
R. Coombes	50·00	
Fees Received		130·00
Sales		25·50
Wages	16·00	
Transport Expenses	4·50	
	£1 197·50	1 197·50

(6) Books of R. Tilehurst (*SPA page 39*)

Capital A/c — L 1

Dr	£	Cr	£
		19..	
		June 1 Sundry Assets	2 870·00

Premises A/c — L 2

Dr	£	Cr	£
19..			
June 1 Capital	1 550·00		

Stock A/c — L 3

Dr	£	Cr	£
19..			
June 1 Capital	820·00		

Equipment A/c — L 4

Dr	£	Cr	£
19..			
June 1 Capital	200·00		
3 Cash	12·25		

Bank A/c — L 5

Dr	£	Cr	£
19..		19..	
June 1 Capital	270·00	June 10 Purchases	27·50
		30 Wages	24·50
		30 Balance	218·00
	£270·00		£270·00
19..			
July 1 Balance	218·00		

Cash A/c — L 6

Dr	£	Cr	£
19..		19..	
June 1 Capital	30·00	June 2 Telephone Expenses	3·50
3 Sales	22·35	3 Fittings	12·25
10 Sales	18·50	4 Wages	10·00
17 Sales	27·35	4 Purchases	3·00
		10 Carriage	5·50
		10 Wages	2·00
		17 Carriage	4·50
		30 Fuel	7·20
		30 Purchases	11·50
		30 Balance	38·75
	£98·20		£98·20
19..			
July 1 Balance	38·75		

Telephone Expenses A/c — L 7

Dr	£	Cr	£
19..			
June 2 Cash	3·50		

Sales A/c — L 8

Dr	£	Cr	£
		19..	
		June 3 Cash	22·35
		4 Ocean Hotel	37·50
		10 Cash	18·50
		17 Alhambro	86·50
		17 Cash	27·35

Imperial Iron Co. Ltd. A/c — L 9

Dr	£	Cr	£
		19..	
		June 3 Purchases	250·00
		23 Purchases	186·50

Purchases A/c — L 10

Dr	£	Cr	£
19..			
June 3 Imperial Iron Co.	250·00		
4 Cash	3·00		
10 Bank	27·50		
23 Imperial Iron Co.	186·50		
30 Cash	11·50		

Wages A/c — L 11

Dr	£	Cr	£
19..			
June 4 Cash	10·00		
10 Cash	2·00		
30 Bank	24·50		

Ocean Hotel A/c — L 12

Dr	£	Cr	£
19..			
June 4 Sales	37·50		

Carriage Outwards A/c — L 13

Dr	£	Cr	£
19..			
June 10 Cash	5·50		
17 Cash	4·50		

Alhambro Garden Works A/c — L 14

Dr	£	Cr	£
19..			
June 17 Sales	86·50		

Light and Heat A/c — L 15

Dr	£	Cr	£
19..			
June 30 Cash	7·20		

Trial Balance (as at June 30th 19..)

	Dr. £	Cr. £
Capital		2 870·00
Premises	1 550·00	
Stock	820·00	
Equipment	212·25	
Bank	218·00	
Cash	38·75	
Telephone Expenses	3·50	
Sales		192·20
Imperial Iron Co. Ltd.		436·50
Purchases	478·50	
Wages	36·50	
Ocean Hotel	37·50	
Carriage Out	10·00	
Alhambro Garden Works	86·50	
Light and Heat	7·20	
	£3 498·70	3 498·70

Unit Four

Accounting to Final-Accounts Level
Part One: The Trial Balance

Exercises Set 5: Drawing up Trial Balances

(1) Books of R. Fowler (*SPA page 43*)

Trial Balance (as at March 31st 19..)

Accounts	Dr. £	Cr. £
Discount Allowed	26·45	
Capital		1 500·00
Rent and Rates	250·00	
Office Expenses	142·50	
Loan from M. Castle		1 000·00
Stock in Hand at April 1st	600·00	
Sundry Creditors		845·00
Bank	1 970·55	
Plant and Machinery	1 750·00	
Returns Inwards	45·50	
Trade Expenses	248·50	
Sales		6 560·00
Purchases	1 580·50	
Cash in Hand	65·50	
Freehold Property	2 000·00	
Sundry Debtors	1 225·50	
	£9 905·00	9 905·00

(2) Books of A. Dealer (*SPA page 43*)

Trial Balance (as at April 30th 19..)

Accounts	Dr. £	Cr. £
Sundry Debtors	2 516·50	
Sundry Creditors		4 826·50
Plant and Machinery	11 550·00	
Furniture and Fittings	825·00	
Land and Buildings	13 000·00	
Opening Stock at April 1st 19..	3 266·00	
Cash	175·00	
Bank	2 475·00	
Purchases	16 875·00	
Sales		38 265·00
Office Salaries	265·50	
Light and Heat	104·40	
Telephone Expenses	76·70	
Warehouse Wages	1 595·50	
General Expenses	295·50	
Rates	462·90	
Insurance	380·50	
Drawings	228·00	
Loan (R. Thomas)		1 000·00
Capital A/c		10 000·00
	£54 091·50	54 091·50

(3) Books of J. Brown (*SPA page 43*)

Trial Balance (as at December 31st 19..)

Accounts	Dr. £	Cr. £
Returns Inwards	175·50	
Returns Outwards		195·90
Cash in Hand	40·00	
Machinery	1 640·00	
Salaries	1 522·00	
Audit Fee	27·50	
Sales		7 261·40
Stock at July 1st	800·00	
Telephone	45·20	
Bank Overdraft		506·00
Factory Wages	4 676·00	
Discount Received		27·50
Creditors		4 726·50
Debtors	3 871·60	
Carriage Outwards	42·40	
Bad Debts	165·60	
Capital at July 1st		5 000·00
Rent and Rates	240·00	
Purchases	2 535·50	
Commission Received		1 864·00
Furniture	300·00	
Premises	3 500·00	
	£19 581·30	19 581·30

(4) Books of J. Fisher (*SPA page 43*)

Trial Balance (as at December 31st 19..)

Accounts	Dr. £	Cr. £
Warehouse Wages	850·00	
Office Salaries	1 750·00	
Debtors	2 462·50	
Creditors		4 861·50
Furniture and Fittings	250·00	
Commission Received		1 755·00
Capital		4 000·00
Drawings	1 500·00	
Returns Outwards		75·00
Returns Inwards	250·00	
Rent and Rates	450·00	
Light and Heat	600·00	
Carriage In	48·50	
Carriage Out	72·60	
Opening Stock at January 1st	1 575·00	
Cash in Hand	42·50	
Cash at Bank	1 664·60	
Purchases	11 160·50	
Sales		17 404·70
Motor Vehicles	1 420·00	
Land and Buildings	5 000·00	
Loan from Bank		1 000·00
	£29 096·20	29 096·20

(5) Books of I. Cooper (*SPA page 44*)

Trial Balance (as at December 31st 19..)

Accounts	Dr. £	Cr. £
Purchases	37 000·00	
Sales		56 000·00
Sales Returns	2 004·00	
Purchases Returns		194·50
Opening Stock (at January 1st 19..)	8 850·50	
Warehouse Wages	250·90	
Warehouse Expenses	56·00	
Discount Allowed	36·50	
Discount Received		79·80
Light and Heat	198·40	
Travelling Expenses	34·50	
Repairs	18·50	
Rent Paid	450·00	
Rent Received		150·00
Commission Received		185·55
Furniture and Fittings	2 650·00	
Plant and Machinery	13 840·70	
Motor Vehicles	6 825·50	
Debtors	675·50	
Creditors		12 133·00
Cash	1 383·50	
Bank	4 718·35	
Mortgage		3 000·00
Loan (Bank Finance Ltd.)		1 000·00
Drawings (I. Cooper)	1 750·00	
Capital (I. Cooper)		8 000·00
	£80 742·85	80 742·85

(6) Books of David Cann (*SPA page 44*)

Trial Balance (as at December 31st 19..)

Accounts	Dr. £	Cr. £
Goodwill	5 000·00	
Bad Debts	426·00	
Commission Received		1 285·00
Motor Vehicles	750·00	
Furniture	450·00	
Premises	3 800·00	
Warehouse Wages	1 150·00	
Discount Received		24·50
Creditors		1 284·00
Debtors	2 562·00	
Carriage In	82·00	
Returns In	141·00	
Returns Out		60·50
Cash in Hand	248·00	
Machinery	1 250·00	
Office Salaries	2 376·00	
Sales		17 987·00
Stock (at start of year)	1 450·00	
Postage	56·50	
Office Expenses	275·50	
Bank Loan		2 000·00
Capital		6 916·50
Rates and Insurance	450·50	
Light and Heat	276·80	
Purchases	8 572·60	
General Factory Expenses	240·60	
	£29 557·50	29 557·50

Unit Five

Accounting to Final-Accounts Level
Part Two: The Gross Profit on Trading

Exercises Set 6: The Trading Account

(1) Books of R. Hudson (*SPA page 54*)

Trading A/c (for year ending December 31st 19..)   L 177

	£	£		£
Opening Stock		325·00	Sales	2 725·00
Purchases	785·00		*Less* Sales Returns	125·00
Less Purchases Returns	15·00			
			Net Turnover	2 600·00
Net Purchases		770·00		
Total Stock Available		1 095·00		
Less Closing Stock		295·00		
Cost of Stock Sold		800·00		
Gross Profit (to Profit and Loss A/c)		1 800·00		
		£2 600·00		£2 600·00

(2) Books of I. Brunel (*SPA page 54*)

Trading A/c (for year ending June 30th 19..)   L 195

	£	£		£
Opening Stock		1 500·00	Sales	17 250·00
Purchases	12 520·00		*Less* Sales Returns	120·00
Less Purchases Returns	1 520·00			
			Net Turnover	17 130·00
Net Purchases		11 000·00		
Total Stock Available		12 500·00		
Less Closing Stock		2 370·00		
Cost of Stock Sold		10 130·00		
Gross Profit		7 000·00		
		£17 130·00		£17 130·00

(3) Books of T. Turner (*SPA page 55*)

Trading A/c (for year ending March 31st 19..)

	£	£		£
Opening Stock		17 280·00	Sales	184 000·00
Purchases	66 275·00		*Less* Sales Returns	2 500·00
Less Purchases Returns	1 275·00			
			Net Turnover	181 500·00
Net Purchases		65 000·00		
Total Stock Available		82 280·00		
Less Closing Stock		14 180·00		
Cost of Stock Sold		68 100·00		
Warehouse Wages		3 400·00		
Cost of Sales		71 500·00		
Gross Profit		110 000·00		
		£181 500·00		£181 500·00

(4) Books of J. Metcalfe (*SPA page 55*)

Trading A/c (for year ending March 31st 19..)

	£	£		£
Opening Stock		12 500·00	Sales	175 200·00
Purchases	105 000·00		*Less* Sales Returns	3 700·00
Carriage In	500·00			
			Net Turnover	171 500·00
	105 500·00			
Less Purchases Returns	1 800·00			
Net Purchases		103 700·00		
Total Stock Available		116 200·00		
Less Closing Stock		14 700·00		
Cost of Stock Sold		101 500·00		
Warehouse Wages	3 500·00			
Warehouse Expenses	1 500·00			
		5 000·00		
Cost of Sales		106 500·00		
Gross Profit (to Profit and Loss A/c)		65 000·00		
		£171 500·00		£171 500·00

(5) Books of R. Miller (*SPA page 55*)

Trading A/c (for year ending March 31st 19..)

	£	£		£
Opening Stock		2 350·50	Sales	65 700·00
Purchases	38 440·00		*Less* Sales Returns	255·50
Carriage In	130·00			
			Net Turnover	65 444·50
	38 570·00			
Less Purchases Returns	262·75			
Net Purchases		38 307·25		
Total Stock Available		40 657·75		
Less Closing Stock		2 535·40		
Cost of Stock Sold		38 122·35		
Warehouse Wages	2 565·00			
Trade Expenses	370·35			
		2 935·35		
Cost of Sales		41 057·70		
Gross Profit (to Profit and Loss A/c)		24 386·80		
		£65 444·50		£65 444·50

(6) Books of G. Poole (*SPA page 55*)

Trading A/c (for year ending June 30th 19..)

	£	£		£
Opening Stock		15 750·00	Sales	196 000·00
Purchases	105 002·00		*Less* Sales Returns	2 500·00
Carriage In	150·00			
Customs Duty	620·00		Net Turnover	193 500·00
	105 772·00			
Less Purchases Returns	1 280·50			
Net Purchases		104 491·50		
Total Stock Available		120 241·50		
Less Closing Stock		16 726·60		
Cost of Stock Sold		103 514·90		
Warehouse Expenses	752·30			
Warehouse Wages	1 650·70			
Warehouse Redecorations	249·60			
Total Expenses		2 652·60		
Cost of Sales		106 167·50		
Gross Profit (to Profit and Loss A/c)		87 332·50		
		£193 500·00		£193 500·00

Accounting to Final-Accounts Level
Part Three: The Net Profit of the Enterprise

Exercises Set 7: Profit and Loss Accounts

(1) Accounts of M. Lawrence (*SPA page 59*)

Profit and Loss A/c (for year ending December 31st 19..)

	£		£
Rent and Rates	850·00	Gross Profit	2 755·00
Light and Heat	230·50		
Office Salaries	945·00		
	2 025·50		
Net Profit (to Capital A/c)	729·50		
	£2 755·00		£2 755·00

(2) Accounts of W. Sandon (*SPA page 59*)

Profit and Loss A/c (for year ending March 31st 19..)

	£		£
Rent and Rates	2 560·00	Gross Profit	18 655·00
Light and Heat	426·00	Commission Received	2 065·00
Office Salaries	7 956·00	Rent Received	240·00
Telephone Expenses	236·50		
Sundry Expenses	32·50		20 960·00
Postage	125·50		
	11 336·50		
Net Profit (to Capital A/c)	9 623·50		
	£20 960·00		£20 960·00

(3) Accounts of M. Chesterfield (*SPA page 59*)

Profit and Loss A/c (for year ending June 30th 19..)

	£		£
Rent Paid	2 865·50	Gross Profit	78 561·75
Office Salaries	9 589·50	Rent Received	525·25
Office Expenses	2 361·00		
Office Light and Heat	854·60		79 087·00
Advertising	7 965·50		
Interest on Loans	450·00		
Interest on Overdraft	65·50		
Entertainment of Visitors	2 725·50		
Total Expenses	26 877·10		
Net Profit (to Capital A/c)	52 209·90		
	£79 087·00		£79 087·00

(4) Accounts of R. Burton (*SPA page 60*)

Profit and Loss A/c (for year ending December 31st 19..)

	£		£
Rent and Rates	800·00	Gross Profit	12 840·00
Office Expenses	1 440·00	Discount Received	60·00
Light and Heat	240·00	Commission Received	180·00
Loan Interest	400·00	Rent Received	360·00
Mortgage Interest	664·00		
Discount Allowed	400·00	Total Profit	13 440·00
Advertising Expenses	886·00		
Transport	1 106·00		
Total Expenses	5 936·00		
Net Profit (to Capital A/c)	7 504·00		
	£13 440·00		£13 440·00

(5) Books of L. Lucerne (*SPA page 60*)

Trading A/c (for year ending March 31st 19..)

	£	£		£
Stock at Start		3 521·10	Sales	17 033·20
Purchases	9 101·00		*Less* Sales Returns	33·67
Less Purchases Returns	24·25			
				16 999·53
Net Purchases		9 076·75		
Total Stock Available		12 597·85		
Less Closing Stock		3 171·30		
Cost of Stock Sold		9 426·55		
Gross Profit		7 572·98		
		£16 999·53		£16 999·53

Profit and Loss A/c (for year ending March 31st 19..)

	£		£
Discount Allowed	34·50	Gross Profit	7 572·98
Insurance	8·30	Discount Received	4·00
Office Expenses	853·50		
Printing and Stationery	51·76		7 576·98
Rents and Rates	885·00		
General Expenses	649·80		
Telephone Expenses	51·00		
Interest Paid	61·10		
Light and Heat	49·20		
	2 644·16		
Net Profit (to Capital A/c)	4 932·82		
	£7 576·98		£7 576·98

(6) Books of B. Grant (*SPA page 60*)

Trading A/c (for year ending December 31st 19..)

	£	£		£
Stock		12 000·00	Sales	82 500·00
Purchases	46 550·00		*Less* Sales Returns	350·00
Less Purchases Returns	1 500·00			
				82 150·00
Net Purchases		45 050·00		
Total Stock Available		57 050·00		
Less Closing Stock		11 500·00		
Cost of Stock Sold		45 550·00		
Gross Profit		36 600·00		
		£82 150·00		£82 150·00

Profit and Loss A/c (for year ending December 31st 19..)

	£		£
Rent and Rates	1 000·00	Gross Profit	36 600·00
Bad Debts	1 150·00		
Carriage Out	1 300·00		
Office Salaries	9 450·00		
Telephone Expenses	750·00		
	13 650·00		
Net Profit (to Capital A/c)	22 950·00		
	£36 600·00		£36 600·00

Unit Seven

Accounting to Final-Accounts Level Part Four: The Balance Sheet of the Business

Exercises Set 8: The Balance Sheet of a Business

(1) Books of R. Long (*SPA page 70*)

Balance Sheet (as at December 31st 19..)

	£	£		£	£
Fixed Assets			Capital		
Land and Buildings		10 500·00	At Start		30 000·00
Office Equipment		4 500·00	Net Profit	5 000·00	
Motor Vehicles		2 000·00	*Less* Drawings	2 500·00	
					2 500·00
		17 000·00			
					32 500·00
Current Assets			Long-term Liabilities		
Stock	10 000·00		Bank Loan		5 000·00
Debtors	2 000·00		Current Liabilities		
Cash at Bank	9 000·00		Creditors		1 500·00
Cash in Hand	1 000·00				
		22 000·00			
		£39 000·00			£39 000·00

(2) Books of J. Triton (*SPA page 71*)

Balance Sheet (as at December 31st 19..)

	£	£		£	£
Fixed Assets			Capital		
Land and Buildings		10 000·00	At Start		25 000·00
Plant and Machinery		3 000·00	Net Profit	3 000·00	
Office Equipment		2 000·00	*Less* Drawings	1 750·00	
Motor Vehicles		5 000·00			1 250·00
		20 000·00			
					26 250·00
Current Assets			Long-term Liabilities		
Stock	4 500·00		Mortgage on Premises		5 000·00
Debtors	1 600·00		Current Liabilities		
Cash at Bank	6 850·00		Creditors		1 850·00
Cash in Hand	150·00				
		13 100·00			
		£33 100·00			£33 100·00

(3) **Books of T. North** (*SPA page 71*)

Balance Sheet (as at December 31st 19..)

	£	£		£	£
Current Assets			Current Liabilities		
Cash in Hand		36·50	Creditors		997·20
Cash at Bank		548·50	Long-term Liabilities		
Trade Debtors		1 036·50	Bank Loan	3 000·00	
Stock		1 245·00	Mortgage on Premises	1 000·00	
Investments		400·00			4 000·00
		3 266·50			
Fixed Assets			Capital		
Motor Vehicles	1 500·75		At Start		4 185·00
Furniture and Fittings	515·55		Net Profit	2 250·60	
Plant and Machinery	1 400·00		*Less* Drawings	1 750·00	
Land and Buildings	3 000·00			500·60	
		6 416·30			4 685·60
		£9 682·80			£9 682·80

(4) **Books of M. Twain** (*SPA page 72*)

Balance Sheet (as at March 31st 19..)

	£	£		£	£
Current Assets			Current Liabilities		
Cash in Hand		38·50	Creditors		919·25
Cash at Bank		720·50			
Debtors		1 434·25	Long-term Liabilities		
Closing Stock		1 500·00	Mortgage on Premises		4 000·00
		3 693·25			
Fixed Assets			Capital		
Motor Vehicles	1 675·50		At Start		11 765·00
Furniture and Fittings	2 565·50		Net Profit	1 750·00	
Land and Buildings	9 000·00		*Less* Drawings	1 500·00	
		13 241·00		250·00	
					12 015·00
		£16 934·25			£16 934·25

Unit Eight

Accounting to Final-Accounts Level
Part Five: Exercises to Final-Accounts Level

Exercises Set 9: Accounting to Final-Accounts Level— Part One

(1) Books of R. Todd (*SPA page 79*)

Capital A/c (R. Todd)   L 1

19..		£	19..		£
July 6	Drawings	50·00	July 1	Bank	500·00
6	Balance	585·25	6	Profit and Loss A/c	135·25
		£635·25			£635·25
			19..		£
			July 7	Balance	585·25

Bank A/c   L 2

19..		£	19..		£
July 1	Capital	500·00	July 1	Stall and Equipment	25·00
5	Cash	50·00	1	Purchases	34·00
			1	Stall and Equipment	12·50
			5	Purchases	16·50
			6	Balance	462·00
		£550·00			£550·00
19..		£			
July 7	Balance	462·00			

Stall and Equipment A/c   L 3

19..		£
July 1	Bank	25·00
1	Bank	12·50

Purchases A/c   L 4

19..		£	19..		£
July 1	Bank	34·00	July 6	Trading A/c	106·50
2	Cash	8·00			
3	Cash	26·50			
4	Cash	21·50			
5	Cash	16·50			
		£106·50			£106·50

Cash A/c   L 5

19..		£	19..		£
July 2	Sales	36·00	July 2	Purchases	8·00
3	Sales	42·00	2	Wages	2·00
4	Sales	13·00	3	Purchases	26·50
5	Sales	84·00	3	Light and Heat	2·00
6	Sales	62·50	3	Sundry Expenses	0·25
			4	Purchases	21·50
			4	Wages	2·00
			5	Wages	3·50
			5	Bank	50·00
			6	Wages	3·50
			6	Drawings	50·00
			6	Balance	68·25
		£237·50			£237·50
19..		£			
July 7	Balance	68·25			

Sales A/c   L 6

19..		£	19..		£
July 6	Trading A/c	237·50	July 2	Cash	36·00
			3	Cash	42·00
			4	Cash	13·00
			5	Cash	84·00
			6	Cash	62·50
		£237·50			£237·50

	Wages A/c		L 7
19..	£	19..	£
July 2 Cash	2·00	July 6 Profit and	
4 Cash	2·00	Loss A/c	11·00
5 Cash	3·50		
6 Cash	3·50		
	£11·00		£11·00

	Sundry Expenses A/c		L 8
19..	£	19..	£
July 3 Cash	0·25	July 6 Profit and	
		Loss A/c	0·25
	£0·25		£0·25

	Light and Heat A/c		L 9
19..	£	19..	£
July 3 Cash	2·00	July 6 Profit and	
		Loss A/c	2·00
	£2·00		£2·00

	Drawings A/c		L 10
19..	£	19..	£
July 6 Cash	50·00	July 6 Capital	50·00
	£50·00		£50·00

	Stock A/c	L 11
19..	£	
July 6 Trading A/c	17·50	

Trial Balance (as at July 1st 19..)

	Dr.	Cr.
	£	£
Capital		500·00
Bank	462·00	
Stall and Equipment	37·50	
Purchases	106·50	
Cash	68·25	
Sales		237·50
Wages	11·00	
Sundry Expenses	0·25	
Light and Heat	2·00	
Drawings	50·00	
	£737·50	737·50

Trading A/c (for week ending July 6th 19..)   L 12

19..	£	19..	£
Purchases	106·50	Sales	237·50
Less			
Closing Stock	17·50		
Cost of Stock			
Sold	89·00		
Gross Profit	148·50		
	£237·50		£237·50

Profit and Loss A/c (for week ending July 6th 19..)   L 13

19..	£	19..	£
Wages	11·00	Gross Profit	148·50
Light and Heat	2·00		
Sundry Expenses	0·25		
	13·25		
Net Profit	135·25		
(to Capital)			
	£148·50		£148·50

Balance Sheet (as at July 6th 19..)

	£	£		£	£
Fixed Assets			Capital		
Stall and Equipment		37·50	At Start		500·00
Current Assets			Net Profit	135·25	
Stock	17·50		*Less* Drawings	50·00	
Bank	462·00				85·25
Cash	68·25				
		547·75			585·25
		£585·25			£585·25

(2) Books of E. Carr (*SPA page* 79)

Capital (E. Carr) A/c   L 1

19..		£	19..		£
July 6	Drawings	40·00	July 1	Bank	1 500·00
	Balance		6	Profit and	
		1 735·05		Loss A/c	275·05
		£1 775·05			£1 775·05
			19..		£
			July 7	Balance	1 735·05

Bank A/c   L 2

19..		£	19..		£
July 1	Capital	1 500·00	July 1	Stall and	
4	Cash	100·00		Equipment	75·00
			1	Purchases	120·00
			1	Equipment	67·50
			4	Purchases	85·00
			6	Balance	1 252·50
		£1 600·00			£1 600·00
19..		£			
July 7	Balance	1 252·50			

Stall and Equipment A/c   L 3

19..		£
July 1	Bank	75·00
1	Bank	67·50

Purchases A/c   L 4

19..		£	19..		£
July 1	Bank	120·00	July 6	Trading A/c	322·00
2	Cash	18·00			
3	Cash	36·50			
4	Bank	85·00			
5	Cash	62·50			
		£322·00			£322·00

Cash A/c   L 5

19..		£	19..		£
July 2	Sales	84·00	July 2	Purchases	18·00
3	Sales	142·00	2	Wages	3·00
4	Sales	113·00	3	Purchases	36·50
5	Sales	94·00	3	Light and	
6	Sales	164·00		Heat	3·00
			3	Sundry	
				Expenses	0·25
			4	Wages	2·00
			4	Bank	100·00
			5	Purchases	62·50
			5	Wages	8·50
			6	Wages	17·20
			6	Drawings	40·00
			6	Balance	306·05
		£597·00			£597·00
19..		£			
July 7	Balance	306·05			

Sales A/c   L 6

19..		£	19..		£
July 6	Trading		July 2	Cash	84·00
	A/c	597·00	3	Cash	142·00
			4	Cash	113·00
			5	Cash	94·00
			6	Cash	164·00
		£597·00			£597·00

Wages A/c			L 7
19..	£	19..	£
July 2 Cash	3·00	July 6 Profit and	
4 Cash	2·00	Loss A/c	30·70
5 Cash	8·50		
6 Cash	17·20		
	£30·70		£30·70

Sundry Expenses A/c			L 8
19..	£	19..	£
July 3 Cash	0·25	July 6 Profit and	
		Loss A/c	0.25

Light and Heat A/c			L 9
19..	£	19..	£
July 3 Cash	3·00	July 6 Profit and	
		Loss A/c	3·00

Drawings A/c			L 10
19..	£	19..	£
July 6 Cash	40·00	July 6 Capital	40·00
	£40·00		£40·00

Stock A/c		L 11
19..	£	
July 6 Trading		
A/c	34·00	

Trial Balance (as at July 6th 19..)

	Dr.	Cr.
	£	£
Capital		1 500·00
Bank	1 252·50	
Stalls and Equipment	142·50	
Purchases	322·00	
Cash	306·05	
Sales		597·00
Wages	30·70	
Light and Heat	3·00	
Sundry Expenses	0·25	
Drawings	40·00	
	£2 097·00	2 097·00

Trading A/c L 12
(week ending July 6th 19..)

	£		£
Purchases	322·00	Sales	597·00
Less			
Closing Stock	34·00		
Cost of Stock			
Sold	288·00		
Gross Profit	309·00		
	£597·00		£597·00

Profit and Loss A/c L 13
(week ending July 6th 19..)

	£		£
Wages	30·70	Gross Profit	309·00
Light and Heat	3·00		
Sundry Expenses	0·25		
	33·95		
Net Profit	275·05		
(to Capital A/c)			
	£309·00		£309·00

Balance Sheet (as at July 6th 19..)

	£	£		£	£
Fixed Assets			Capital		
Stalls and Equipment		142·50	At Start		1 500·00
Current Assets			Net Profit	275·05	
Stock	34·00		*Less* Drawings	40·00	
Bank	1 252·50				235·05
Cash	306·05				1 735·05
		1 592·55			
		£1 735·05			£1 735·05

(3) Books of M. Tapley (*SPA page 79*)

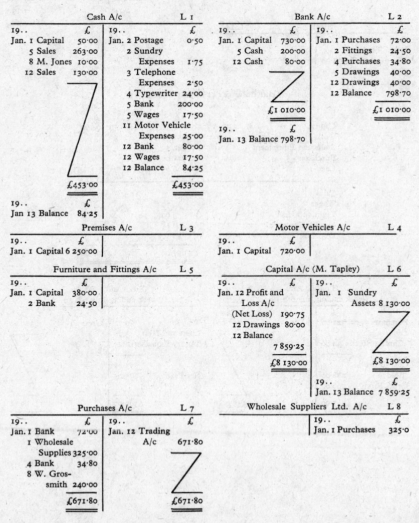

Cash A/c				L 1
19..	£	19..		£
Jan. 1 Capital	50·00	Jan. 2 Postage		0·50
5 Sales	263·00	2 Sundry		
8 M. Jones	10·00	Expenses		1·75
12 Sales	130·00	3 Telephone		
		Expenses		2·50
		4 Typewriter	24·00	
		5 Bank	200·00	
		5 Wages	17·50	
		11 Motor Vehicle		
		Expenses	25·00	
		12 Bank	80·00	
		12 Wages	17·50	
		12 Balance	84·25	
	£453·00		£453·00	
19..	£			
Jan 13 Balance	84·25			

Bank A/c				L 2
19..	£	19..		£
Jan. 1 Capital	730·00	Jan. 1 Purchases		72·00
5 Cash	200·00	2 Fittings		24·50
12 Cash	80·00	4 Purchases		34·80
		5 Drawings		40·00
		12 Drawings		40·00
		12 Balance		798·70
	£1 010·00			£1 010·00
19..	£			
Jan. 13 Balance	798·70			

Premises A/c		L 3
19..	£	
Jan. 1 Capital	6 250·00	

Motor Vehicles A/c		L 4
19..	£	
Jan. 1 Capital	720·00	

Furniture and Fittings A/c		L 5
19..	£	
Jan. 1 Capital	380·00	
2 Bank	24·50	

Capital A/c (M. Tapley)			L 6
19..	£	19..	£
Jan. 12 Profit and		Jan. 1 Sundry	
Loss A/c		Assets	8 130·00
(Net Loss)	190·75		
12 Drawings	80·00		
12 Balance			
7 859·25			
£8 130·00		£8 130·00	
		19..	£
		Jan. 13 Balance	7 859·25

Purchases A/c				L 7
19..	£	19..		£
Jan. 1 Bank	72·00	Jan. 12 Trading		
1 Wholesale		A/c		671·80
Supplies	325·00			
4 Bank	34·80			
8 W. Gros-				
smith	240·00			
	£671·80		£671·80	

Wholesale Suppliers Ltd. A/c		L 8
	19..	£
	Jan. 1 Purchases	325·0

	Postage A/c		L 9
19..	£	19..	£
Jan. 2 Cash	0·50	Jan. 12 Profit and	
		Loss A/c	0·50
	£0·50		£0·50

	Sundry Expenses A/c		L 10
19..	£	19..	£
Jan. 2 Cash	1·75	Jan. 12 Profit and	
		Loss A/c	1·75
	£1·75		£1·75

	M. Jones A/c		L 11
19..	£	19..	£
Jan. 3 Sales	42·50	Jan. 8 Cash	10·00
9 Sales	62·30	12 Balance	94·80
	£104·80		£104·80
19..	£		
Jan. 13 Balance	94·80		

	Sales A/c		L 12
19..	£	19..	£
Jan. 12 Trading		Jan. 3 M. Jones	42·50
A/c	497·80	5 Cash	263·00
		9 M. Jones	62·30
		12 Cash	130·00
	£497·80		£497·80

	Telephone Expenses A/c		L 13
19..	£	19..	£
Jan. 3 Cash	2·50	Jan. 12 Profit and	
		Loss A/c	2·50
	£2·50		£2·50

	Typewriter A/c		L 14
19..	£		
Jan. 4 Cash	24·00		

	Wages A/c		L 15
19..	£	19..	£
Jan. 5 Cash	17·50	Jan. 12 Profit and	
12 Cash	17·50	Loss A/c	35·00
	£35·00		£35·00

	Drawings A/c		L 19
19..	£	19..	£
Jan. 5 Bank	40·00	Jan. 12 Capital	80·00
12 Bank	40·00		
	£80·00		£80·00

	W. Grossmith A/c		L 17
		19..	£
		Jan. 8 Purchases	240·00

	Motor Vehicle Expenses A/c		L 18
19..	£	19..	£
Jan. 11 Cash	25·00	Jan. 12 Profit and	
		Loss A/c	25·00
	£25·00		£25·00

	Stock A/c		L 19
19..	£		
Jan. 12 Trading			
A/c	48·00		

Trial Balance (as at January 12th 19..)

	Dr. £	Cr. £
Cash	84·25	
Bank	798·70	
Premises	6 250·00	
Motor Vehicles	720·00	
Furniture and Fittings	404·50	
Capital		8 130·00
Purchases	671·80	
Wholesale Suppliers Ltd.		325·00
Postage	0·50	
Sundry Expenses	1·75	
M. Jones	94·80	
Sales		497·80
Telephone Expenses	2·50	
Typewriter	24·00	
Wages	35·00	
Drawings	80·00	
W. Grossmith		240·00
Motor Vehicle Expenses	25·00	
	£9 192·80	9 192·80

Trading A/c — L 19
(for fortnight ending January 12th 19..)

	£		£
Purchases	671·80	Sales	497·80
Less		Gross Loss	126·00
Closing Stock	48·00		
Cost of			
Stock Sold	£623·80		£623·80

Profit and Loss A/c — L 20
(for fortnight ending January 12th 19..)

	£		£
Gross Loss	126·00	Net Loss (to	
Wages	35·00	Capital A/c)	190·75
Postage	0·50		
Sundry Expenses	1·75		
Telephone			
Expenses	2·50		
Motor Vehicle			
Expenses	25·00		
	£190·75		£190·75

Balance Sheet (as at January 12th 19..)

	£	£		£	£
Fixed Assets			Capital		
Premises		6 250·00	At Start		8 130·00
Furniture and Fittings		404·50	Less Net Loss	190·75	
Typewriters		24·00	and Drawings	80·00	
Motor Vehicles		720·00			270·75
		7 398·50			7 859·25
Current Assets					
Stock	48·00				
M. Jones	94·80		Current Liabilities		
Bank	798·70		Creditors		565·00
Cash	84·25				
		1 025·75			
		£8 424·25			£8 424·25

Advice to M. Tapley

This short trading period has proved unprofitable. Tapley should question the causes of this. In the early stages of a business enterprise it may be necessary to sustain losses while the business is built up, but at least what is sold should be profitable. In this case it is not (see Trading Account). Selling prices are too low, and must be raised. If this is impossible because the trade is very competitive, Tapley should insist on cheaper prices from his suppliers, or cease trading.

(4) Books of R. Quilp (SPA page 80)

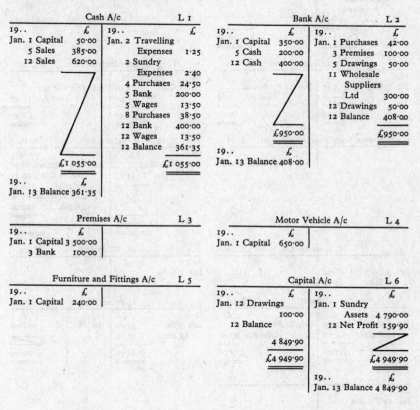

Cash A/c			L 1
19..	£	19..	£
Jan. 1 Capital	50·00	Jan. 2 Travelling	
5 Sales	385·00	Expenses	1·25
12 Sales	620·00	2 Sundry	
		Expenses	2·40
		4 Purchases	24·50
		5 Bank	200·00
		5 Wages	13·50
		8 Purchases	38·50
		12 Bank	400·00
		12 Wages	13·50
		12 Balance	361·35
	£1 055·00		£1 055·00
19..	£		
Jan. 13 Balance	361·35		

Bank A/c			L 2
19..	£	19..	£
Jan. 1 Capital	350·00	Jan. 1 Purchases	42·00
5 Cash	200·00	3 Premises	100·00
12 Cash	400·00	5 Drawings	50·00
		11 Wholesale	
		Suppliers	
		Ltd	300·00
		12 Drawings	50·00
	£950·00	12 Balance	408·00
19..	£		£950·00
Jan. 13 Balance	408·00		

Premises A/c			L 3
19..	£		
Jan. 1 Capital	3 500·00		
3 Bank	100·00		

Motor Vehicle A/c			L 4
19..	£		
Jan. 1 Capital	650·00		

Furniture and Fittings A/c			L 5
19..	£		
Jan. 1 Capital	240·00		

Capital A/c			L 6
19..	£	19..	£
Jan. 12 Drawings		Jan. 1 Sundry	
	100·00	Assets	4 790·00
12 Balance		12 Net Profit	159·90
	4 849·90		
	£4 949·90		£4 949·90
		19..	£
		Jan. 13 Balance	4 849·90

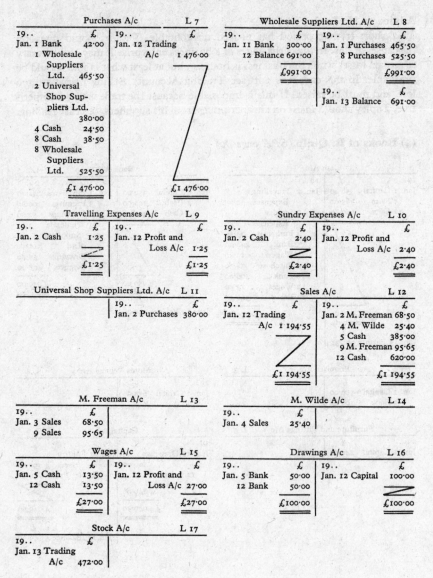

	Purchases A/c		L 7
19..	£	19..	£
Jan. 1 Bank	42·00	Jan. 12 Trading	
1 Wholesale		A/c	1 476·00
Suppliers			
Ltd.	465·50		
2 Universal			
Shop Sup-			
pliers Ltd.			
	380·00		
4 Cash	24·50		
8 Cash	38·50		
8 Wholesale			
Suppliers			
Ltd.	525·50		
	£1 476·00		£1 476·00

	Wholesale Suppliers Ltd. A/c		L 8
19..	£	19..	£
Jan. 11 Bank	300·00	Jan. 1 Purchases	465·50
12 Balance	691·00	8 Purchases	525·50
	£991·00		£991·00
		19..	£
		Jan. 13 Balance	691·00

	Travelling Expenses A/c		L 9
19..	£	19..	£
Jan. 2 Cash	1·25	Jan. 12 Profit and	
		Loss A/c	1·25
	£1·25		£1·25

	Sundry Expenses A/c		L 10
19..	£	19..	£
Jan. 2 Cash	2·40	Jan. 12 Profit and	
		Loss A/c	2·40
	£2·40		£2·40

	Universal Shop Suppliers Ltd. A/c		L 11
		19..	£
		Jan. 2 Purchases	380·00

	Sales A/c		L 12
19..	£	19..	£
Jan. 12 Trading		Jan. 2 M. Freeman	68·50
A/c	1 194·55	4 M. Wilde	25·40
		5 Cash	385·00
		9 M. Freeman	95·65
		12 Cash	620·00
	£1 194·55		£1 194·55

	M. Freeman A/c		L 13
19..	£		
Jan. 3 Sales	68·50		
9 Sales	95·65		

	M. Wilde A/c		L 14
19..	£		
Jan. 4 Sales	25·40		

	Wages A/c		L 15
19..	£	19..	£
Jan. 5 Cash	13·50	Jan. 12 Profit and	
12 Cash	13·50	Loss A/c	27·00
	£27·00		£27·00

	Drawings A/c		L 16
19..	£	19..	£
Jan. 5 Bank	50·00	Jan. 12 Capital	100·00
12 Bank	50·00		
	£100·00		£100·00

	Stock A/c		L 17
19..	£		
Jan. 13 Trading			
A/c	472·00		

Trial Balance (as at January 12th 19..)

	Dr. £	Cr. £
Cash	361·35	
Bank	408·00	
Premises	3 600·00	
Motor Vehicles	650·00	
Furniture and Fittings	240·00	
Capital		4 790·00
Purchases and Sales	1 476·00	1 194·55
Wholesale Suppliers Ltd.		691·00
Travelling Expenses	1·25	
Sundry Expenses	2·40	
Universal Shop Suppliers Ltd.		380·00
M. Freeman	164·15	
M. Wilde	25·40	
Wages	27·00	
Drawings	100·00	
	£7 055·55	7 055·55

Trading A/c   L 18
(for 2 weeks ending January 12th 19..)

	£		£
Purchases	1 476·00	Sales	1 194·55
Less			
Closing Stock	472·00		
	1 004·00		
Gross Profit	190·55		
	£1 194·55		£1 194·55

Profit and Loss A/c   L 19
(for 2 weeks ending January 12th 19..)

	£		£
Travelling Expenses	1·25	Gross Profit	190·55
Sundry Expenses	2·40		
Wages	27·00		
	30·65		
Net Profit (to Capital A/c)	159·90		
	£190·55		£190·55

Balance Sheet (as at January 12th 19..)

Fixed Assets	£	£	£	Capital		£	£
Premises			3 600·00	At Start			4 790·00
Furniture and Fittings			240·00	Net Profit		159·90	
Motor Vehicles			650·00	Less Drawings		100·00	
			4 490·00				59·90
							4 849·90
Current Assets							
Stock		472·00					
Debtors				Current Liabilities			
M. Freeman	164·15			Creditors			
M. Wilde	25·40			Wholesale Suppliers Ltd.		691·00	
		189·55		Universal Shop Suppliers			
Cash at Bank		408·00		Ltd.		380·00	
Cash in Hand		361·35					1 071·00
			1 430·90				
			£5 920·90				£5 920·90

Advice to Quilp

This short trading period has proved profitable, and he should carry on trading, but he has taken on large debts to two suppliers. As he has insufficient funds to cover these debts he should watch the situation carefully and not re-order until his cash position improves.

(5) Books of R. Bingham (*SPA page 81*)

Motor Vehicles A/c		L 1
19..	£	
Apr. 1 Capital	530·00	

Furniture and Fittings A/c		L 2
19..	£	
Apr. 1 Capital	275·00	
1 Bank	25·50	
2 Bank	70·00	

Premises A/c		L 3
19..	£	
Apr. 1 Capital	3 800·00	

Cash A/c				L 4
19..	£	19..		£
Apr. 1 Capital	24·50	Apr. 6 Travelling		
6 Sales	165·50		Expenses	1·25
13 Sales	238·25	10 Typewriter		32·50
20 Sales	167·75	10 Stationery		6·55
27 Sales	245·50	13 Bank		200·00
		16 Wages		42·00
		23 Fares		2·25
		27 Bank		200·00
		29 Postage		0·25
		29 Repairs		1·65
		30 Wages		42·00
		30 Balance		313·05
	£841·50			£841·50
19..	£			
May 1 Balance	313·05			

Bank A/c			L 5
19..	£	19..	£
Apr. 1 Capital	725·50	Apr. 1 Purchases	150·00
13 Cash	200·00	1 Furniture and	
27 Cash	200·00	Fittings	25·50
		2 Furniture and	
		Fittings	70·00
		8 Purchases	65·50
		12 Purchases	240·00
		30 Drawings	120·00
		30 T. Lines	75·00
		30 Balance	379·50
	£1 125·50		£1 125·50
19..	£		
May 1 Balance	379·50		

Capital A/c			L 6
19..	£	19..	£
Apr. 30 Drawings		Apr. 1 Sundry	
	120·00	Assets	5 355·00
30 Balance		30 Net Profit	189·05
	5 424·05		
	£5 544·05		£5 544·05
		19..	£
		May 1 Balance	5 424·05

Purchases A/c			L 7
19..	£	19..	£
Apr. 1 Bank	150·00	Apr. 30 Trading	
2 T. Lines	75·00	A/c	716·00
8 Bank	65·50		
12 Bank	240·00		
20 T. Lines	185·50		
	£716·00		£716·00

T. Lines A/c			L 8
19..	£	19..	£
Apr. 30 Bank	75·00	Apr. 2 Purchases	75·00
30 Balance	185·50	20 Purchases	185·50
	£260·50		£260·50
		19..	£
		May 1 Balance	185·50

	Sales A/c		L 9
19..	£	19..	£
Apr. 30 Trading		Apr. 6 Cash	165·50
A/c	885·00	8 R. French	25·50
		12 T. Tozer	42·50
		13 Cash	238·25
		20 Cash	167·75
		27 Cash	245·50
	£885·00		£885·00

	Travelling Expenses A/c		L 10
19..	£	19..	£
Apr. 6 Cash	1·25	Apr. 30 Profit and	
23 Cash	2·25	Loss A/c	3·50
	£3·50		£3·50

	R. French A/c	L 11
19..	£	
Apr. 8 Sales	25·50	

	Typewriter A/c	L 12
19..	£	
Apr. 10 Cash	32·50	

	Stationery A/c		L 13
19..	£	19..	£
Apr. 10 Cash	6·55	Apr. 30 Profit and	
		Loss A/c	6·55
	£6·55		£6·55

	T. Tozer A/c	L 14
19..	£	
Apr. 12 Sales	42·50	

	Wages A/c		L 15
19..	£	19..	£
Apr. 16 Cash	42·00	Apr. 30 Profit and	
30 Cash	42·00	Loss A/c	84·00
	£84·00		£84·00

	Postage A/c		L 16
19..	£	19..	£
Apr. 29 Cash	0·25	Apr. 30 Profit and	
		Loss A/c	0·25
	£0·25		£0·25

	Repairs A/c		L 17
19..	£	19..	£
Apr. 29 Cash	1·65	Apr. 30 Profit and	
		Loss A/c	1·65
	£1·65		£1·65

	Drawings A/c		L 18
19..	£	19..	£
Apr. 30 Bank	120·00	Apr. 30 Capital	
		A/c	120·00
	£120·00		£120·00

	Stock A/c	L 19
19..	£	
Apr. 30 Trading		
A/c	116·00	

Trial Balance (as at April 30th 19..)

	Dr. £	Cr. £
Motor Vehicles	530·00	
Furniture and Fittings	370·50	
Premises	3 800·00	
Cash	313·05	
Bank	379·50	
Capital		5 355·00
Purchases	716·00	
T. Lines		185·50
Sales		885·00
Travelling Expenses	3·50	
R. French	25·50	
Typewriters	32·50	
Stationery	6·55	
T. Tozer	42·50	
Wages	84·00	
Postage	0·25	
Repairs	1·65	
Drawings	120·00	
	£6 425·50	6 425·50

Trading A/c
(for month ended April 30th 19..)

	£		£
Purchases	716·00	Sales	885·00
Less			
Closing Stock	116·00		
Cost of Stock Sold	600·00		
Gross Profit	285·00		
	£885·00		£885·00

Profit and Loss A/c
(for month ended April 30th 19..)

	£		£
Travelling Expenses	3·50	Gross Profit	285·00
Stationery	6·55		
Wages	84·00		
Postage	0·25		
Repairs	1·65		
	95·95		
Net Profit	189·05		
(to Capital A/c)			
	£285·00		£285·00

Balance Sheet (as at April 30th 19..)

	£	£		£	£
Fixed Assets			Capital		
Premises		3 800·00	At Start		5 355·00
Furniture and Fittings		370·50	Net Profit	189·05	
Motor Vehicles		530·00	Less Drawings	120·00	
Typewriters		32·50			69·05
		4 733·00			5 424·05
Current Assets					
Stock	116·00				
Debtors	68·00				
Cash at Bank	379·50		Current Liabilities		
Cash in Hand	313·05		Creditors		185·50
		876·55			
		£5 609·55			£5 609·55

(6) Books of M. Day (*SPA page 81*)

Motor Vehicles A/c		L 1
19..	£	
Jan. 1 Capital	650·00	

Furniture and Fittings A/c		L 2
19..	£	
Jan. 1 Capital	230·00	
1 Cash	3·55	
12 Cash	12·25	
23 Cash	27·50	

Premises A/c		L 3
19..	£	
Jan. 1 Capital	4 200·00	

Cash A/c				L 4
19..	£	19..		£
Jan. 1 Capital	35·00	Jan .1 Fittings		3·55
6 Sales	84·75	6 Postage		0·25
13 Sales	172·50	8 Sundry		
20 Sales	163·80		Expenses	2·55
27 Sales	236·50	10 Repairs		2·25
		12 Fittings		12·25
		13 Bank		150·00
		20 Bank		100·00
		22 Wages		3·25
		23 Fittings		27·50
		27 Bank		200·00
		29 Postage		0·35
		30 Wages		7·50
		31 Balance		183·10
	£692·55			£692·55
19..	£			
Feb. 1 Balance	183·10			

Bank A/c				L 5
19..	£	19..		£
Jan. 1 Capital	475·00	Jan. 1 Purchases		250·00
13 Cash	150·00	6 Telephone		
20 Cash	100·00		Expenses	2·50
27 Cash	200·00	30 Drawings		100·00
		30 Advertise-		
			ment	12·10
		30 Remington		
			Ltd.	48·50
		31 Balance		511·90
	£925·00			£925·00
19..	£			
Feb. 1 Balance	511·90			

Capital A/c				L 6
19..	£	19..		£
Jan. 31 Drawings		Jan. 1 Sundry		
	100·00		Assets	5 590·00
31 Balance		31 Net Profit		294·30
	5 784·30			
	£5 884·30			£5 884·30
		19..		£
		Feb. 1 Balance		5 784·30

Purchases A/c			L 7
19..	£	19..	£
Jan. 1 Bank	250·00	Jan. 31 Trading A/c	
2 R. Lyons	75·50		485·50
16 R. Lyons	160·00		
	£485·50		£485·50

R. Lyons A/c		L 8
	19..	£
	Jan. 2 Purchases	75·50
	16 Purchases	160·00

Typwriters A/c		L 9
19..	£	
Jan. 2 Remington's		
	48·50	

Remington's A/c			L 10
19..	£	19..	£
Jan. 30 Bank	48·50	Jan. 2 Typewriters	48·50
	£48·50		£48·50

	Sales A/c		L 11
19..	£	19..	£
Jan. 31 Trading		Jan. 6 Cash	84·75
A/c	755·05	8 Mowler, Tooth	
		and Co.	42·50
		13 Cash	172·50
		20 Cash	163·80
		27 Cash	236·50
		29 R. White	55·00
	£755·05		£755·05

	Postage A/c		L 12
19..	£	19..	£
Jan. 6 Cash	0·25	Jan. 31 Profit and	
29 Cash	0·35	Loss A/c	0·60
	£0·60		£0·60

	Telephone A/c		L 13
19..	£	19..	£
Jan. 6 Bank	2·50	Jan. 31 Profit and	
		Loss A/c	2·50
	£2·50		£2·50

	Sundry Expenses A/c		L 14
19..	£	19..	£
Jan. 8 Cash	2·55	Jan. 31 Profit and	
		Loss A/c	2·55
	£2·55		£2·55

	Mowler, Tooth and Co. A/c		L 15
19..	£		
Jan. 8 Sales	42·50		

	Repairs A/c		L 16
19..	£	19..	£
Jan. 10 Cash	2·25	Jan. 31 Profit and	
		Loss A/c	2·25
	£2·25		£2·25

	Wages A/c		L 17
19..	£	19..	£
Jan. 22 Cash	3·25	Jan. 31 Profit and	
30 Cash	7·50	Loss A/c	10·75
	£10·75		£10·75

	R. White A/c		L 18
19..	£		
Jan. 29 Sales	55·00		

	Advertising A/c		L 19
19..	£	19..	£
Jan. 30 Bank	12·10	Jan. 31 Profit and	
		Loss A/c	12·10
	£12·10		£12·10

	Drawings A/c		L 20
19..	£	19..	£
Jan. 30 Bank	100·00	Jan. 31 Capital	100·00

	Stock A/c		L 21
19..	£		
Jan. 31 Trading			
A/c	55·50		

Trial Balance (as at January 31st 19..)

	Dr. £	Cr. £
Motor Vehicles	650·00	
Furniture and Fittings	273·30	
Premises	4 200·00	
Cash	183·10	
Bank	511·90	
Capital		5 590·00
Purchases	485·50	
R. Lyons		235·50
Typewriters	48·50	
Sales		755·05
Postage	0·60	
Telephone	2·50	
Sundry Expenses	2·55	
Mowler, Tooth and Co.	42·50	
Repairs	2·25	
Wages	10·75	
R. White	55·00	
Advertising	12·10	
Drawings	100·00	
	£6 580·55	6 580·55

Trading A/c   L 22
(for month ending January 31st 19..)

	£		£
Purchases	485·50	Sales	755·05
Less			
Closing Stock	55·50		
	430·00		
Gross Profit	325·05		
	£755·05		£755·05

Profit and Loss A/c   L 23
(for month ending January 31st 19..)

	£		£
Postage	0·60	Gross Profit	325·05
Telephone	2·50		
Sundry Expenses	2·55		
Repairs	2·25		
Wages	10·75		
Advertising	12·10		
	30·75		
Net Profit	294·30		
	£325·05		£325·05

Balance Sheet (as at January 31st 19..)

	£	£		£	£
Fixed Assets			Capital		
Premises		4 200·00	At Start		5 590·00
Furniture and Fittings		273·30	Net Profit	294·30	
Motor Vehicles		650·00	Less Drawings	100·00	
Typewriters		48·50			194·30
		5 171·80			5 784·30
Current Assets					
Closing Stock	55·50				
R. White	55·00				
Mowler, Tooth and Co.	42·50		Current Liability		
Bank	511·90		R. Lyons		235·50
Cash	183·10				
		848·00			
		£6 019·80			£6 019·80

Exercises Set 10: Accounting to Final-Accounts Level—Part Two

(1) Books of M. Davies (*SPA page 83*)

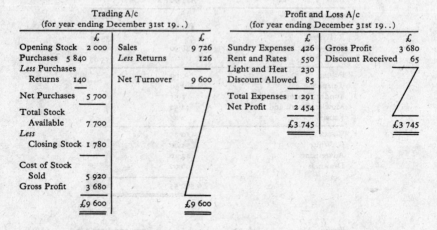

	Trading A/c (for year ending December 31st 19..)		
	£		£
Opening Stock	2 000	Sales	9 726
Purchases 5 840		*Less* Returns	126
Less Purchases			
Returns 140		Net Turnover	9 600
Net Purchases	5 700		
Total Stock			
Available	7 700		
Less			
Closing Stock 1 780			
Cost of Stock			
Sold	5 920		
Gross Profit	3 680		
	£9 600		£9 600

	Profit and Loss A/c (for year ending December 31st 19..)		
	£		£
Sundry Expenses	426	Gross Profit	3 680
Rent and Rates	550	Discount Received	65
Light and Heat	230		
Discount Allowed	85		
Total Expenses	1 291		
Net Profit	2 454		
	£3 745		£3 745

Balance Sheet (as at December 31st 19..)					
	£	£		£	£
Fixed Assets			Capital		
Land and Buildings		4 500	At Start		6 656
Furniture and Fittings		380	Net Profit	2 454	
Motor Vehicles		750	*Less* Drawings	1 500	
		5 630			954
Current Assets					7 610
Stock	1 780				
Debtors	495				
Cash at Bank	800		Current Liabilities		
Cash in Hand	200		Creditors		1 295
		3 275			
		£8 905			£8 905

(2) Books of P. Robinson (*SPA page 84*)

Trading A/c
(for year ended March 31st 19..)

	£		£
Opening Stock 2 175		Sales	21 155
Purchases 10 250		*Less* Returns	355
Less Returns 650			
			20 800
Net Purchases 9 600			
Total Stock			
Available 11 775			
Less			
Closing Stock 2 250			
Cost of Stock			
Sold 9 525			
Warehouse			
Wages 2 135			
Warehouse			
Expenses 108			
	2 243		
Cost of Sales 11 768			
Gross Profit 9 032			
	£20 800		£20 800

Profit and Loss A/c
(for year ended March 31st 19..)

	£			£
Sundry Expenses 2 640		Gross Profit		9 032
Selling Expenses 1 255		Discount Received		88
Interest Paid 65		Commission		
Discount Allowed 172		Received		255
Total Expenses 4 132				9 375
Net Profit 5 243				
	£9 375			£9 375

Balance Sheet (as at March 31st 19..)

	£	£		£	£
Fixed Assets			Capital		
Premises		5 240	At Start		4 937
Fixtures and Fittings		430	Net Profit	5 243	
Motor Vehicles		1 850	*Less* Drawings	950	
		7 520			4 293
					9 230
Current Assets					
Stock	2 250		Long-term Liabilities		
Debtors	1 555		Loan (A. Colleague)		1 300
Cash at Bank	950		Current Liabilities		
Cash in Hand	50		Creditors		1 795
		4 805			
		£12 325			£12 325

(3) Books of T. Ford (*SPA page 85*)

Trading A/c
(for year ending December 31st 18..)

	£		£
Opening Stock	1 850	Sales	17 550
Purchases	11 800	*Less* Returns	150
Carriage In	40		
			17 400
	11 840		
Less Purchases			
Returns	100		
Net Purchases	11 740		
Total Stock			
Available	13 590		
Less			
Closing Stock	2 000		
Cost of Stock			
Sold	11 590		
Warehouse Ex-			
penses	895		
Cost of Sales	12 485		
Gross Profit	4 915		
	£17 400		£17 400

Profit and Loss A/c
(for year ending December 31st 19..)

	£		£
Rent, Rates and		Gross Profit	4 915
Insurance	725	Commission	
Heat, Light and		Received	285
Fuel	480	Fees Received	1 245
Petrol and Oil	254		
Motor Vehicle			6 445
Repairs	126		
Cleaning Expenses	72		
Repairs and			
Redecorations	234		
Interest Paid	420		
Total Expenses	2 311		
Net Profit	4 134		
	£6 445		£6 445

Balance Sheet (as at December 31st 19..)

	£	£		£	£
Fixed Assets			Capital		
Land and Buildings		5 000	At Start		3 816
Furniture and Fittings		840	Net Profit	4 134	
Fork Lift Trucks		1 220	*Less* Drawings	1 850	
					2 284
		7 060			6 100
Current Assets					
Closing Stock	2 000		Long-term Liabilities		
Debtors	425		Mortgage on Premises		3 000
Cash at Bank	850		Current Liabilities		
Cash in Hand	150		Creditors		1 385
		3 425			
		£10 485			£10 485

(4) Books of R. Maycock (*SPA page 86*)

Trading A/c
(for year ending December 31st 19..)

	£		£
Opening Stock	850·75	Sales	11 246·50
Purchases		*Less* Returns	146·50
	5 725·50		
Carriage			11 100·00
In	35·75		
	5 761·25		
Less			
Rtns	125·50		
Net Purchases	5 635·75		
Total Stock			
Available	6 486·50		
Less Closing			
Stock	1 000·00		
Cost of Stock			
Sold	5 486·50		
Warehouse			
Expenses	425·25		
Cost of Sales	5 911·75		
Gross Profit	5 188·25		
	£11 100·00		£11 100·00

Profit and Loss A/c
(for year ending December 31st 19..)

	£		£
Rents, Rates and		Gross Profit	5 188·25
Insurance	136·50	Commission	
Light, Heat and		Received	175·50
Fuel	149·75	Fees Received	1 250·00
Petrol and Oil	235·25		
Motor Vehicle			6 613·75
Repairs	62·50		
Cleaning			
Expenses	148·50		
Repairs and			
Redecorations	230·65		
Interest Paid	336·50		
Total Expenses			
	1 299·65		
Net Profit	5 314·10		
	£6 613·75		£6 613·75

Balance Sheet (as at December 31st 19..)

	£			£
Fixed Assets		Capital		
Land and Buildings	6 250·00	At Start		2 848·05
Furniture and Fittings	1 385·80	Net Profit	5 314·10	
Fork Lift Trucks	1 485·50	*Less* Drawings	1 450·00	
	9 121·30			3 864·10
				6 712·15
Current Assets				
Stock	1 000·00	Long-term Liability		
Debtors	247·35	Mortgage (secured on premises)		4 000·00
Cash at Bank	975·00	Current Liabilities		
Cash in Hand	25·00	Creditors		656·50
	2 247·35			
	£11 368·65			£11 368·65

(5) Books of A. Brewis (*SPA page 87*)

Trading A/c
(for year ending March 31st 19..)

	£		£
Opening Stock	4 650	Sales	44 725
Purchases 27 246		*Less* Returns	725
Carriage In			
180			44 000
27 426			
Less			
Returns 1 266			
Net Purchases	26 160		
Total Stock			
Available	30 810		
Less			
Closing Stock	5 450		
Cost of Stock			
Sold	25 360		
Gross Profit	18 640		
	£44 000		£44 000

Profit and Loss A/c
(for year ending March 31st 19..)

	£		£
Carriage Out	325	Gross Profit	18 640
Rent and Rates	1 420	Discount Received	86
Insurance	148	Commission	
Light and Heat	1 630	Received	2 469
Discount Allowed	125		21 195
Commission Paid			
	1 095		
Salaries	5 854		
	10 597		
Net Profit	10 598		
	£21 195		£21 195

Balance Sheet (as at March 31st 19..)

	£	£		£	£
Fixed Assets			Capital		
Land and Buildings		10 750	At Start		9 600
Furniture and Fittings		1 250	Net Profit	10 598	
Motor Vehicles		1 480	*Less* Drawings	1 625	
		13 480			8 973
Current Assets					18 573
Stock	5 450		Long-term Liabilities		
Debtors	2 760		Loan (R. Petworth)		5 000
Cash at Bank	2 745		Current Liabilities		
Cash in Hand	138		Creditors		1 000
		11 093			
		£24 573			£24 573

(6) Books of E. London (*SPA page 88*)

<table>
<tr><td colspan="2" align="center">Trading A/c
(for year ending December 31st 19..)</td><td colspan="2" align="center">Profit and Loss A/c
(for year ending December 31st 19..)</td></tr>
</table>

	£		£
Opening Stock		Sales	25 624·30
	2 000·00	*Less* Returns	624·30
Purchases			
12 580·50			25 000·00
Carriage			
In 120·50			
12 701·00			
Less			
Rtns 580·50			
Net Pur-			
chases 12 120·50			
Total Stock			
Available 14 120·50			
Less Closing			
Stock 2 500·00			
Cost of Stock			
Sold 11 620·50			
Warehouse Wages			
1 480·50			
Warehouse Expenses			
338·75			
	1 819·25		
Cost of Sales 13 439·75			
Gross Profit 11 560·25			
£25 000·00		**£25 000·00**	

	£		£
Light and Heat 240·50		Gross Profit	11 560·25
Rent and Rates		Rent Received	240·00
	1 248·00		
Telephone			11 800·25
Expenses 86·55			
Insurance 48·50			
Selling Expenses			
	726·30		
Motor Vehicle			
Expenses 241·55			
Travellers'			
Salaries 3 865·25			
Office Salaries			
	1 585·50		
Total Expenses			
	8 042·15		
Net Profit 3 758·10			
	£11 800·25		**£11 800·25**

Balance Sheet (as at December 31st 19..)

	£	£		£	£
Fixed Assets			Capital		
Land and Buildings		11 250·00	At Start		7 811·10
Furniture and Fittings		870·50	Net Profit	3 758·10	
Plant and Machinery		3 150·00	*Less* Drawings	1 650·00	
		15 270·50			2 108·10
					9 919·20
Current Assets			Long-term Liabilities		
Stock	2 500·00		Mortgage	7 250·00	
Debtors	842·00		Bank Loan	1 000·00	
Cash at Bank	1 150·00				8 250·00
Cash in Hand	142·70		Current Liabilities		
		4 634·70	Creditors		1 736·00
		£19 905·20			**£19 905·20**

Unit Nine

Books of Original Entry
Part One: The Journal

Exercises Set 11: Opening Journal Entries

(1) Books of R. Marshall (*SPA page 94*)

19..				£	£
Jan.	1	Bank A/c Dr.	L 1	1 000·00	
		Capital A/c (R. Marshall)	L 2		1 000·00
		Being capital contributed by the proprietor, R. Marshall, at this date		£1 000·00	£1 000·00

Bank A/c	L 1		Capital A/c (R. Marshall)	L 2
19.. £			19.. £	
Jan. 1 Capital 1 000·00			Jan. 1 Capital 1 000·00	

(2) Books of M. Leghorn (*SPA page 94*)

19..				£	£
June	1	Bank A/c Dr.	L 1	2 500·00	
		Capital A/c (M. Leghorn)	L 2		2 500·00
		Being capital contributed by the proprietor, M. Leghorn, at this date		£2 500·00	£2 500·00

Bank A/c	L 1		Capital A/c (M. Leghorn)	L 2
19.. £			19.. £	
June 1 Capital 2 500·00			June 1 Bank 2 500·00	

(3) Books of M. Tyler (*SPA page 94*)

19..				£	£
Jan.	1	Cash A/c Dr.	L 1	24·00	
		Bank A/c Dr.	L 2	125·00	
		Premises A/c Dr.	L 3	2 500·00	
		Motor Vehicles A/c Dr.	L 4	472·00	
		Office Equipment A/c Dr.	L 5	350·00	
		Capital A/c (M. Tyler	L 6		3 471·00
		Being assets contributed at this date by M. Tyler, the proprietor		£3 471·00	£3 471·00

(4) Books of R. Lucas (*SPA page 94*)

19.. Jan.	1				£	£
		Cash A/c	Dr.	L 1	48·00	
		Bank A/c	Dr.	L 2	225·00	
		Premises A/c	Dr.	L 3	3 800·00	
		Motor Vehicles A/c	Dr.	L 4	740·00	
		Office Equipment A/c	Dr.	L 5	520·00	
		Capital A/c (R. Lucas)		L 6		5 333·00
		Being assets contributed as capital by the proprietor R. Lucas, at this date			£5 333·00	£5 333·00

(5) Books of G. Porter (*SPA page 94*)

19.. Jan.	1				£	£
		Cash A/c	Dr.	L 1	32·00	
		Bank A/c	Dr.	L 2	250·00	
		Premises A/c	Dr.	L 3	3 300·00	
		Motor Vehicles A/c	Dr.	L 4	655·00	
		Office Equipment A/c	Dr.	L 5	256·00	
		Capital A/c (G. Porter)		L 6		4 493·00
		Being assets contributed as capital by the proprietor, G. Porter, at this date			£4 493·00	£4 493·00

(6) Books of M. Larkin (*SPA page 94*)

19.. Apr.	1				£	£
		Cash A/c	Dr.	L 1	256·00	
		Bank A/c	Dr.	L 2	325·00	
		Premises A/c	Dr.	L 3	7 000·00	
		Plant and Machinery A/c	Dr.	L 4	485·00	
		Stock A/c	Dr.	L 5	480·00	
		P. Rose A/c	Dr.	L 6	52·00	
		M. Groves A/c	Dr.	L 7	37·00	
		R. Beeden A/c		L 8		285·50
		Capital A/c (M. Larkin)		L 9		8 349·50
		Being assets and liabilities at this date, when business commenced			£8 635·00	£8 635·00

Cash A/c		L 1		Bank A/c		L 2
19..	£			19..	£	
Apr. 1 Capital	256·00			Apr. 1 Capital	325·00	

Premises A/c		L 3		Plant and Machinery A/c		L 4
19..	£			19..	£	
Apr. 1 Capital	7 000·00			Apr. 1 Capital	485·00	

Stock A/c		L 5		P. Rose A/c		L 6
19..	£			19..	£	
Apr. 1 Capital	480·00			Apr. 1 Capital	52·00	

	M. Groves A/c	L 7
19..	£	
Apr. 1 Capital	37·00	

	R. Beeden A/c	L 8
	19..	£
	Apr. 1 Sundry	
	Assets	285·50

	Capital A/c	L 9
	19..	£
	Apr. 1 Sundry	
	Assets 8 349·50	

(7) Books of M. Lawson *(SPA page 94)*

19..					£	£
Apr.	1	Cash A/c	Dr.	L 1	8·00	
		Bank A/c	Dr.	L 2	192·00	
		Premises A/c	Dr.	L 3	1 600·00	
		Plant and Machinery A/c	Dr.	L 4	85·00	
		Stock A/c	Dr.	L 5	240·00	
		P. Rogers A/c	Dr.	L 6	47·00	
		M. Graves A/c	Dr.	L 7	29·00	
		R. Bell A/c		L 8		162·50
		Capital A/c (M. Lawson)		L 9		2 038·50
		Being assets and liabilities at this date, on commencement of business			£2 201·00	£2 201·00

	Cash A/c	L 1
19..	£	
Apr. 1 Capital	8·00	

	Bank A/c	L 2
19..	£	
Apr. 1 Capital	192·00	

	Premises A/c	L 3
19..	£	
Apr. 1 Capital 1	600·00	

	Plant and Machinery A/c	L 4
19..	£	
Apr. 1 Capital	85·00	

	Stock A/c	L 5
19..	£	
Apr. 1 Capital	240·00	

	P. Rogers A/c	L 6
19..	£	
Apr. 1 Capital	47·00	

	M. Graves A/c	L 7
19..	£	
Apr. 1 Capital	29·00	

	R. Bell A/c	L 8
	19..	£
	Apr. 1 Sundry	
	Assets	162·50

	Capital A/c (M. Lawson)	L 9
	19..	£
	Apr. 1 Sundry	
	Assets 2 038·50	

(3) Books of S. Thompson (*SPA page 94*)

19.. Apr.	1				£	£
		Cash A/c	Dr.	L 1	82·00	
		Bank A/c	Dr.	L 2	1 156·00	
		Premises A/c	Dr.	L 3	2 958·00	
		Plant and Machinery A/c	Dr.	L 4	440·00	
		Stock A/c	Dr.	L 5	650·00	
		R. Lyons A/c	Dr.	L 6	276·50	
		A. Moore A/c	Dr.	L 7	550·50	
		Lyle Finance Co. A/c		L 8		268·50
		Capital A/c		L 9		5 844·50
		Being assets and liabilities on commencement of business at this date			£6 113·00	£6 113·00

	Cash A/c	L 1		Bank A/c	L 2
19..	£		19..	£	
Apr. 1 Capital	82·00		Apr. 1 Capital 1 156·00		

	Premises A/c	L 3		Plant and Machinery A/c	L 4
19..	£		19..	£	
Apr. 1 Capital 2 958·00			Apr. 1 Capital 440·00		

	Stock A/c	L 5		R. Lyons A/c	L 6
19..	£		19..	£	
Apr. 1 Capital 650·00			Apr. 1 Capital 276·50		

	A. Moore A/c	L 7		Lyle Finance Co. A/c	L 8
19..	£			19..	£
Apr. 1 Capital 550·50				Apr. 1 Sundry Assets 268·50	

	Capital A/c	L 9
	19..	£
	Apr. 1 Sundry Assets 5 844·50	

(9) Books of Peter Martin (*SPA page 94*)

19.. Jan.	1				£	£
		Cash A/c	Dr.	L 1	24·00	
		Bank A/c	Dr.	L 2	1 756·00	
		Premises A/c	Dr.	L 3	8 500·00	
		Stock A/c	Dr.	L 4	1 750·00	
		Motor Vehicles A/c	Dr.	L 5	840·00	
		R. Long A/c	Dr.	L 6	27·50	
		B. Short A/c	Dr.	L 7	42·75	
		T. Wide A/c	Dr.	L 8	36·85	
		Imperial Loan Co. A/c		L 9		1 500·00
		Longlife Finance Co. A/c		L 10		800·00
		Capital A/c		L 11		10 677·10
		Being assets and liabilities at this date			£12 977·10	£12 977·10

(10) Books of Steptoe and Son (*SPA page 95*)

19..						£	£
July	1	Cash A/c	Dr.	L	1	85·00	
		Bank A/c	Dr.	L	2	1 876·00	
		Premises A/c	Dr.	L	3	2 800·00	
		Stock A/c	Dr.	L	4	185·00	
		Motor Vehicles A/c	Dr.	L	5	1 050·00	
		Equipment A/c	Dr.	L	6	42·50	
		A. Scrapiron A/c	Dr.	L	7	285·00	
		B. Ragdealer A/c	Dr.	L	8	155·50	
		A. Welder A/c		L	9		25·00
		Capital A/c /Steptoe, Senior)		L	10		5 000·00
		Capital A/c (Steptoe, Junior)		L	11		1 454·00
		Being assets and liabilities at this date				£6 479·00	£6 479·00

Books of Original Entry
Part Two: The Purchases and Sales
Day Books

Exercises Set 12: The Purchases Day Book

(1) Books of M. Sibthorpe (*SPA page 101*)

19..					£	£
May	1	F. Ball				
		3 sets of golf clubs at £42·50 per set	L 1			127·50
	2	B. Bannerman				
		20 badminton sets at £1·55 each			31·00	
		20 comeback tennis trainers at £2·25 each			45·00	
			L 2			76·00
	11	R. Downs				
		100 golf balls at 25p each	L 3			25·00
	17	P. Roberts				
		40 leather footballs at £1·80 each			72·00	
		200 plastic footballs at 85p each			170·00	
			L 4			242·00
	24	G. Wright				
		200 'Homesocca' games at £2·35 each	L 5			470·00
			L 6			£940·50

F. Ball A/c	L 1
	19.. £
	May 1 Purchases 127·50

B. Bannerman A/c	L 2
	19.. £
	May 2 Purchases 76·00

R. Downs A/c	L 3
	19.. £
	May 11 Purchases 25·00

P. Roberts A/c	L 4
	19.. £
	May 17 Purchases
	242·00

G. Wright A/c	L 5
	19.. £
	May 24 Purchases
	470·00

Purchases A/c	L 6
19.. £	
May 31 Sundry	
Creditors	
940·50	

(2) Books of R. Beech (*SPA page 102*)

19.					£	£
May	1	M. Benton				
		5 sets 'Home Painter' equipment at £5·50 each	L 1			27·50
	3	D. Cade				
		20 drums paint at £1·85 each			37·00	
		20 gallons thinners at 65p per gallon			13·00	
			L 2			50·00
	14	S. Carter				
		100 rolls wallpaper at 55p each	L 3			55·00
	27	D. Cade				
		40 tins white gloss paint at £1·60 each			64·00	
		200 plastic trays at 45p each			90·00	
			L 2			154·00
	29	G. Wright				
		100 rolls wallpaper at 85p each	L 4			85·00
			L 5			£371·50

M. Benton A/c	L 1		D. Cade A/c	L 2
19..	£		19..	£
May 1 Purchases	27·50		May 3 Purchases	50·00
			27 Purchases	154·00

S. Carter A/c	L 3		G. Wright A/c	L 4
19..	£		19..	£
May 14 Purchases	55·00		May 29 Purchases	85·00

Purchases A/c	L 5
19..	£
May 31 Sundry Creditors	
	371·50

(3) Books of M. Lawson (*SPA page 102*)

19..					£	£
Jan.	4	R. Davy				
		12 Barracuda fish tanks at £3·20 each	L 1			38·40
	10	K. Adcock				
		12 mini-tank aeration pumps at £1·55 each	L 2			18·60
	13	M. Bridger				
		Tropical fish			18·50	
		Submarine landscape features 24 sets at 85p			20·40	
			L 3			38·90
	21	D. De'ath				
		Garden fish tanks	L 4			184·50
	23	R. Lawrence				
		Freshwater fish			12·50	
		Weed (assorted)			6·00	
			L 5			18·50
			L 6			£298·90

R. Davy A/c	L 1
19..	£
Jan 4 Purchases	38·40

K. Adcock A/c	L 2
19..	£
Jan. 10 Purchases	18·60

M. Bridger A/c	L 3
19..	£
Jan. 13 Purchases	38·90

D. De'ath A/c	L 4
19..	£
Jan. 21 Purchases	184·50

R. Lawrence A/c	L 5
19..	£
Jan. 23 Purchases	18·50

Purchases A/c		L 6
19..	£	
Jan. 31 Sundry		
Creditors		
298·90		

(4) Books of R. J. Upfold (*SPA page 102*)

19.. May				£	£
1	R. Biggs				
	Tomatoes			17·50	
	Eggs (2 000 dozen at 1·5p per dozen)			30·00	
			L 1		47·50
7	Golden Freezers Ltd.				
	Butter			42·50	
	Margarine			36·50	
	Bacon packs			45·00	
			L 2		124·00
8	California Fruit Co. Ltd.				
	Tinned peaches			40·00	
	Tinned pears			36·00	
	Blueberries			5·50	
			L 3		81·50
11	Danish Produce Ltd.				
	Bacon			50·00	
	Cheeses			32·00	
	Butter			43·50	
			L 4		125·50
17	Shropshire Co-operative Producers Ltd.				
	Eggs			48·50	
	Milk products			32·50	
	Cheese			16·50	
			L 5		97·50
29	London Import Co.				
	Canadian produce		L 6		248·00
			L 7		£724·00

R. Biggs A/c	L 1
19..	£
May 1 Purchases	47·50

Golden Freezers Ltd. A/c	L 2
19..	£
May 7 Purchases	124·00

California Fruit Co. Ltd. A/c	L 3
19..	£
May 8 Purchases	81·50

Danish Produce Ltd. A/c	L 4
19..	£
May 11 Purchases	125·50

Shropshire Co-operative Producers Ltd. A/c	**L 5**	London Import Co. A/c	**L 6**

Shropshire Co-operative Producers Ltd. A/c — L 5

	£
19..	
May 17 Purchases	97·50

London Import Co. A/c — L 6

	£
19..	
May 29 Purchases	248·00

Purchases A/c — L 7

	£
19..	
May 31 Sundry Creditors	724·00

(5) Books of R. Davison (*SPA page 103*)

19..			£	£
June	1	*P. Ketley*		
		Brassware	15·60	
		Ironware	27·30	
		L 1		42·90
	7	*Safety Fires Ltd.*		
		12 oil stoves at £3·75 each	45·00	
		10 cooking stoves at £7·95 each	79·50	
		Spare wicks and mantles	8·55	
		L 2		133·05
	11	*Sheffield Cutlers Ltd.*		
		Stainless steel cutlery L 3		185·00
	13	*Plastico Ltd.*		
		Tea Sets	42·00	
		Bowls	36·00	
		Buckets	32·00	
		L 4		110·00
	23	*A. E. Plant*		
		Tools and equipment L 5		234·50
	29	*K. J. Adlam*		
		Copper fittings	48·50	
		Chromium fittings	77·50	
		Mirror wares	12·85	
		L 6		138·85
		L 7		£844·30

P. Ketley A/c — L 1

	£
19..	
June 1 Purchases	42·90

Safety Fires Ltd. A/c — L 2

	£
19..	
June 7 Purchases	133·05

Sheffield Cutlers Ltd. A/c — L 3

	£
19..	
June 11 Purchases	185·00

Plastico Ltd. A/c — L 4

	£
19..	
June 13 Purchases	110·00

A. E. Plant A/c — L 5

	£
19..	
June 23 Purchases	234·50

K. J. Adlam A/c — L 6

	£
19..	
June 29 Purchases	138·85

Purchases A/c — L 7

	£
19..	
June 30 Sundry Creditors	844·30

Exercises Set 13: The Sales Day Book

(1) Books of R. Hall (*SPA page 105*)

19..				£	£
May	1	R. *Whitechurch* 2 chicken sheds at £45·50	L 1		91·00
	13	M. *Lamb* Peep-proof fencing 20 × 2-metre panels at £2·50 3 × 1-metre panels at £1·50		50·00 4·50	
			L 2		54·50
	17	R. *Marshall* Lean-to greenhouse frame	L 3		13·50
	19	R. *Shaw* 12 kits for garden sheds at £13·80	L 4		165·60
	27	M. *Lever* 4 chicken sheds at £45·50	L 5		182·00
			L 6		£506·60

R. Whitechurch A/c	L 1		M. Lamb A/c	L 2
19..	£		19..	£
May 1 Sales	91·00		May 13 Sales	54·50

R. Marshall A/c	L 3		R. Shaw A/c	L 4
19..	£		19..	£
May 17 Sales	13·50		May 19 Sales	165·60

M. Lever A/c	L 5		Sales A/c	L 6
19..	£			
May 27 Sales	182·00		19..	£
			May 31 Sundry Debtors	506·60

(2) Books of M. Thomas (*SPA page 106*)

19..				£	£
June	4	M. *Allen* 200 assorted sandwiches at 5p each 400 pastries at 5p each 1 three-tier cake		10·00 20·00 18·50	
			L 1		48·50
	11	R. *Cross* 400 bridge rolls at 1p each 300 assorted sandwiches at 5p each 300 pastries at 5p each 1 single-tier cake		4·00 15·00 15·00 12·00	
			L 2		46·00
	4	R. *Diamond Ltd.* 200 filled rolls at 4p each 200 sandwiches at 5p each 500 pastries at 5p each Decorated *petit fours*		8·00 10·00 25·00 10·00	
			L 3		53·00
			L 4		£147·50

	M. Allen A/c	L 1			R. Cross A/c	L 2
19..	£			19..	£	
June 4 Sales	48·50			June 11 Sales	46·00	

	R. Diamond Ltd. A/c	L 3			Sales A/c	L 4
19..	£				19..	£
June 24 Sales	53·00				June 30 Sundry	
					Debtors	147·50

(3) Books of R. Larch (*SPA page 106*)

				£	£
19..					
Apr.	2	*Garden Traders Ltd.*			
		25 boxes antirrhinums at 20p each		5·00	
		25 boxes salvias at 25p each		6·25	
			L 1		11·25
	9	*Fine Gardens Co.*			
		200 boxes dahlias at 20p each	L 2		40·00
	21	*Green, Finger and Co.*			
		100 boxes dahlias at 20p each		20·00	
		100 boxes salvias at 25p each		25·00	
		100 boxes lobelia at 20p each		20·00	
		100 boxes mesembryanthemums at 20p each		20·00	
		100 boxes alyssum at 20p each		20·00	
			L 3		105·00
	28	*Garden Traders Ltd.*			
		50 boxes alyssum at 20p each		10·00	
		50 boxes lobelia at 20p each		10·00	
			L 1		20·00
			L 4		£176·25

	Garden Traders Ltd. A/c	L1			Fine Gardens Co. A/c	L 2
19..	£			19..	£	
Apr. 2 Sales	11·25			Apr. 9 Sales	40·00	
28 Sales	20·00					

	Green, Finger and Co. A/c	L 3			Sales A/c	L 4
19..	£				19..	£
Apr. 21 Sales	105·00				Apr. 30 Sundry	
					Debtors	176·25

(4) Books of M. Paterson (*SPA page 106*)

19.. May				£	£
	4	*Colossal Insurance Co.*			
		Assorted plant stands	L 1		85·00
	11	*Pharmaceutical Specialities Ltd.*			
		1 display cabinet at £90·50		90·50	
		2 display cabinets at £35 each		70·00	
			L 2		160·50
	19	*Re-proofed Concrete Ltd.*			
		1 Fish tank display	L 3		250·50
	27	*International Exporters Ltd.*			
		1 world map wall display		234·00	
		1 motorway display model		165·00	
			L 4		399·00
			L 5		£895·00

Colossal Insurance Co. A/c L 1		Pharmaceutical Specialities Ltd. A/c L 2	
19.. May 4 Sales	£ 85·00	19.. May 11 Sales	£ 160·50

Re-proofed Concrete Ltd. A/c L 3		International Exporters Ltd. A/c L 4	
19.. May 19 Sales	£ 250·50	19.. May 27 Sales	£ 399·00

Sales A/c L 5	
	19.. May 31 Sundry Debtors 895·00

(5) Books of R. Lawes (*SPA page 107*)

19.. Jan.				£	£
	3	*R. Smith*			
		200 tins Kumficat at 5p each		10·00	
		60 packets dog biscuits at 25p per packet		15·00	
			L 1		25·00
	7	*M. Lyons*			
		144 packets fish food at 5p per packet		7·20	
		1 litre live daphnia at £3·15		3·15	
			L 2		10·35
	8	*R. Jayson*			
		200 tins Kumficat at 5p each		10·00	
		120 tins Bestfriend dogmeat at 25p per tin		30·00	
			L 3		40·00
	19	*M. Lord*			
		60 packets dog biscuits at 25p per packet		15·00	
		120 tins Bestfriend at 25p per tin		30·00	
			L 4		45·00
	29	*R. Countryman*			
		Assorted pet foods		15·00	
		120 packets dog biscuits at 25p per packet		30·00	
			L 5		45·00
			L 6		£165·35

Books of Original Entry
Part Three: The Purchases and Sales Returns Books

Exercises Set 14: The Purchases Returns Book

(1) Books of R. Lutterworth (*SPA page 110*)

19..				£	£
May	4	*Lustre Colour Ltd.*			
		1 set curtains (colour faded)	L 1		27·50
	11	*C. E. Montrose*			
		3 sets sheets at £2·25 per set (faulty design pattern)	L 2		6·75
	29	*E. A. Phillips*			
		Curtain lining (damaged by water)	L 3		5·50
			L 4		£39·75

Lustre Colour Ltd. A/c	L 1
19.. £	
May 4 Purchases	
Returns 27·50	

C. E. Montrose A/c	L 2
19.. £	
May 11 Purchases	
Returns 6·75	

E. A. Phillips A/c	L 3
19.. £	
May 19 Purchases	
Returns 5·50	

Purchases Returns A/c	L 4
	19.. £
	May 31 Sundry
	Creditors 39·75

(2) Books of E. S. Oliver (*SPA page 111*)

19..				£	£
July	7	*Miniparts Ltd.*			
		1 set chrome-plated mudguards (chrome defective)	L 1		8·75
	22	*Accessories Ltd.*			
		1 chronometer (defective mechanism)		8·95	
		1 oil-pressure gauge (poorly machined)		4·25	
			L 2		13·20
	30	*Battery Wholesale Supply Co. Ltd.*			
		1 12-volt battery (leaking)	L 3		4·35
			L 4		£26·30

Miniparts Ltd. A/c		L 1
19..	£	
July 7 Purchases		
Returns	8·75	

Accessories Ltd. A/c		L 2
19..	£	
July 22 Purchases		
Returns	13·20	

Battery Wholesale Supply Co. Ltd. A/c		L 3
19..	£	
July 30 Purchases		
Returns	4·35	

Purchases Returns A/c		L 4
	19..	£
	July 31 Sundry	
	Creditors	26·30

(3) Books of C. Hosking (*SPA page 111*)

19..				£	£
June	1	Seager's Sweet Co.			
		1 jar bullseyes at £2·50 (contaminated)	L 1		2·50
	13	Liquorice Allsorts Co.			
		Empty jars and tins	L 2		3·45
	14	Read's Liqueur Chocolates Ltd.			
		1 box (damaged in transit)	L 3		0·55
	27	Seager's Sweet Co.			
		Empty jars and tins	L 1		3·20
			L 4		£9·70

Seager's Sweet Co. A/c		L 1
19..	£	
June 1 Purchases		
Returns	2·50	
27 Purchases		
Returns	3·20	

Liquorice Allsorts Co. A/c		L 2
19..	£	
June 13 Purchases		
Returns	3·45	

Read's Liqueur Chocolates Ltd. A/c		L 3
19..	£	
June 14 Purchases		
Returns	0·55	

Purchases Returns A/c		L 4
	19..	£
	June 30 Sundry	
	Creditors	9·70

(4) Books of R. Robertson (*SPA page 111*)

19..				£	£
Aug.	4	Norwich Traders Ltd.			
		1 pair brown size 12 children's shoes (stitching faulty)	L 1		2·25
	5	Northampton Leather Dealers			
		1 pair 'country cumfi' boots (discoloured)		4·35	
		1 pair dress boots (inner lining defective)		7·25	
			L 2		11·60
	25	Shoe Importers Ltd.			
		1 case plastic beach sandals (no buckles)	L 3		25·00
			L 4		£38·85

Norwich Traders Ltd. A/c		L 1
19..	£	
Aug. 4 Purchases		
Returns	2·25	

Northampton Leather Dealers A/c		L 2
19..	£	
Aug. 5 Purchases		
Returns	11·60	

		Shoe Importers Ltd. A/c L 3			Purchases Returns A/c L 4
19..		£	19..		£
Aug. 25	Purchases		Aug. 31	Sundry	
	Returns 25·00			Creditors 38·85	

(5) Books of T. New and Son (*SPA page 111*)

19..				£	£
Nov.	13	*Hall Bros.*			
		1 blazer (machined imperfectly)	L 1		4·75
	22	*Lamark Trading Company*			
		1 car coat (badly torn)		6·50	
		1 pair car blankets (wrong colour)		8·95	
			L 2		15·45
	25	*Lutz and Co.*			
		3 sets men's underwear (not as ordered)	L 3		2·75
	29	*Hall Bros.*			
		1 blazer (pocket torn)	L 1		3·35
			L 4		£26·30

	Hall Bros. A/c L 1		Lamark Trading Company A/c L 2
19..	£	19..	£
Nov. 13 Purchases		Nov. 22 Purchases	
Returns 4·75		Returns 15·45	
29 Purchases			
Returns 3·35			

	Lutz and Co. A/c L 3		Purchases Returns A/c L 4
19..	£		19.. £
Nov. 25 Purchases			Nov. 30 Sundry
Returns 2·75			Creditors 26·30

Exercises Set 15: The Sales Returns Book

(1) Books of T. Cratchett (*SPA page 113*)

19..				£	£
June	4	*Pram Centre Co.*			
		1 Slumbercot (damaged in transit)	L 1		14·50
	6	*E. Proctor and Co. Ltd.*			
		1 coach-built pram (wheels strained)		13·45	
		1 pram basket (damaged in transit)		3·00	
			L 2		16·45
	16	*R. Rudd*			
		1 electric toaster (faulty switch)	L 3		3·25
	27	*T. W. Russell*			
		1 Vacumetric cleaner (motor burnt out)	L 4		34·65
			L 5		£68·85

	Pram Centre Co. A/c L 1		E. Proctor and Co. Ltd. A/c L 2
	19.. £		19.. £
	June 4 Sales		June 6 Sales
	Returns 14·50		Returns 16·45

R. Rudd A/c	L 3
	19.. £
	June 16 Sales
	Returns 3·25

T. W. Russell A/c	L 4
	19.. £
	June 27 Sales
	Returns 34·65

Sales Returns A/c	L 5
19.. £	
June 30 Sundry	
Debtors 68·85	

(2) Books of Paul Luscombe (*SPA page 114*)

19..				£
Jan.	4	Macaulay and Co,		
		Train set (faulty motor)	L 1	8·25
	11	Petersen and Co.		
		1 Hobbyhorse, scooter and trailer (painting defective)	L 2	7·25
	19	T. Barr		
		12 boxes bricks (incorrectly packed)	L 3	8·58
	29	T. R. Portray Ltd.		
		1 train set (faulty motor)	L 4	8·25
			L 5	£32·33

Macaulay and Co. A/c	L 1
	19.. £
	Jan. 4 Sales
	Returns 8·25

Petersen and Co. A/c	L 2
	19.. £
	Jan. 11 Sales
	Returns 7·25

T. Barr A/c	L 3
	19.. £
	Jan. 19 Sales
	Returns 8·58

T. R. Portray Ltd. A/c	L 4
	19.. £
	Jan. 29 Sales
	Returns 8·25

Sales Returns A/c	L 5
19.. £	
Jan. 31 Sundry	
Debtors 32·33	

(3) Books of A. Robens (*SPA page 114*)

19..				£	£
Feb.	1	T. MacAndrew and Co. Ltd.			
		1 typist's chair (metalwork rough)		5·50	
		1 filing cabinet (lock faulty)		19·75	
			L 1		25·25
	4	R. Robertson			
		1 cabinet (wrong colour)	L 2		33·95
	14	M. Loach			
		Returned crates	L 3		5·50
	25	R. Ingrams			
		1 filing cabinet (lock faulty)		19·75	
		Metal trays (swivel mechanism faulty)		5·50	
			L 4		25·25
			L 5		£89·95

T. MacAndrew and Co. Ltd. A/c   L 1
19..	£
Feb. 1 Sales	
Returns	25·25

R. Robertson A/c   L 2
19..	£
Feb. 4 Sales	
Returns	33·95

M. Loach A/c   L 3
19...	£
Feb. 14 Sales	
Returns	5·50

R. Ingrams A/c   L 4
19..	£
Feb. 25 Sales	
Returns	25·25

Sales Returns A/c   L 5
19..	£
Feb. 28 Sundry	
Debtors 89·95	

(4) Books of A. W. Manser (*SPA page 114*)

19..				£	£
July	4	*John Mansfield*			
		Seeds (sale or return basis)	L 1		5·48
	11	*Garden Beauty Co.*			
		2 fruit trees at £0·40 (dead)		0·80	
		6 Standard roses at £0·60 (dead)		3·60	
			L 2		4·40
	19	*Kilmuir Landscape Co. Ltd.*			
		24 bedding plants at £0·20 (wrong variety)	L 3		4·80
	29	*Kent Window Box Co.*			
		Plants (allowance against poor quality)	L 4		5·00
			L 5		£19·68

John Mansfield A/c   L 1
19..	£
July 4 Sales	
Returns	5·48

Garden Beauty Co. A/c   L 2
19..	£
July 11 Sales	
Returns	4·40

Kilmuir Landscape Co. A/c   L 3
19..	£
July 19 Sales	
Returns	4·80

Kent Window Box Co. A/c   L 4
19..	£
July 29 Sales	
Returns	5·00

Sales Returns A/c   L 5
19..	£
July 31 Sundry	
Debtors 19·68	

(5) Books of M. Lancaster (*SPA page 114*)

19..				£
June	7	*M. Rooselar*		
		Allowance (Argentine Beef)	L 1	65·00
	19	*M. Candler*		
		Allowance (English beef)	L 2	8·00
	21	*R. T. Jones*		
		Allowance (frozen produce defrosted)	L 3	44·00
	29	*M. Johnson*		
		Allowance (poor quality Australian mutton)	L 4	10·50
			L 5	£127·50

	M. Rooselar A/c	L 1
	19..	£
	June 7 Sales	
	Returns	65·00

	M. Candler A/c	L 2
	19..	£
	June 19 Sales	
	Returns	8·00

	R. T. Jones A/c	L 3
	19..	£
	June 21 Sales	
	Returns	44·00

	M. Johnson A/c	L 4
	19..	£
	June 29 Sales	
	Returns	10·50

Sales Returns A/c	L 5
19..	£
June 30 Sundry	
Debtors	
127·50	

Unit Twelve

Books of Original Entry
Part Four: More Journal Proper Entries—
Assets and Depreciation

Exercises Set 16: The Purchase of Assets

(1) Books of R. Lever (*SPA page 117*)

19.. Jan.	1	Furniture and Fittings A/c Dr. Bank A/c Being purchase of 12 display cabinets (serial nos. A1856–67) at this date)	L 12 L 5	£ 156·00	£ 156·00

Furniture and Fittings A/c L 12	Bank A/c L 5
19.. Jan. 1 Bank £ 156·00	19.. Jan. 1 Furniture and Fittings 156·00

(2) Books of M. Robertson (*SPA page 117*)

19.. July	16	Typewriters A/c Dr. British Olivetti Ltd. A/c Being purchase of an electric typewriter (ref. No. E1/20785)	L 17 L 49	£ 186·00	£ 186·00

Typewriters A/c L 17	British Olivetti Ltd. L 49

19..
July 16 British
   Olivetti 186·00   £
	19..
	July 16 Typewriters
	    186·00 £

(3) Books of A. Printz (*SPA page 117*)

19.. Aug.	1	Motor Vehicles A/c Dr. Heavy Autos Ltd. A/c Being purchase of vehicle AJN 187L (engine ref. No. 32Z/7146, chassis No. E8/47.625) at this date	L 15 L 95	£ 9 500·00	£ 9 500·00

Motor Vehicles A/c L 15	Heavy Autos Ltd. A/c L 95

19..
Aug. 1 Heavy
   Autos Ltd.
    9 500·00   £
	19..
	Aug. 1 Motor
	    Vehicles
	    9 500·00 £

(4) Books of S. Debbotista (*SPA page 117*)

| 19..
May | 31 | Motor Vehicles A/c   Dr.
  Bank A/c
  Special Motors Ltd. A/c
Being purchase of security vehicle RJO 125M
at this date | L 17
L 5
L 96 | £
1 656·00 | £

828·00
828·00 |

(5) Books of J. Scaggs (*SPA page 117*)

| 19..
June | 1 | Fixtures and Fittings A/c   Dr.
  Cash A/c
  Shop Fittings Ltd. A/c
Being purchase of automatic till (Ref. No.
Automatic 38.754) at this date | L 13
L 4
L 80 | £
220·00 | £

110·00
110·00 |

(6) Books of M. Lucien (*SPA page 118*)

| 19..
Dec. | 1 | Furniture and Fittings A/c   Dr.
Typewriters A/c   Dr.
  General Supplies Co. A/c
Being purchase of desks, chairs, filing cabinets
and typewriters at this date. (Ref. Nos. filing
cabinets E 12 745/6 and typewriters A 1 075–80) | L 27
L 28
L 162 | £
495·00
540·00 | £

1 035·00 |

Furniture and Fittings A/c   L 27
19..   £
Dec. 1 General
Supplies 495·00

Typewriters A/c   L 28
19..   £
Dec. 1 General
Supplies 540·00

General Supplies Co. A/c   L 162
19..   £
Dec. 1 Furniture
and
Fittings 1 035·00

Exercises Set 17: Simple Depreciation Exercises

(1) Books of A. Reeve (*SPA page 119*)

| 19..
Dec. | 31 | Depreciation A/c   Dr.
  Executive Motor Car A/c
Being depreciation for year written off | L 127
L 86 | £
1 830·00 | £
1 830·00 |

	Depreciation A/c	L 127
19..	£	
Dec. 31 Exec.		
Motor		
Car 1 830·00		

	Executive Motor Car A/c	L 86
19..	£	19..	£
Jan. 1 Bank 5 500·00		Dec. 31 Deprec-	iation 1 830·00
		31 Balance	
		c/d 3 670·00
	£5 500·00		£5 500·00
19..	£		
Jan. 1 Balance			
B/d 3 670·00			

(2) Books of P. Senior (*SPA page 119*)

19..					£	£
Dec.	31	Depreciation A/c	Dr.	L 85	270·00	
		Office Equipment A/c		L 12		270·00
		Being depreciation at 20 per cent on value at start of year				

	Depreciation A/c	L 85
19..	£	
Dec. 31 Office		
Equip-		
ment 270·00		

	Office Equipment A/c	L 12
19..	£	19..	£
Jan. 1 Balance 1 350·00		Dec 31 Depreciation	
			270·00
		31 Balance	
		c/d 1 080·00
	£1 350·00		£1 350·00
19..	£		
Jan. 1 Balance			
B/d 1 080·00			

(3) Books of C. Blythe (*SPA page 119*)

19..					£	£
Dec.	31	Depreciation A/c	Dr.	L 47	600·00	
		Fittings and Equipment A/c		L 5		600·00
		Being one-third of original cost written off in accordance with agreed policy				

(4) Books of M. Larkins (*SPA page 119*)

19..					£	£
Dec.	31	Depreciation A/c	Dr.	L 186	1 600·00	
		Motor Vehicles A/c		L 47		1 600·00
		Being depreciation for year to reduce value of motor vehicles to valuation at this date				

	Motor Vehicles A/c		L 47
19..	£		£
Jan. 1 Balance B/d	6 300·00	Dec. 31 Depreciation	1 600·00
		31 Balance c/d	4 700·00
	£6 300·00		£6 300·00
19..	£		
Dec. 31 Balance B/d	4 700·00		

(5) Books of Howden Ironware Co. (*SPA page 120*)

19..					£	£
Dec.	31	Depreciation A/c	Dr.	L 175	1 500·00	
		Premises A/c		L 14		1 500·00
		Being depreciation on premises for year at 10 per cent per annum				

		Premises A/c			L 14
19..		£	19..		£
Jan. 1 Balance B/d		12 000·00	Dec. 31 Depreciation		1 500·00
July 1 Bank		6 000·00	31 Balance c/d		16 500·00
		£18 000·00			£18 000·00
19..		£			
Jan. 1 Balance B/d		16 500·00			

(6) Books of M. Burns (*SPA page 120*)

19..					£	£
Dec.	31	Depreciation A/c	Dr.	L 127	5 800·00	
		Quarry A/c		L 5		3 800·00
		Capital A/c		L 2		2 000·00
		Being depreciation of rock quarried (5 800 tons) and increased reserves (2 000 tons)				

Exercises Set 18: The Disposal of Assets

(1) Books of John Kelleher (*SPA page 122*)

19..					£	£
Dec.	31	Bank A/c	Dr.	L 1	50·00	
		Motor Vehicles A/c		L 9		50·00
		Being sale of motor vehicle XYT997H at this date, for the book value				

(2) Books of A. Hancock (*SPA page 122*)

19..					£	£
July	31	Cash A/c	Dr.	L 2	45·00	
		Shop Equipment A/c		L 15		45·00
		Being sale of mechanized till to A. Streetseller at the book value				

(3) Books of D. Heywood (*SPA page 122*)

19..					£	£
Jan.	1	Cash A/c	Dr.	L 1	85·00	
		Sale of Fittings A/c	Dr.	L 172	215·00	
		Furniture and Fittings A/c		L 14		300·00
		Being sale of shop fittings to A. Junkbuyer prior to re-organization				

D

(4) Books of J. Scaggs (*SPA page 122*)

19..					£	£
Aug.	1	Bank A/c	Dr.	L 2	2 800·00	
		Sale of Premises A/c	Dr.	L 173	450·00	
		Premises A/c		L 15		3 250·00
		Being disposal of premises rendered inconvenient by road changes				

(5) Books of Allen Motors Ltd. (*SPA page 122*)

19..					£	£
Aug.	31	Bank A/c	Dr.	L 1	38 000·00	
		Premises A/c		L 17		10 000·00
		Site Appreciation A/c		L 142		28 000·00
		Being sale of premises at greatly increased value at this date				

	Bank A/c		L 1			Premises A/c		L 17
19..		£			19..	£	19..	£
Aug. 31	Premises	38 000·00			Jan. 1 Balance	10 000·00	Aug. 31 Bank	10 000·00
						£10 000·00		£10 000·00

	Site Appreciation A/c		L 142
		19..	£
		Aug. 31 Bank	28 000·00

(6) Books of John Briggs (*SPA page 122*)

19..					£	£
Jan.	1	Cash A/c	Dr.	L 1	230·00	
		Motor Vehicles A/c		L 22		180·00
		Sale of Vehicles A/c		L 173		50·00
		Being sale of motor vehicle above book value at this date. Profit on disposal of vehicle treated as fortuitous				

(7) Books of Paul Watts (*SPA page 123*)

19..					£	£
Dec.	31	National Industrial Museum of America A/c	Dr.	L 192	380·00	
		Plant and Machinery A/c		L 5		30·00
		Sale of Machinery A/c		L 76		350·00
		Being sale of steam engine at a figure above book value				

(8) Books of F. Azouqua (*SPA page 123*)

19.. Sept.	15	Greek Liners Ltd. Dr.	L 187	£ 5 900·00	£
		Vessels A/c	L 42		2 800·00
		Sale of Vessels A/c	L 95		3 100·00
		Being diposal of vessel above current book value at this date			

Books of Original Entry
Part Five: More Journal Proper Entries—
Bad Debts

Exercises Set 19: Bad Debts

(1) (*SPA page 128*)

19.. July	19	Bad-Debts A/c Dr. R. Porter A/c Being debt written off on Mr. Porter's death, as a gesture of sympathy	L 75 L 36	£ 50·40	£ 50·40

Bad-Debts A/c	L 75		R. Porter A/c	L 36
19.. July 19 R. Porter 50·40	£	19.. July 1 Balance 50·40 £50·40	£	19.. July 19 Bad Debts 50·40 £50·40

(2) (*SPA page 128*)

19.. June	29	Bad-Debts A/c Dr. A. Student A/c Being uneconomic debt written off at this date, in view of likely collection costs	L 48 L 174	£ 3·50	£ 3·50

Bad-Debts A/c	L 48		A. Student A/c	L 174
19.. June 29 A. Student 3·50	£	19.. July 1 Balance 3·50	£	19.. June 29 Bad Debts 3·50

(3) (*SPA page 128*)

19.. Oct.	19	Bank A/c Dr. Bad-Debts A/c Dr. Anne Oldlady A/c Being final settlement of debt by the Aged Persons' Charitable Association	L 1 L 49 L 72	£ 17·50 17·50	£ 35·00

Bank A/c	L 1		Bad-Debts A/c	L 49
19.. Oct. 19 A. Oldlady 17·50	£		19.. Oct. 19 A. Oldlady 17·50	£

Anne Oldlady A/c	L 72
19.. Oct. 1 Balance 35·00	£	19.. Oct. 19 Bank and Bad Debt 35·00	£

(4) (*SPA page 128*)

19..						£	£
July	4	Bank A/c	Dr.	L 1		575·00	
		Bad-Debts A/c	Dr.	L 47		1 725·00	
		Solar Ventures (Moortown) Ltd.		L 56			2 300·00
		Being final settlement of £0·25 in the £1 on liquidation					

Bank A/c	L 1
19..	£
July 4 Solar	
Ventures	
575·00	

Bad-Debts A/c	L 47
19..	£
July 4 Solar	
Ventures	
1 725·00	

Solar Ventures (Moortown) Ltd. A/c		L 56
19..	£	19..	£
July 1 Balance 2 300·00		July 4 Bank and
		Bad Debts
		2 300·00
£2 300·00		£2 300·00

(5) (*SPA page 128*)

19..						£	£
Aug.	31	Bad-Debts A/c	Dr.	L 35		1·50	
		R. Pettifogger A/c		L 72			1·50
		Being balance of debt written off—disputed by debtor					

Bad-Debts A/c	L 35
19..	£
Aug. 31 R. Petti-	
fogger 1·50	

R. Pettifogger A/c		L 72
19..	£	19..	£
Aug. 1 Sales	100·00	Aug. 29 Bank	98·50
		31 Bad Debts 1·50
	£100·00	£100·00

(6) (*SPA page 128*)

19..						£	£
July	11	Bank A/c	Dr.	L 1		27·60	
		Bad-Debts A/c	Dr.	L 49		6·90	
		Carnival Productions (Westlake) Ltd.		L 76			34·50
		Being settlement of debt at £0·80 in the £1, by liquidator, at this date					

Bank A/c	L 1
19..	£
July 11 Carnival	
Produc-	
tions 27·60	

Bad-Debts A/c	L 49
19..	£
July 11 Carnival	
Produc-	
tions 6·90	

Carnival Productions (Westlake) Ltd. A/c   L 76

19..	£	19..	£
July 1 Balance	34·50	July 11 Bank and Bad Debts	34·50

(7) (*SPA page 128*)

19.. Feb.	14	Bank A/c Dr. Bad-Debts Recovered A/c Being settlement of debt by a debtor, A. Slowsettler, whose a/c has been written off	L 1 L 54	£ 3·50	£ 3·50

Bank A/c	L 1
19.. £	
Feb. 14 Bad Debts Recovered 3·50	

	Bad-Debts Recovered A/c L 54
	19.. £
	Feb. 14 Bank 3·50

(8) (*SPA page 128*)

19.. Apr.	5	Bank A/c Dr. Interest-Received A/c Bad-Debts Recovered A/c Being 10 per cent of debt previously written off as bad, refunded by M. Lipsey	L 1 L 84 L 85	£ 42·00	£ 2·00 40·00

Bank A/c	L 1
19.. £	
Apr. 5 Bad-Debts Recovered and Interest Received 42·00	

	Interest-Received A/c L 84
	19.. £
	Apr. 5 Bank 2·00

	Bad-Debts Recovered A/c L 85
	19.. £
	Apr. 5 Bank 40·00

(9) *(SPA page 129)*

19..						£	£
Dec.	8	Bank A/c	Dr.	L 1		38·25	
		Interest-Received A/c		L 45			8·25
		Bad-Debts Recovered A/c		L 62			30·00
		Being settlement in full of a debt previously written off as bad					

	Bank A/c	L 1			Interest Received A/c	L 45
19..	£				19..	£
Dec. 8 Bad-Debts Recovered and Interest Received					Dec. 8 Bank	8·25
	38·25					

	Bad-Debts Recovered A/c	L 62
	19..	£
	Dec. 8 Bank	30·00

(10) *(SPA page 129)*

19..						£	£
June	1	Bank A/c	Dr.	L 1		113·00	
		Bad-Debts Recovered A/c		L 75			100·00
		Interest-Received A/c		L 79			5·00
		Legal-Charges Recovered A/c		L 108			8·00
		Being complete recovery of a bad debt written off a year ago (A. Sloman)					

	Bank A/c	L 1			Bad-Debts Recovered A/c	L 75
19..	£				19..	£
June 1 Bad Debts Recovered					June 1 Bank	100·00
	113·00					

	Interest-Received A/c	L 79			Legal-Charges Recovered A/c	L 108
	19..	£			19..	£
	June 1 Bank	5·00			June 1 Bank	8·00

Unit Fourteen
Books of Original Entry
Part Six: The Three-Column Cash Book

Exercises Set 20: The Three-column Cash Book

(1) Books of D. Swann (SPA page 140)

Dr.

19.. Mar.	Particulars	F	£	£	£
1	Balances	B/d		72·50	1 550·75
4	R. Hope		0·25		4·75
5	Sales	C		103·55	
5	Cash				100·00
			£0·25	176·05	1 655·50
Mar. 8	Balances	B/d		62·75	1 507·75

Cr.

19.. Mar.	Particulars	F	£	£	£
1	A. Driver		5·00		95·00
2	R. Jones		2·00		38·00
3	Travelling Expenses			3·23	
3	Rates (U.D.C.)				14·75
4	Carriage In			1·55	
5	Bank	C		100·00	
5	Wages			8·50	
5	Balance	c/d		62·75	1 507·75
			£7·00	176·05	1 655·50

(2) Books of D. Hunter (SPA page 140)

Dr.

19.. May	Particulars	F	£	£	£
1	Balances	B/d		28·55	275·65
2	R. Long	L 17	4·50		80·00
4	Bank	C		50·00	
5	D. Lester	L 12			85·50
5	Sales	L 36		275·50	
5	Cash	C			180·00
			£4·50	354·05	621·15
May 8	Balance	B/d		92·65	477·75

Cr.

19.. May	Particulars	F	£	£	£
1	R. Benjamin	L 15		6·50	
1	Postage	L 19		1·25	
3	Rent	L 20			25·00
3	M. Morgan	L 48	3·60		68·40
4	Cash	C			50·00
4	Purchases	L 35		45·00	
5	Bank	C		180·00	
5	Wages	L 21		27·50	
5	Postage	L 19		1·15	
5	Balance	c/d L 28		92·65	477·75
			£3·60	354·05	621·15

(3) Books of B. Gale (SPA page 140)

19..			£	£	£
Nov. 11	Balances	B/d		72·65	1 250·50
12	R. Levis	L 5	0·25	9·75	
14	Bank	C		80·00	
14	D. Delderfield	L 71	2·37		92·63
		L 18	£ 2·62	162·40	1 343·13
19..				£	£
Nov. 16	Balances	B/d		62·13	1 220·63

19..			£	£	£
Nov. 11	Purchases	L 16		36·50	
12	L. Robbins	L 32	2·25		42·50
13	Light and Heat	L 29		7·50	
13	Sundry Expenses	L 30		0·42	
13	Postage	L 31		0·85	
14	Cash	C			80·00
15	Wages	L 34		35·00	
15	Light and Heat	L 29		17·50	
15	Postage	L 31		2·50	
15	Balances	c/d		62·13	1 220·63
		L 19	£ 2·25	162·40	1 343·13

(4) Books of E. Stapleton (SPA page 141)

19.. Dec.		Folio	£	£	£
1	Balance	B/d			
1	Bank Loan A/c	L 21			500·00
2	M. Giles	L 22	1·00		39·00
2	Bank	C		30·00	
3	R. Lawton	L 56	3·00		117·00
5	Sales	L 18		275·00	
5	Cash	C			250·00
		L 40	£ 4·00	330·00	906·00
19.. Dec. 6	Balances	B/d		39·45	346·79

19.. Dec.		Folio	£	£	£
1	Balance	B/d			326·55
2	R. Hopkinson	L 38	2·24		42·56
2	Cash	C			30·00
3	Repairs	L 19		5·35	
3	M. Glyndeborne	L 67		7·25	5·60
3	Stationery	L 20			
4	Travelling Expenses	L 21		3·35	
4	Purchases	L 17			29·50
5	P. Roche	L 84	5·00		95·00
5	Drawings	L 25			30·00
5	Wages	L 23		24·60	
5	Bank	C		250·00	
5	Balances	c/d		39·45	346·79
		L 41	£ 7·24	330·00	906·00

(5) Books of W. Allen (SPA page 141)

Dr.

19..	Particulars	Fol.	£ (Discount)	£ (Cash)	£ (Bank)
July 15	Balances	B/d		5·00	1 047·15
15	M. Long	L 42	1·25		23·75
15	Bank	C		20·00	
17	R. Lightfoot	L 40	5·00		195·00
18	R. Thomas	L 73			5·65
19	Cash Sales	L 19		112·75	
		L 34	£ 6·25	137·75	1 271·55
19.. July 20	Balances	B/d		97·80	1 021·60

Cr.

19..	Particulars	Fol.	£ (Discount)	£ (Cash)	£ (Bank)
July 15	Postage	L 30		1·35	
15	Cash	C			20·00
16	Cash Purchases	L 20		12·50	
16	Travelling Expenses	L 31		3·50	
17	M. Treegrove	L 45			128·70
17	Postage	L 30		1·85	
17	Repairs	L 32		4·25	
18	M. Hudson	L 49	1·50		28·50
19	R. Johnson	L 46	2·25		42·75
19	Drawings	L 24			30·00
19	Wages	L 33		16·50	
19	Balances	c/d		97·80	1 021·60
		L 35	£ 3·75	137·75	1 271·55

	M. Long A/c		L 42
19..	£	19..	£
July 1 Balance	25·00	July 15 Bank	23·75
		15 Discount	1·25

	R. Lightfoot A/c		L 40
19..	£	19..	£
July 1 Balance	200·00	July 17 Bank	195·00
		17 Discount	5·00

	R. Thomas A/c		L 73
19..	£	19..	£
July 1 Balance	5·65	July 18 Bank	5·65

	Sales A/c		L 19
		19..	£
		July 19 Cash	112·75

	Postage A/c		L 30
19..	£		
July 15 Cash	1·35		
17 Cash	1·85		

	Purchases A/c		L 20
19..	£		
July 15 Cash	12·50		

	Travelling Expenses A/c		L 31
19..	£		
July 16 Cash	3·50		

	M. Treegrove A/c		L 45
19..	£	19..	£
July 17 Bank	128·70	July 1 Balance	128·70

	Repairs A/c		L 32
19..	£		
July 17 Cash	4·25		

	M. Hudson A/c		L 49
19..	£	19..	£
July 18 Bank	28·50	July 1 Balance	30·00
18 Discount	1·50		

	R. Johnson A/c		L 46
19..	£	19..	£
July 19 Bank	42·75	July 1 Balance	45·00
19 Discount	2·25		

	Drawings A/c		L 24
19..	£		
July 19 Bank	30·00		

	Wages A/c		L 33
19..	£		
July 19 Cash	16·50		

	Discount-Allowed A/c		L 34
19..	£		
July 19 Sundry			
Discounts			
6·25			

	Discount-Received A/c		L 35
		19..	£
		July 19 Sundry	
		Discounts	3·75

(6) Books of Joseph Cotton (*SPA page 142*)

19.. Mar.	Particulars	F.	£	£	£	19.. Mar.	Particulars	F.	£	£	£
1	Balances	B/d		10·00	540·00	4	Cash	C			40·00
4	Bank	C		40·00		8	K. Jones	L 1	3·00		67·00
14	S. Rolf	L 2	2·00		72·00	8	Wages	L 3		10·00	
29	Cash	C			25·00	22	Wages	L 3		20·00	
29	S. Rolf	L 2		15·00		28	Office Expenses	L 4		8·00	
29	Rent Received	L 5			13·00	29	Bank	C		25·00	
						29	Bank Charges	L 8			7·00
						31	Balance	c/d		2·00	536·00
		L 7	£2·00	£65·00	£650·00			L 6	£3·00	£65·00	£650·00
19.. Apr. 1	Balances	B/d		2·00	536·00						

Unit Fifteen

Books of Original Entry
Part Seven: The Petty-Cash Book

Exercises Set 21: The Petty-cash Book

(1) (*SPA page 149*)

The chief points are:

(a) Check the arithmetical accuracy of the book-keeping, by long-totting and cross-totting the figures.

(b) Check that the receipts from the main cash book correspond with the chief cashier's entries in that book.

(c) Check that the sums spent correspond with the petty-cash vouchers which authorize the payments.

(d) Check the postings made to the ledger accounts.

(2) (*SPA page 149*)

Advantages:

(i) It saves the chief cashier's time, since a junior handles these trifling sums.

(ii) It saves time in posting because analysis columns collect similar items together.

(iii) It develops and trains young staff.

(iv) It is a secure system, since the small sums impressed for petty cash purposes do not represent a temptation either to the petty cashier or to other staff.

Postings:

(a) The total of the postage column is debited to Postage Account, and the Folio No. is inserted below the column total.

(b) The Ledger Account column entry, L. Shire, is debited to L. Shire's Account and the Folio No. is inserted in the folio column alongside.

(c) The 'Restored Imprest' entry is credited in the Main Cash Book.

(d) The entry 'Staff Purchases' is credited to Purchases Account, since it represents goods sold to staff at cost price.

(3) Books of D. Benson (*SPA page 149*)

Dr. £	19..	Details	PCV	Total £	Postage £	Travel £	Stationery £	Sundry Expenses £	Cleaning £	F £	Cr. Ledger Accounts £
4·35	Apr. 7	Balance	B/d								
5·65	7	Restored Imprest	CB 5								
	7	Postage	1	0·22	0·22						
	7	Bus Fares	2	0·08		0·08					
	7	R. Collins	3	1·32						L 56	1·32
0·57	8	Private Telephone Call	L 20								
	8	Postage	4	0·36	0·36						
	8	Stationery	5	0·10			0·10				
	9	Postage	6	0·24	0·24						
	9	Train Fares	7	0·65		0·65					
	9	Gratuities	8	0·10				0·10			
	10	Office Equipment	9	1·27						L 87	1·27
	10	Office Cleaner	10	1·25					1·25		
	10	Cleaning Materials	11	0·26					0·26		
	11	Postage	12	0·49	0·49						
	11	Cakes	13	0·28				0·28			
				6·62	1·31	0·73	0·10	0·38	1·51		2·59
	11	Balance	c/d	3·95	L 27	L 28	L 29	L 30	L 31		
£10·57				£10·57							
3·95	12	Balance	B/d								

(4) Books of R. Norris (*SPA page 150*)

Dr. £	19..			PCV	Total £	Postage £	Fares £	Office Sundries £	Repairs £	£	F	Cr. Ledger Accounts £
25·00	July 15	Imprest		CB 27								
	15	Postage		1	3·50	3·50						
	16	Fares		2	0·28		0·28					
	16	String		3	0·25			0·25				
	16	Plumbing Repairs		4	2·75				2·75			
	16	T. Bright		5	4·75						L 27	4·75
	17	Postage		6	1·55	1·55						
	17	Stationery		7	0·50			0·50				
	17	Cleaning Materials		8	0·25			0·25				
	18	R. Jones		9	1·45						L 43	1·45
0·35	18	Private Telephone Call		L 20								
	18	Fares		10	0·16		0·16					
	19	Fares		11	2·35		2·35					
	19	Repairs		12	0·85				0·85			
	19	M. Knight		13	3·25						L 47	3·25
	19	Postage		14	0·50	0·50						
					22·39	5·55	2·79	1·00	3·60			9·45
	19	Balance		c/d	2·96	L 21	L 22	L 23	L 24			
£25·35					£25·35							
£					£							
2·96	20	Balance		B/d								
22·04	20	Restored Imprest		CB 30								

(5) Books of M. Jobbing (*SPA page 150*)

(a)

Dr. £	19..	Particulars	PCV	Total £	Postage £	Travel Expenses £	Cleaning £	Sundry Expenses £	F	Cr. Ledger Accounts £
20·00	Mar. 19	Balance	B/d							
5·00	19	Restored Imprest	CB 7							
	19	Postage	1	0·45	0·45					
	19	Bus Fares	2	0·65		0·65				
	20	Postage	3	0·36	0·36					
1·35	20	Tom Jones	L 42							
	21	Fares	4	0·15		0·15				
	21	Postage	5	0·05	0·05					
	21	Stationery	6	0·23				0·23		
	22	Soap, etc.	7	1·65			1·65			
	22	M. Brogan	8	3·75					L 67	3·75
	22	Office Equipment	9	0·65					L 72	0·65
	23	Postage	10	1·25	1·25					
	23	Telegram	11	0·65	0·65					
				9·84	2·76	0·80	1·65	0·23		4·40
	23	Balance	c/d	16·51	L 21	L 22	L 23	L 24		
£26·35				£26·35						
16·51	24	Balance	B/d							
8·49	24	Restored Imprest	CB 12							

(5) *continued*

(b)

The entries on March 20th would be posted as follows:

(i) Postage of £0·36 would be added in with the other postage items and debited to Postage Account.

(ii) The payment received from Tom Jones would be credited in Tom's ledger account—clearing the small account he owed.

(iii) Fares of £0·15 would be added in with other items of travelling expenses and debited to Travelling Expenses Account.

(6) Books of M. Clarke (SPA page 150)

Dr. £	19..	Details	PCV	Total £	Postage £	Travel Expenses £	Stationery £	General Expenses £	L	F	Cr. Ledger Accounts £
20·00	Jan. 11	Imprest	CB 12								
	11	Postage	1	1·45	1·45						
	11	M. Hemstock	2	2·48						L 84	2·48
	12	Fares	3	0·26		0·26					
	12	Notepaper	4	0·55			0·55				
2·32	12	Private Telephone Calls	L 25								
	13	Cleaning Materials	5	0·28				0·28			
	13	Tea and Cakes	6	0·36				0·36			
	14	L. Smith	7	2·25						L 76	2·25
	14	Cleaning Materials	8	1·30				1·30			
	15	Cleaner's Wages	9	5·00				5·00			
	15	Fares	10	0·12		0·12					
	15	Window Cleaner	11	0·25				0·25			
				14·30	1·45	0·38	0·55	7·19			4·73
	15	Balance	c/d	8·02	L 20	L 21	L 22	L 23			
£22·32				£22·32							
8·02	Jan. 16	Balance	B/d								
11·98	16	Restored Imprest	CB 17								

(7) (*SPA page 151*)

(*a*) The cashier should hand the petty cashier sums as follows:

February 1st £22·09 (i.e. £25 — £2·91 which is left from January).

March 1st £22·52 (i.e. £25 — £2·48 which is left from February).

(*b*) Double entries should be as follows:

£7·12. This figure should be debited to General Expenses Account. It is one of the losses of the business.

£4·13. This sum should be debited to the account of E. Robbins. The petty cash spent on the container must be reclaimed from Robbins, on whose behalf it was expended. He thus becomes a debtor for this amount.

(8) (SPA page 151)

Dr. £	19..		PCV	Total £	Postage and Stationery £	Travel Expenses £	Carriage £	Office Expenses £	£	F	Cr. Ledger Accounts £
2·25	Jan. 14	Balance	B/d								
7·75	14	Restored Imprest	CB 19								
	14	Stamps	1	2·00	2·00						
	15	Train Fares	2	0·25		0·25					
	15	Bus Fares	3	0·85		0·85					
	15	Telegrams	4	0·25	0·25						
	16	Carriage	5	0·45			0·45				
	16	Train Fares	6	0·86		0·86					
	16	Stationery	7	0·68	0·68						
	17	Repairs (window)	8	1·65				1·65			
	17	T. Smith	9	2·55						L 47	2·55
	18	Tea Lady	10	0·16				0·16			
				9·70	2·93	1·96	0·45	1·81			2·55
£10·00	18	Balance	c/d	0·30	L 36	L 37	L 38	L 39			
				£10·00							
0·30	19	Balance	B/d								

(9) Books of R. Duncan (*SPA page 151*)

Dr.   **Cr.**

£	19..		Particulars	PCV	Total £	Postage £	Cleaning £	Sundries £	£	£	F	£
10·00	June	29	Balances	B/f	6·30	4·14	1·22	0·94				
		29	Postage	19	0·13	0·13						
		30	Window Cleaner	20	0·22		0·22					
		30	Bus Fares	21	0·07			0·07				
		30	Postage	22	0·15	0·15						
					6·87	4·42	1·44	1·01				
		30	Balance	c/d	3·13	L 51	L 52	L 53				
£10·00					£10·00							
3·13	July	1	Balance	B/d								
6·87		1	Restored Imprest	CB 17								

Postage A/c   L 51
	£
19..	
June 30 Petty Cash	4·42

Cleaning A/c   L 52
	£
19..	
June 20 Petty Cash	1·44

Sundries A/c   L 53
	£
19..	
June 30 Petty Cash	1·01

(10) Books of R. Lyons (SPA page 152)

(a)

Dr. £	19..		Details	PCV	Total £	Fares £	Postage £	Sundry Expenses £	Cleaning £	£	F	Ledger Accounts £	Cr.
25·00	Jan.	21	Imprest	CB 11									
		21	Postage	1	2·50		2·50						
		22	Repairs	2	2·45			2·45					
		22	Window Cleaner	3	0·30				0·30				
		22	Postage	4	0·25		0·25						
		23	Sundry Expenses	5	0·50			0·50					
		23	Cleaner's Wages	6	1·50				1·50				
		23	R. Thompson	7	2·35						L 17	2·35	
		24	Postage	8	0·36		0·36						
		24	Travelling Expenses	9	0·25	0·25							
		25	Sundry Expenses	10	0·55			0·55					
		25	Stamps	11	1·25		1·25						
		25	Postage	12	1·43		1·43						
		25	Travelling Expenses	13	2·25	2·25							
					15·94	2·50	5·79	3·50	1·80			2·35	
		25	Balance	c/d	9·06	L 19	L 20	L 21	L 22				
£25·00					£25·00							2·35	
9·06		26	Balance	B/d									
15·94		26	Restored Imprest	CB 18									

(10) *continued*

(b)

(i) The double entry for this receipt in the Petty-cash Book is in the main cash book: a credit entry in the cash column of £25·00.

(ii) The double entry for this payment of cash is in R. Thompson's account, where it has been debited to reduce the amount R. Lyons owes R. Thompson (who is clearly a creditor of R. Lyons).

(iii) The double entry for this payment is a debit in Travelling Expenses Account, where it appears as part of the £2·50 posted on January 25th.

More Journal Proper Entries— Unusual Bank Transactions

Exercises Set 22: Bank Loans, Interest and Charges

(1) Books of R. Piggott (*SPA page 157*)

19..				£	£
Dec. 15	Bank A/c	Dr.	CB 1	500·00	
	Interest-Payable A/c	Dr.	L 27	70·00	
	Lloyd's Bank Loan A/c		L 56		570·00
	Being loan negotiated at this date for two years at 7 per cent				

Cash Book (Bank A/c) L 1		Interest-Payable A/c L 27	
19.. £		19.. £	
Dec. 15 Loan A/c 500·00		Dec. 15 Loan A/c 70·00	

Lloyd's Bank Loan A/c L 56	
	19.. £
	Dec 15 Bank and Interest-Payable A/cs 570·00

Note: In the second edition of *SPA* the interest figure on this loan was changed to 16 per cent. Readers using this edition should note that the interest is therefore £160 and the Loan A/c total is £660.

(2) Books of M. Smith (*SPA page 157*)

19..				£	£
Aug. 4	Bank A/c	Dr.	CB 17	150·00	
	Interest-Payable A/c	Dr.	L 18	12·00	
	Bank Loan A/c		L 76		162·00
	Being Bank Loan arranged at this date repayable over one year at 8 per cent				

Cash Book (Bank A/c) L 17		Interest-Payable A/c L 18	
19.. £		19.. £	
Aug. 4 Bank Loan 150·00		Aug. 4 Bank Loan 12·00	

Bank Loan A/c L 76	
	19.. £
	Aug. 4 Bank and Interest-Payable A/cs 162·00

(3) Books of Loamshire Quarry Co. (*SPA page 157*)

19..					£	£
Apr.	8	Bank A/c	Dr.	CB 1	300 000·00	
		Interest-Due A/c	Dr.	L 30	72 000·00	
		Bank Loan A/c		L 96		372 000·00
		Being loan granted to clear overdraft, interest calculated at 8 per cent per annum for three years				

	Cash Book (Bank A/c)	L 1
19..	£	
Apr. 8 Bank		
Loan		
300 000·00		

	Interest-Due A/c	L 30
19..	£	
Apr. 8 Bank		
Loan 72 000·00		

	Bank Loan A/c	L 96
	19..	£
	Apr. 8 Bank and	
	Interest	
	Due	
	A/cs 372 000·00	

(4) Books of M. Dawson (*SPA page 157*)

19..					£	£
May	7	P. Hawkins A/c	Dr.	L 137	120·25	
		Bank A/c		CB 1		120·25
		Being dishonoured cheque removed from Bank A/c, and debt restored to the debtor's account				

(5) Books of B. Barnard (*SPA page 158*)

19..					£	£
July	21	M. Rookes A/c	Dr.	L 72	40·00	
		Bank A/c		CB 1		38·50
		Discount-Allowed A/c		L 25		1·50
		Being bad debt restored in full to debtor's account. Cheque dishonoured, and discount cancelled				

	M. Rookes A/c		L 72	
19..	£	19..	£	
July 1 Balance	40·00	July 17 Bank	38·50	
21 Bank, etc.	40·00	17 Discount	1·50	

	Cash Book (Bank A/c)	L 1
	19..	£
	July 21 M. Rookes 38·50	

	Discount-Allowed A/c	L 25
	19..	£
	July 21 M. Rookes 1·50	

(6) Books of M. Kelley (*SPA page 158*)

19..					£	£
May	17	R. Boniface A/c	Dr.	L 84	76·00	
		Bank A/c		CB 1		72·20
		Discount-Allowed A/c		L 35		3·80
		Being dishonoured cheque restored to debtor, including discount now disallowed				

	R. Boniface A/c	L 84		Cash Book (Bank A/c)	L 1

19..	£	19..	£	19..	£
May 1 Balance	76·00	May 12 Bank	72·20	May 17 R.Boniface	
17 Bank,etc.	76·00	12 Discount Allowed	3·80		72·20

	Discount-Allowed A/c	L 35
	19..	£
	May 17 R. Boniface	3·80

(7) Books of R. Hope (*SPA page 158*)

19..					£	£
July	15	Bank Charges A/c	Dr.	L 27	8·75	
		Bank A/c		CB 1		8·75
		Being bank charges deducted in June as per Bank Statement received today				

(8) Books of M. Hall (*SPA page 158*)

19..					£	£
Mar.	31	Bank charges A/c	Dr.	L 37	4·25	
		Bank A/c		CB 1		4·25
		Being bank charges as per Bank Statement received today				
Mar.	31	Bank Deposit A/c	Dr.	L 96	6·25	
		Interest-Received A/c		L 58		6·25
		Being interest on Deposit A/c credited by bank as per Bank Statement				

(9) Books of R. Homberger (*SPA page 158*)

19..					£	£
Dec.	27	Bank Deposit A/c	Dr.	L 58	6·50	
		Interest-Received A/c		L 28		6·50
		Being interest on Deposit A/c as notified by bank				

(10) Books of B. Charles (*SPA page 158*)

19..					£	£
Mar.	31	Home Loans (London) Ltd. Deposit A/c Dr.	L 175		42·80	
		Interest-Received A/c	L 26			42·80
		Being interest notified by Building Society at this date				

Unit Seventeen

A Full Set of Accounts

Exercises Set 23: Accounting with a Full Set of Books to Final-Accounts Level

(1) Books of Paul Brickhill (*SPA page 169*)

19..		Journal Proper			£	£
May	1	Cash A/c	Dr.	CB 1	12·00	
		Bank A/c	Dr.	CB 1	132·00	
		Premises A/c	Dr.	L 1	4 800·00	
		Furniture A/c	Dr.	L 2	450·00	
		R. Lyons A/c	Dr.	L 3	56·50	
		B. Forte A/c	Dr.	L 4	116·25	
		Stock A/c	Dr.	L 5	1 450·00	
		M. Hague A/c		L 6		420·00
		R. Wright A/c		L 7		270·00
		Capital A/c		L 8		6 326·75
		Being assets and liabilities at this date			£7 016·75	£7 016·75
	4	Bank A/c	Dr.	CB 1	500·00	
		Bank Loan A/c		L 9		500·00
		Being loan arranged at this date				
	11	Typewriter A/c	Dr.	L 10	55·00	
		Bank A/c		CB 1		55·00
		Being purchase of typewriter (Ref. No. D/71258) at this date				

19..		Sales Day Book			£
May	5	R. Lyons			
		Goods		L 3	36·50
	18	B. Forte			
		Goods		L 4	25·50
				L 11	£62·00

19..		Sales Returns Book			£
May	25	B. Forte			
		Goods		L 4	25·50
				L 12	£25·50

19..			**Purchases Day Book**					£
May	10		M. Hague					
			Goods		L 6			325·00
	15		R. Wright					
			Goods		L 7			125·00
					L 13			£450·00

(Continued on page 108.)

Cash Book

Dr.

19.. May	Particulars	Folio	£	£	£
1	Balances		—	12·00	132·00
1	Sales	J 1		42·50	
4	Bank Loan	L 11			500·00
8	Sales	J 1		262·50	
8	Cash	L 11			200·00
16	R. Lyons	C 3			56·50
19	Sales	L 11		245·00	
19	Cash	C			200·00
26	Sales	L 11		148·50	
30	Cash	C			200·00
31	Sales	L 11		49·50	
			—	760·00	1 288·50
19.. June 1	Balances	B/d		72·10	528·00

Cr.

19.. May	Particulars	Folio	£	£	£
5	Wages	L 14		9·30	
8	Bank	C		200·00	
10	Typewriter	J 1			55·00
12	Wages	L 14		9·30	
12	M. Hague	L 6	21·00		399·00
19	Wages	L 14		9·30	
22	Bank	C		200·00	
23	R. Wright	L 7	13·50		256·50
23	Office Expenses	L 15		5·25	
26	Wages	L 14		10·00	
29	Purchases	L 13		37·50	
30	Cleaning Expenses	L 16		7·25	
30	Bank	C		200·00	
31	Drawings	L 17			50·00
31	Balances	c/d		72·10	528·00
			34·50	760·00	1 288·50
			L 18		

Premises A/c   L 1

19..	£
May 1 Opening	
Balance	
4 800·00	

Furniture and Fittings A/c   L 2

19..	£
May 1 Opening	
Balance	450·00

R. Lyons A/c   L 3

19..	£	19..	£
May 1 Opening		May 16 Bank	56·50
Balance	56·50	31 Balance	36·50
2 Sales	36·50		
	£93·00		£93·00
19..	£		
June 1 Balance	36·50		

B. Forte A/c   L 4

19..	£	19..	
May 1 Opening		May 25 Sales Returns	
Balance	116·25		25·50
18 Sales	25·50	31 Balance	116·25
	£141·75		£141·75
19..	£		
June 1 Balance	116·25		

Stock A/c   L 5

19..	£	19..	£
May 1 Opening		May 31 Trading	
Balance		A/c	1 450·00
	1 450·00	31 Balance	1 300·00
31 Trading			
A/c	1 300·00		
	£2 750·00		£2 750·00
19..	£		
June 1 Balance	1 300·00		

M. Hague A/c   L 6

19..	£	19..	£
May 12 Bank	399·00	May 1 Opening	
12 Discount	21·00	Balance	420·00
31 Balance	325·00	10 Purchases	325·00
	£745·00		£745·00
		19..	£
		June 1 Balance	325·00

R. Wright A/c   L 7

19..	£	19..	£
May 22 Bank	256·50	May 1 Opening	
22 Discount	13·50	Balance	270·00
31 Balance	125·00	15 Purchases	125·00
	£395·00		£395·00
		19..	£
		June 1 Balance	125·00

Capital A/c   L 8

19..	£	19..	£
May 31 Drawings		May 1 Opening Bal-	
	50·00	ance	6 326·75
31 Balance		31 Net	
	6 407·85	Profit	131·10
	£6 457·85		£6 457·85
		19..	£
		June 1 Balance	6 407·85

Bank Loan A/c   L 9

		19..	£
		May 4 Bank	500·00

Typewriter A/c   L 10

19..	£		
May 11 Bank	55·00		

Sales A/c   L 11

19..	£	19..	£
May 31 Trading		May 1 Cash	42·50
A/c	810·00	8 Cash	262·50
		19 Cash	245·00
		26 Cash	148·50
		31 Cash	49·50
		31 Sundry	
		Debtors	62·00
	£810·00		£810·00

Sales–Returns A/c   L 12

19..	£	19..	£
May 31 Sundry		May 31 Trading	
Debtors	25·50	A/c	25·50
	£25·50		£25·50

	Purchases A/c	L 13		
19..	£	19..		£
May 29 Cash	37·50	May 31 Trading		
31 Sundry		A/c		487·50
Creditors	450·00			
	£487·50			£487·50

	Wages A/c	L 14		
19..	£	19..		£
May 5 Cash	9·30	May 31 Trading		
12 Cash	9·30	A/c		37·90
19 Cash	9·30			
26 Cash	10·00			
	£37·90			£37·90

	Office Expenses A/c	L 15		
19..	£	19..		£
May 23		May 31 Profit and		
Cash	5·25	Loss A/c	5·25	

	Cleaning Expenses A/c	L 16		
19..	£	19..		£
May 30		May 31 Profit and		
Cash	7·25	Loss A/c	7·25	

	Drawings A/c	L 17		
19..	£	19..		£
May 31 Bank	50·00	May 31 Capital A/c	50·00	

	Discount Received A/c	L 18		
19..	£	19..		£
May 31 Profit and		May 31 Sundry		
Loss		Dis-		
A/c	34·50	counts	34·50	

Trial Balance (as at May 31st 19..)

	Dr.	Cr.
	£	£
Cash	72·10	
Bank	528·00	
Premises	4 800·00	
Fixtures and Fittings	450·00	
R. Lyons	36·50	
B. Forte	116·25	
Stock	1 450·00	
M. Hague		325·00
R. Wright		125·00
Capital		6 326·75
Bank Loan		500·00
Typewriter	55·00	
Sales		810·00
Sales Returns	25·50	
Purchases	487·50	
Wages	37·90	
Office Expenses	5·25	
Cleaning Expenses	7·25	
Drawings	50·00	
Discount Received		34·50
	£8 121·25	8 121·25

Trading A/c (for month ended May 31st 19..)			
19..	£	19..	£
Open Stock	1 450·00	Sales	810·00
Purchases	487·50	*Less* Returns	25·50
Total Stock Available	1 937·50		784·50
Less Closing Stock	1 300·00		
Cost of Stock Sold	637·50		
Wages	37·90		
Cost of Sales	675·40		
Gross Profit	109·10		
	£784·50		£784·50

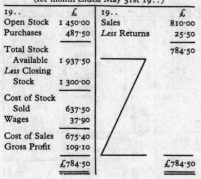

Profit and Loss A/c (for month ended May 31st 19..)			
19..	£	19..	£
Office Expenses	5·25	Gross Profit	109·10
Cleaning Expenses	7·25	Discount Received	34·50
Total Expenses	12·50		143·60
Net Profit (to Capital A/c)	131·10		
	£143·60		£143·60

Balance Sheet (as at May 31st 19..)

	£	£		£	£
Fixed Assets			Capital		
Premises		4 800·00	At Start		6 326·75
Fixtures and Fittings		450·00	*Add* Net Profit	131·10	
Typewriter		55·00	*Less* Drawings	50·00	
					81·10
		5 305·00			
Current Assets					6 407·85
Stock	1 300·00				
Debtors	152·75		Long-term Liability		
Bank	528·00		Bank Loan		500·00
Cash	72·10		Current Liability		
		2 052·85	Creditors		450·00
		£7 357·85			£7 357·85

(2) Books of Martin Lawrence (*SPA page 169*)

Journal Proper

19..					£	£
Oct.	1	Cash A/c	Dr.	CB 1	27·00	
		Bank A/c	Dr.	CB 1	525·00	
		Premises A/c	Dr.	L 1	9 500·00	
		Furniture A/c	Dr.	L 2	850·00	
		M. Lowe A/c	Dr.	L 3	27·50	
		R. Lark A/c	Dr.	L 4	38·60	
		Stock A/c	Dr.	L 5	1 500·00	
		M. Thomas A/c		L 6		272·60
		R. Peacock A/c		L 7		162·50
		Capital A/c		L 8		12 033·00
		Being assets and liabilities at this date			£12 468·10	12 468·10
	4	Furniture A/c	Dr.	L 2	86·50	
		Office Display Co. A/c		L 9		86·50
		Being purchase of new showcase at this date				
	11	Office Equipment A/c	Dr.	L 10	34·00	
		Bank A/c		CB 1		34·00
		Being purchase of calculator (Ref. No. M/727a) at this date				

Sales Day Book

19..				£	£
Oct.	2	*M. Lowe*			
		Goods	L 3		85·50
	15	*R. Lark*			
		Goods	L 4		16·50
			L 11		£102·00

Purchases Day Book

19..				£	£
Oct.	10	*M. Thomas*			
		Goods	L 6		28·75
	22	*R. Peacock*			
		Goods	L 7		140·00
			L 12		£168·75

Sales Returns Book

19..				£	£
Oct.	25	*M. Lowe*	L 3		45·00
		Goods			
			L 13		£45·00

Cash Book

19.. Oct.	Particulars	Folio	£	£	£
1	Balance	J 1		27·00	525·00
1	Sales	L 11		127·50	
8	Sales	L 11		136·50	
8	Cash	C			200·00
18	R. Lark	L 4	1·93	172·75	
19	Sales	L 11		175·50	
26	Cash	C			200·00
26	Sales	L 11		38·50	
31	Sales	L 11			36·67
		£	1·93	677·75	961·67
19.. Nov. 1	Balance	B/d L 14		132·50	386·20

19.. Oct.	Particulars	Folio	£	£	£
5	Wages	L 15		44·50	
8	Bank	C		200·00	
11	Office Equipment A/c	J 1			34·00
12	Wages	L 15		44·50	
16	M. Thomas	L 6	13·63		258·97
19	Wages	L 15		44·50	
23	R. Peacock	L 7			162·50
26	Bank	C		200·00	
29	Repairs	L 16		4·25	
30	Cleaning Expenses	L 17		7·50	
31	Drawings	L 18			120·00
31	Balance	c/d		132·50	386·20
		£ L 19	13·63	677·75	961·67

Premises A/c		L 1
19..	£	
Oct. 1 Opening		
Balance		
9 500·00		

Furniture A/c		L 2
19..	£	
Oct. 1 Opening		
Balance 850·00		
4 Office Display		
Co. 86·50		

M. Lowe A/c — L 3

19..	£	19..	£
Oct. 1 Opening		Oct. 25 Sales	
Balance	27·50	Returns	45·00
2 Sales	85·50	31 Balance	68·00
	£113·00		£113·00
19..	£		
Nov. 1 Balance	68·00		

R. Lark A/c — L 4

19..	£	19..	£
Oct. 1 Opening		Oct. 18 Bank	36·67
Balance	38·60	18 Discount	1·93
15 Sales	16·50	31 Balance	16·50
	£55·10		£55·10
19..	£		
Nov. 1 Balance	16·50		

Stock A/c — L 5

19..	£	19..	£
Oct. 1 Opening		Oct. 31 Trading	
Balance		A/c	1 500·00
1 500·00			
1 500·00		1 500·00	
Oct. 31 Trading A/c			
1 400·00			

M. Thomas A/c — L 6

19..	£	19..	£
Oct. 16 Bank	258·97	Oct. 1 Opening	
16 Discount	13·63	Balance	272·60
31 Balance	28·75	31 Purchases	28·75
	£301·35		£301·35
		19..	£
		Nov. 1 Balance	28·75

R. Peacock A/c — L 7

19..	£	19..	£
Oct. 23 Bank	162·50	Oct. 1 Opening	
31 Balance	140·00	Balance	162·50
		22 Purchases	140·00
	£302·50		£302·50
		19..	£
		Nov. 1 Balance	140·00

Capital A/c — L 8

19..	£	19..	£
Oct. 31 Drawings		Oct. 1 Opening	
	120·00	Balance	
31 Balance			12 033·00
	12 218·45	31 Net Profit	305·45
	£12 338·45		£12 338·45
		19..	£
		Nov. 1 Balance	12 218·45

Office Display Co. A/c — L 9

19..	£
Oct. 4 Furniture	86·50

Office Equipment A/c — L 10

19..	£
Oct. 11 Bank	34·00

Sales A/c — L 11

19..	£	19..	£
Oct. 31 Trading		Oct. 1 Cash	127·50
A/c	752·75	8 Cash	136·50
		19 Cash	172·75
		26 Cash	175·50
		31 Cash	38·50
		31 Sundry Debtors	
			102·00
	£752·75		£752·75

Purchases A/c — L 12

19..	£	19..	£
Oct. 31 Sundry		Oct. 31 Trading	
Creditors		A/c	168·75
	168·75		
	£168·75		£168·75

Sales-Returns A/c — L 13

19..	£	19..	£
Oct. 31 Sundry		Oct. 31 Trading	
Debtors	45·00	A/c	45·00
	£45·00		£45·00

Discount-Allowed A/c — L 14

19..	£	19..	£
Oct. 31 Sundry		Oct. 31 Profit and	
Discounts	1·93	Loss A/c	1·93
	£1·93		£1·93

	Wages A/c	L 15	
19..	£	19..	£
Oct. 5 Cash	44·50	Oct. 31 Trading	
12 Cash	44·50	A/c	133·50
19 Cash	44·50		
	£133·50		£133·50

	Repairs A/c	L 16	
19..	£	19..	£
Oct. 29 Cash	4·25	Oct. 31 Profit and	
		Loss A/c	4·25
	£4·25		£4·25

	Cleaning Expenses A/c	L 17	
19..	£	19..	£
Oct. 30 Cash		Oct. 31 Profit and	
	7·50	Loss A/c	7·50

	Drawings A/c	L 18	
19..	£	19..	£
Oct. 31 Bank		Oct. 31 Capital	
	120·00	A/c	120·00

	Discount-Received A/c	L 19	
19..	£	19..	£
Oct. 31 Profit and		Oct. 31 Sundry	
Loss A/c		Discounts	
	13·63		13·63

Trial Balance (as at October 31st 19..)

	Dr.	Cr.
	£	£
Cash	132·50	
Bank	386·20	
Premises	9 500·00	
Furniture	936·50	
M. Lowe	68·00	
R. Lark	16·50	
Stock	1 500·00	
M. Thomas		28·75
R. Peacock		140·00
Capital		12 033·00
Office Display Co.		86·50
Office Equipment	34·00	
Sales		752·75
Purchases	168·75	
Sales Returns	45·00	
Discount Allowed	1·93	
Wages	133·50	
Repairs	4·25	
Cleaning Expenses	7·50	
Drawings	120·00	
Discount Received		13·63
	£13 054·63	13 054·63

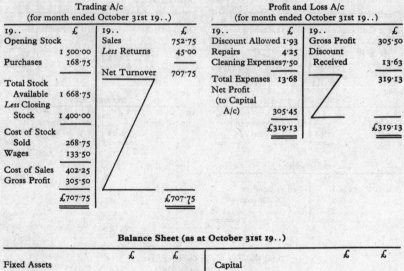

Trading A/c
(for month ended October 31st 19..)

19..	£	19..	£
Opening Stock		Sales	752·75
	1 500·00	Less Returns	45·00
Purchases	168·75		
		Net Turnover	707·75
Total Stock			
Available	1 668·75		
Less Closing			
Stock	1 400·00		
Cost of Stock			
Sold	268·75		
Wages	133·50		
Cost of Sales	402·25		
Gross Profit	305·50		
	£707·75		£707·75

Profit and Loss A/c
(for month ended October 31st 19..)

19..	£	19..	£
Discount Allowed	1·93	Gross Profit	305·50
Repairs	4·25	Discount	
Cleaning Expenses	7·50	Received	13·63
Total Expenses	13·68		319·13
Net Profit			
(to Capital			
A/c)	305·45		
	£319·13		£319·13

Balance Sheet (as at October 31st 19..)

	£	£		£	£
Fixed Assets			Capital		
Premises		9 500·00	At Start		12 033·00
Furniture		936·50	Add Net Profit	305·45	
Office Equipment		34·00	Less Drawings	120·00	
		10 470·50			185·45
					12 218·45
Current Assets					
Stock	1 400·00				
Debtors	84·50				
Bank	386·20		Current Liabilities		
Cash	132·50		Creditors		255·25
		2 003·20			
		£12 473·70			£12 473·70

(3) Books of Martin Candler (*SPA page 170*)

Journal Proper

19..					£	£
July	1	Cash A/c	Dr.	CB 1	138·50	
		Bank A/c	Dr.	CB 1	3 250·00	
		Stock A/c	Dr.	L 1	320·00	
		Furniture and Fittings A/c	Dr.	L 2	650·00	
		M. Truelove A/c	Dr.	L 3	15·75	
		R. Carter A/c	Dr.	L 4	21·60	
		M. Perkins A/c		L 5		184·60
		Capital A/c		L 6		4 211·25
		Being assets and liabilities at this date			£4 395·85	4 395·85
	11	Shop Equipment A/c	Dr.	L 7	28·40	
		Truecharge Ltd. A/c		L 8		28·40
		Being purchase of new scales for shop at this date				

Purchases Day Book

19.. July	2	M. Perkins Goods	L 5 L 9	£	£ 68·50 £68·50

Sales Day Book

19.. July	23	R. Carter Goods	L 4 L 10	£	£ 27·80 £27·80

Cash Book

Dr

19.. July		Particulars	Fo.	£	£	£
	1	Balances	J 1		138·50	3 250·00
	1	M. Truelove	L 3			15·75
	5	Sales	L 10		142·46	120·00
	5	Cash	C	1·08		20·52
	9	R. Carter	L 4		165·60	100·00
	12	Sales	L 10		132·80	
	12	Cash	C			50·00
	19	Sales	L 10		224·26	
	22	Cash	C			250·00
	26	Sales	L 10		65·20	
	26	Cash	C			
	31	Sales	L 10			
			£	1·08	868·82	3 806·27
19.. Aug.	1	Balances	B/d L 11		107·27	3502·50

Cr

19.. July		Particulars	Fo.	£	£	£
	1	Purchases	L 9		26·50	175·37
	4	M. Perkins	L 5	9·23	120·00	
	5	Bank	C			
	8	Purchases	L 9		45·50	
	12	Bank	C		100·00	
	15	Purchases	L 9		36·85	
	15	Repairs	L 12		8·25	
	22	Purchases	L 9		72·50	
	22	Bank	C		50·00	
	24	Wages	L 13		5·00	
	25	Accountants' Charges	L 14			
	26	Bank	C		250·00	8·40
	29	Purchases	L 9		40·45	
	30	Wages	L 13		6·50	
	31	Drawings	L 15			120·00
	31	Balance	c/d		107·27	3 502·50
			£	9·23	868·82	3 806·27
			L 16			

Stock A/c   L 1

19..	£	19..	£
July 1 Opening		July 31 Trading	
Balance	320·00	A/c	320·00
31 Trading		31 Balance	165·00
A/c	165·00		
	£485·00		£485·00

19..	£		
Aug. 1 Balance	165·00		

Furniture and Fittings A/c   L 2

19..	£		
July 1 Opening			
Balance	650·00		

M. Truelove A/c   L 3

19..	£	19..	£
July 1 Opening		July 1 Bank	
Balance	15·75		15·75

R. Carter A/c   L 4

19..	£	19..	£
July 1 Opening		July 9 Bank	20·52
Balance	21·60	9 Discount	1·08
23 Sales	27·80	31 Balance	27·80
	£49·40		£49·40

19..	£		
Aug. 1 Balance	27·80		

M. Perkins A/c   L 5

19..	£	19..	£
July 4 Bank	175·37	July 1 Opening	
4 Discount	9·23	Balance	184·60
31 Balance	68·50	2 Purchases	68·50
	£253·10		£253·10

		19..	£
		Aug. 1 Balance	68·50

Capital A/c   L 6

19..	£	19..	£
July 31 Drawings		July 1 Opening	
	120·00	Balance	4 211·25
31 Balance		31 Net	
	4 384·07	Profit	292·82
	£4 504·07		£4 504·07

		19..	£
		Aug. 1 Balance	4 384·07

Shop Equipment A/c   L 7

19..	£		
July 11 True-			
charge	28·40		

Truecharge Ltd. A/c   L 8

		19..	£
		July 11 Shop	
		Equip-	
		ment	28·40

Purchases A/c   L 9

19..	£	19..	£
July 1 Cash	26·50	July 31 Trading A/c	
8 Cash	45·50		290·30
15 Cash	36·85		
22 Cash	72·50		
29 Cash	40·45		
31 Sundry			
Creditors	68·50		
	£290·30		£290·30

Safes A/c   L 10

19..	£	19..	£
July 31 Trading A/c		July 5 Cash	142·46
	758·12	12 Cash	165·60
		19 Cash	132·80
		26 Cash	224·26
		31 Cash	65·20
		31 Sundry	
		Debtors	27·80
	£758·12		£758·12

Discount-Allowed A/c   L 11

19..	£	19..	£
July 31 Sundry		July 31 Profit and	
Discounts	1·08	Loss A/c	1·08

Repairs A/c   L 12

19..	£	19..	£
July 15		July 31 Profit and	
Cash	8·25	Loss A/c	8·25

	Wages A/c	L 13	
19..	£	19..	£
July 24 Cash	5·00	July 31 Trading	
30 Cash	6·50	A/c	11·50
	£11·50		£11·50

	Accountant's Charges A/c	L 14	
19..	£	19..	£
July 25		July 31 Profit and	
Bank	8·40	Loss A/c	8·40

	Drawings A/c	L 15	
19..	£	19..	£
July 31 Bank	120·00	July 31 Capital A/c	120·00

	Discount-Received A/c	L 16	
19..	£	19..	£
July 31 Profit and		July 31 Sundry	
Loss A/c	9·23	Discounts	9·23

Trial Balance (as at July 31st 19..)

	Dr.	Cr.
	£	£
Cash	107·27	
Bank	3 502·50	
Stock	320·00	
Furniture and Fittings	650·00	
R. Carter	27·80	
M. Perkins		68·50
Capital		4 211·25
Shop Equipment	28·40	
Truecharge Ltd.		28·40
Purchases	290·30	
Sales		758·12
Discount Allowed	1·08	
Repairs	8·25	
Wages	11·50	
Accountant's Charges	8·40	
Drawings	120·00	
Discount Received		9·23
	£5 075·50	5 075·50

Trading A/c
(for month ending July 31st 19..)

July 31	£	July 31	£
Opening Stock	320·00	Sales	758·12
Purchases	290·30		
Total Stock			
Available	610·30		
Less Closing			
Stock	165·00		
Cost of Stock			
Sold	445·30		
Wages	11·50		
Cost of Sales	456·80		
Gross Profit	301·32		
	£758·12		£758·12

Profit and Loss A/c
(for month ending July 31st 19..)

July 31	£	July 31	£
Discount Allowed	1·08	Gross Profit	301·32
Repairs	8·25	Discount Received	9·23
Accountants'			
Charges	8·40		310·55
Total Expenses	17·73		
Net Profit	292·82		
	£310·55		£310·55

Balance Sheet (as at July 31st 19..)

	£	£		£	£
Fixed Assets			Capital		
Furniture and Fittings		650·00	At Start		4 211·25
Shop Equipment		28·40	Net Profit	292·82	
		———	Less Drawings	120·00	
		678·40			172·82
Current Assets					4 384·07
Stock	165·00				
Debtors	27·80				
Bank	3 502·50		Current Liabilities		
Cash	107·27		Creditors		96·90
		3 802·57			
		£4 480·97			£4 480·97

(4) Books of John Walker (*SPA page 171*)

Journal Proper

19..					£	£
July	1	Cash	Dr.	CB 1	138·50	
		Bank	Dr.	CB 1	2 752·50	
		Stock	Dr.	L 1	7 250·00	
		Furniture and Fittings	Dr.	L 2	260·00	
		M. Tankerton	Dr.	L 3	275·00	
		R. Cartier	Dr.	L 4	16·50	
		Union Supply Co.		L 5		1 048·80
		Capital		L 6		9 643·70
		Being assets and liabilities at this date			£10 692·50	10 692·50
July	10	Motor Vehicle A/c	Dr.	L 12	650·00	
		Bank A/c		CB 1		650·00
		Being new vehicle purchased at this date				

Purchases Day Book

19..					£
July	1	*Union Supply Co.*			
		Goods		L 5	650·00
	9	*Carson's Furniture Co.*			
		Goods		L 8	828·50
	11	*Union Supply Co.*			
		Goods		L 5	248·50
				L 7	£1 727·00

Purchases Returns Book

19..					£
July	15	*Carson's Furniture Co.*			
		Allowance		L 8	10·00
				L 9	£10·00

Sales Day Book

19..				£
July 23	A. Rotemeyer	Goods	L 10	64·50
30	R. Cartier	Goods	L 4	48·50
			L 11	£113·00

Cash Book

Dr.

19..	Particulars	Folio	£	£	£
July 1	Balance	B/d	—	138·50	2752·50
2	M. Tankerton	L 3			75·00
6	Cash Sales	L 11		825·50	
6	Cash	C			600·00
8	R. Cartier	L 4		630·55	16·50
13	Sales	L 11		525·50	
19	Sales	L 11			
19	Cash	C			1 000·00
26	Sales	L 11		638·50	
26	Cash	C			400·00
31	Sales	L 11		1 252·50	
			—	4 011·05	4 844·00
Aug. 1	Balance	B/d		1 593·55	3 077·64

Cr.

19..	Particulars	Folio	£	£	£
July 4	Purchases	L 7		42·50	996·36
5	Union Supply Co.	L 5	52·44	600·00	650·00
6	Bank	C			
10	Motor Vehicles	J 1		32·50	
12	Wages	L 13		7·50	
16	Security Expenses	L 14		3·25	
17	Office Expenses	L 15			
19	Bank	C		1 000·00	
24	Purchases	L 7		275·00	
25	Wages	L 13		32·75	
26	Bank	C		400·00	
29	Insurance	L 16		24·00	
31	Drawings	L 17			120·00
31	Balance	c/d		1 593·55	3 077·64
			52·44	4 011·05	4 844·00
		L 18			

Stock A/c	L 1
19.. £	19.. £
July 1 Opening	July 31 Trading
Balance	A/c 7 250·00
7 250·00	31 Balance
31 Trading	6 450·00
A/c 6 450·00	
£13 700·00	£13 700·00
19.. £	
Aug. 1 Balance	
6 450·00	

Furniture and Fittings A/c	L 2
19.. £	
July 1 Opening	
Balance 260·00	

M. Tankerton A/c	L 3
19.. £	19.. £
July 1 Opening	July 2 Bank 75·00
Balance 275·00	31 Balance 200·00
£275·00	£275·00
19.. £	
Aug. 1 Balance 200·00	

R. Cartier A/c	L 4
19.. £	19.. £
July 1 Opening	July 8 Bank 16·50
Balance 16·50	30 Balance 48·50
30 Sales 48·50	
£65·00	£65·00
19.. £	
Aug. 1 Balance 48·50	

Union Supply Co. A/c	L 5
19.. £	19.. £
July 5 Bank 996·36	July 1 Opening
5 Discount 52·44	Balance 1 048·80
31 Balance 898·50	1 Purchases 650·00
	11 Purchases 248·50
£1 947·30	£1 947·30
	19.. £
	Aug. 1 Balance 898·50

Capital A/c	L 6
19.. £	19.. £
July 31 Drawings	July 1 Opening
120·00	Balance 9 643·70
31 Balance	31 Net
10 627·19	Profit 1 103·49
£10 747·19	£10 747·19
	19.. £
	Aug. 1 Balance 10 627·19

Purchases A/c	L 7
19.. £	19.. £
July 4 Cash 42·50	July 31 Trading
24 Cash 275·00	A/c 2 044·50
31 Sundry	
Creditors	
1 727·00	
£2 044·50	£2 044·50

Carson's Furniture Co. A/c	L 8
19.. £	19.. £
July 15 Purchases	July 9 Purchases 828·50
Returns 10·00	
31 Balance 818·50	
£828·50	£828·50
	19.. £
	Aug. 1 Balance 818·50

Purchases-Returns A/c	L 9
19.. £	19.. £
July 31 Trading	July 31 Sundry
A/c 10·00	Creditors 10·00

A. Rotemeyer A/c	L 10
19.. £	
July 23 Sales 64·50	

Sales A/c	L 11
19.. £	19.. £
July 31 Trading	July 6 Cash 825·50
A/c 3 985·55	13 Cash 630·55
	19 Cash 525·50
	26 Cash 638·50
	31 Cash 1 252·50
	31 Sundry
	Debtors 113·00
£3 985·55	£3 985·55

Motor Vehicles A/c	L 12
19.. £	19..
July 10 Bank 650·00	

	Wages A/c	L 13			Security Expenses A/c	L 14
19..	£	19..	£	19..	£	19..	£

Wages A/c — L 13

19..		£	19..		£
July 12	Cash	32·50	July 31	Trading	
25	Cash	32·75		A/c	65·25
		£65·25			£65·25

Security Expenses A/c — L 14

19..		£	19..		£
July 16			July 31	Profit and	
	Cash	7·50		Loss A/c	7·50

Office Expenses A/c — L 15

19..		£	19..		£
July 17			July 31	Profit and	
	Cash	3·25		Loss A/c	3·25

Insurance A/c — L 16

19..		£	19..		£
July 29			July 31	Profit and	
	Cash	24·00		Loss A/c	24·00

Drawings A/c — L 17

19..		£	19..		£
July 31			July 31	Capital	
	Bank	120·00		A/c	120·00

Discount-Received A/c — L 18

19..		£	19..		£
July 31	Profit and		July 31	Sundry	
	Loss A/c	52·44		Discount	52·44

Trial Balance (as at July 31st 19..)

	Dr.	Cr.
	£	£
Cash	1 593·55	
Bank	3 077·64	
Stock	7 250·00	
Furniture and Fittings	260·00	
M. Tankerton	200·00	
R. Cartier	48·50	
Union Supply Co.		898·50
Capital		9 643·70
Purchases	2 044·50	
Carson's Furniture Co.		818·50
Purchases Returns		10·00
A. Rotemeyer	64·50	
Sales		3 985·55
Motor Vehicles	650·00	
Wages	65·25	
Security Expenses	7·50	
Office Expenses	3·25	
Insurance	24·00	
Drawings	120·00	
Discount Received		52·44
	£15 408·69	15 408·69

Trading A/c (for month ending July 31st 19..)

19..		£	£	19..		£
July 31	Opening Stock		7 250·00	July 31	Sales	3 985·55
	Purchases	2 044·50				
	Less Returns	10·00				
			2 034·50			
	Total Stock Available		9 284·50			
	Less Closing Stock		6 450·00			
	Cost of Stock Sold		2 834·50			
	Wages		65·25			
			2 899·75			
	Gross Profit		1 085·80			
			£3 985·55			£3 985·55

Profit and Loss A/c (for month ending July 31st 19..)

19..		£	19..		£
July 31	Security Expenses	7·50	July 31	Gross Profit	1 085·80
	Office Expenses	3·25		Discount Received	52·44
	Insurance	24·00			
		34·75			1 138·24
	Net Profit	1 103·49			
		£1 138·24			£1 138·24

Balance Sheet (as at July 31st 19..)

	£	£		£	£
Fixed Assets			Capital		
Furniture and Fittings	260·00		At Start		9 643·70
Motor Vehicles	650·00		Net Profit	1 103·49	
		910·00	Less Drawings	120·00	
					983·49
Current Assets					10 627·19
Stock	6 450·00				
Debtors	313·00		Current Liabilities		
Bank	3 077·64		Creditors		1 717·00
Cash	1 593·55				
		11 434·19			
		£12 344·19			£12 344·19

(5) Books of Paul Dombey (*SPA page 172*)

Journal Proper

19..					£	£
Jan.	1	Cash	Dr.	CB 1	27·50	
		Bank	Dr.	CB 1	1 056·50	
		Stock	Dr.	L 1	500·00	
		Land and Buildings	Dr.	L 2	13 800·00	
		Furniture and Fittings	Dr.	L 3	425·00	
		Plant and Machinery	Dr.	L 4	3 250·50	
		M. Wyatt	Dr.	L 5	72·80	
		C. Dobson	Dr.	L 6	116·50	
		C. Dickens		L 7		175·60
		Capital		L 8		19 073·20
		Assets and liabilities at this date			£19 248·80	19 248·80
	1	Motor Vehicles	Dr.	L 9	725·00	
		Royal Motors Ltd.		L 10		725·00
		Being motor vehicle purchased on credit at this date				
	13	Furniture and Fittings	Dr.	L 3	68·00	
		Bank		CB 1		68·00
		Being purchase of desks and chairs at this date				
	24	C. Dobson	Dr.	L 6	116·50	
		Bank		CB 1		116·50
		Being cheque dishonoured at this date				

Purchases Day Book

19..					£
Jan.	4	C. Dickens			
		Goods	L 7		72·75
	6	M. Culver			
		Goods	L 13		48·50
	17	C. Dickens			
		Goods	L 7		85·50
			L 14		£206·75

Sales Day Book

19..					£
Jan.	31	M. Wyatt			
		Goods	L 5		45·60
			L 12		£45·60

Sales-Returns Book

19..					£
Jan.	3	M. Wyatt			
		Goods	L 5		15·50
			L 11		£15·50

Cash Book

Dr

19.. Jan.	Particulars	Folio	£	£	£
1	Balances	J 1		27.50	1 056.50
2	Sales	L 12		76.50	69.16
9	M. Wyatt	L 5	3.64	89.50	
10	Sales	L 12			100.00
10	Cash	C			116.50
19	C. Dobson	L 6			
		L 15	£ 3.64	£ 193.50	£ 1 342.16
19.. Feb. 1	Balance	B/d		£ 54.65	£ 732.34

Cr

19.. Jan.	Particulars	Folio	£	£	£
2	Purchases	L 14			53.50
5	Stationery	L 16		7.55	
5	Postage	L 17		3.25	
5	Motor Vehicle Expenses	L 18		12.55	
7	C. Dickens	L 7	8.78		166.82
10	Bank	C		100.00	68.00
13	Furniture and Fittings	J 1			68.00
22	Motor Vehicle Expenses	L 18		15.50	
24	C. Dobson	J 1			116.50
29	Salaries	L 19			85.00
31	Drawings	L 20			120.00
31	Balance	c/d		54.65	732.34
		L 21	£ 8.78	£ 193.50	£ 1 342.16

Stock A/c — L 1

19..	£	19..	£
Jan. 1 Opening Balance	500·00	Jan. 31 Trading A/c	500·00
31 Trading A/c	650·00	31 Balance	650·00
	£1 150·00		£1 150·00
19..	£		
Feb 1 Balance	650·00		

Land and Buildings A/c — L 2

19..	£		
Jan. Opening Balance	13 800·00		

Furniture and Fittings A/c — L 3

19..	£		
Jan. 1 Opening Balance	425·00		
13 Bank	68·00		

Plant and Machinery A/c — L 4

19..	£		
Jan. 1 Opening Balance	3 250·50		

M. Wyatt A/c — L 5

19..	£	19..	£
Jan. 1 Opening Balance	72·80	Jan. 3 Sales Returns	15·50
31 Sales	45·60	9 Bank	69·16
		9 Discount	3·64
		31 Balance	30·10
	£118·40		£118·40
19..	£		
Feb. 1 Balance	30·10		

C. Dobson A/c — L 6

19..	£	19..	£
Jan. 1 Opening Balance	116·50	Jan. 19 Bank	116·50
24 Bank	116·50	31 Balance	116·50
	£233·00		£233·00
19..	£		
Feb. 1 Balance	116·50		

C. Dickens A/c — L 7

19..	£	19..	£
Jan. 7 Bank	166·82	Jan. Opening Balance	175·60
7 Discount	8·78	4 Purchase	72·75
31 Balance	158·25	17 Purchase	85·50
	£333·85		£333·85
		19..	£
		Feb. 1 Balance	158·25

Capital A/c — L 8

19..	£	19..	£
Jan. 31 Profit and Loss A/c	32·86	Jan. 1 Opening Balance	19 073·20
31 Drawings	120·00		
31 Balance	18 920·34		
	£19 073·20		£19 073·20
		19..	£
		Feb. 1 Balance	18 920·34

Motor Vehicles A/c — L 9

19..	£		
Jan. 1 Royal Motors	725·00		

Royal Motors Ltd. A/c — L 10

		19..	£
		Jan. 1 Motor Vehicles	725·00

Sales-Returns A/c — L 11

19..	£	19..	£
Jan. 31 Sundry Debtors	15·50	Jan. 31 Trading A/c	15·50

Sales A/c — L 12

19..	£	19..	£
Jan. 31 Trading A/c	211·60	Jan. 2 Cash	76·50
		10 Cash	89·50
		31 Sundry Debtors	45·60
	£211·60		£211·60

M. Culver A/c	L 13		Purchases A/c		L 14

19..	£	19..	£
		Jan. 6 Purchases 48·50	

19..	£	19..	£
Jan. 2 Bank	53·50	Jan. 31 Trading A/c	260·25
31 Sundry Creditors	206·75		
	£260·25		£260·25

Discount-Allowed A/c	L 15		Stationery A/c	L 16

19..	£	19..	£
Jan. 31 Sundry Discounts	3·64	Jan. 31 Profit and Loss A/c	3·64

19..	£	19..	£
Jan. 5 Cash	7·55	Jan. 31 Profit and Loss A/c	7·55

Postage A/c	L 17		Motor-Vehicle Expenses A/c	L 18

19..	£	19..	£
Jan. 5 Cash	3·25	Jan. 31 Profit and Loss A/c	3·25

19..	£	19..	£
Jan. 5 Cash	12·55	Jan. 31 Profit and Loss A/c	28·05
22 Cash	15·50		
	£28·05		£28·05

Salaries A/c	L 19		Drawings A/c	L 20

19..	£	19..	£
Jan. 29 Bank	85·00	Jan. 31 Profit and Loss A/c	85·00

19..	£	19..	£
Jan. 31 Bank	120·00	Jan. 31 Capital A/c	120·00

Discount-Received A/c	L 21

19..	£	19..	£
Jan. 31 Profit and Loss A/c	8·78	Jan. 31 Sundry Discounts	8·78

Trial Balance (as at January 31st 19..)

	Dr. £	Cr. £
Cash	54·65	
Bank	732·34	
Stock	500·00	
Land and Buildings	13 800·00	
Furniture and Fittings	493·00	
Plant and Machinery	3 250·50	
M. Wyatt	30·10	
C. Dobson	116·50	
C. Dickens		158·25
Capital		19 073·20
Motor Vehicles	725·00	
Royal Motors Ltd.		725·00
Sales Return	15·50	
Sales		211·60
M. Culver		48·50
Purchases	260·25	
Discount Allowed	3·64	
Stationery	7·55	
Postage	3·25	
Motor Vehicle Expenses	28·05	
Salaries	85·00	
Drawings	120·00	
Discount Received		8·78
	£20 225·33	20 225·33

Trading A/c (for month ending January 31st 19..)

19..		£	19..		£
Jan. 31	Opening Stock	500·00	Jan. 31	Sales	211·60
	Purchases	260·25		Less Returns	15·50
		760·25		Net Turnover	196·10
	Less Closing Stock	650·00			
	Cost of Stock Sold	110·25			
	Gross Profit	85·85			
		£196·10			£196·10

Profit and Loss A/c (for month ending January 31st 19..)

19..		£	19..		£
Jan. 31	Discount Allowed	3·64	Jan. 31	Gross Profit	85·85
	Stationery	7·55		Discount Received	8·78
	Postage	3·25			94·63
	Motor Vehicle Expenses	28·05			
	Salaries	85·00		Net Loss	32·86
		£127·49			£127·49

Balance Sheet (as at January 31st 19..)

	£	£		£	£
Fixed Assets			Capital		
Land and Buildings		13 800·00	At Start		19 073·20
Plant and Machinery		3 250·50	Less Net Loss	32·86	
Furniture and Fittings		493·00	Add Drawings	120·00	
Motor Vehicles		725·00			152·86
		18 268·50			18 920·34
Current Assets					
Stock	650·00				
Debtors	146·60		Current Liabilities		
Bank	732·34		Creditors		931·75
Cash	54·65				
		1 583·59			
		£19 852·09			£19 852·09

(6) Books of Gerard Eliasson (*SPA page 172*)

Journal Proper

19..					£	£
Jan.	1	Cash	Dr.	CB 1	75·00	
		Bank	Dr.	CB 1	1 534·50	
		Stock	Dr.	L 1	1 525·00	
		Land and Buildings	Dr.	L 2	7 500·00	
		Furniture and Fittings	Dr.	L 3	850·00	
		Plant and Machinery	Dr.	L 4	2 250·00	
		J. Van Eyck	Dr.	L 5	296·00	
		M. Wittenhagen	Dr.	L 6	350·00	
		G. Van Swieten		L 7		1 550·00
		Capital		L 8		12 830·50
		Being assets and liabilities at this date			£14 380·50	14 380·50
	1	Motor Vehicles	Dr.	L 9	850·00	850·00
		Hague Motors Ltd.		L 10		
		Being purchase of motor vehicle RTN 176 at this date.				
	7	Bank A/c	Dr.	CB 1	1 000·00	
		Mercantile Bank Loan A/c		L 11		1 000·00
		Being loan arranged at this date				

Purchases Day Book

19..					£
Jan.	4	*G. Van Swieten*			
		Goods		L 7	240·00
	6	*J. Denys*			
		Goods		L 12	100·00
				L 13	£340·00

Purchases-Returns Book

19..					£
Jan.	3	*G. Van Swieten*			
		Goods		L 7	150·00
				L 15	£150·00

Sales Day Book

19..					£
Jan.	13	*M. Wittenhagen*			
		Goods		L 6	425·00
				L 14	£425·00

Cash Book

Dr.

19..		Particulars	Folio	£	£	£
Jan.	1	Opening Balance	J 1		75·00	1 534·50
	7	Mercantile Bank Loan	J 1			1 000·00
	9	J. Van Eyck	L 5	14·80		281·20
	10	Sales	L 14		480·00	
	10	Cash	C			400·00
	17	M. Wittenhagen	L 6	17·50		332·50
	19	Sales	L 14		236·50	
	19	Cash	C			200·00
			L 16	£ 32·30	791·50	3 748·20
					£	£
					150·50	1 945·70
Feb.	1	Balance				

Cr.

19..		Particulars	Folio	£	£	£
Jan.	2	Purchases	L 13			175·00
	5	Stationery	L 17		17·50	
	5	Postage	L 18		3·50	
	5	Repairs	L 19		4·25	
	7	G. Van Swieten	L 7	77·50		1 472·50
	10	Bank	C		400·00	
	19	Bank	C		200·00	
	22	Sundry Expenses	L 20		1·25	
	24	Purchases	L 13		14·50	
	29	Salaries	L 21			95·00
	31	Drawings	L 22			60·00
	31	Balance	c/d		150·50	1 945·70
				£ 77·50	791·50	3 748·20
				L 23		

Stock A/c   L 1

19..	£	19..	£
Jan. 1 Opening Balance	1 525·00	Jan. Trading A/c	1 525·00
31 Trading A/c	1 750·00	31 Balance	1 750·00
	£3 275·00		£3 275·00
19..	£		
Feb. 1 Balance	1 750·00		

Land and Buildings A/c   L 2

19..	£
Jan. 1 Opening Balance	7 500·00

Furniture and Fittings A/c   L 3

19..	£
Jan. 1 Opening Balance	850·00

Plant and Machinery A/c   L 4

19..	£
Jan. 1 Opening Balance	2 250·00

J. Van Eyck A/c   L 5

19..	£	19..	£
Jan. 1 Opening Balance	296·00	Jan. 9 Cash	281·20
		9 Discount	14·80
	£296·00		£296·00

M. Wittenhagen A/c   L 6

19..	£	19..	£
Jan. 1 Opening Balance	350·00	Jan. 17 Bank	332·50
13 Sales	425·00	17 Discount	17·50
		31 Balance	425·00
	£775·00		£775·00
19..	£		
Feb. 1 Balance	425·00		

G. Van Swieten A/c   L 7

19..	£	19..	£
Jan. 3 Purchases Returns	150·00	Jan. 1 Opening Balance	1 550·00
7 Bank	1 472·50	4 Purchases	240·00
7 Discount	77·50		
31 Balance	90·00		
	£1 790·00		£1 790·00
		19..	£
		Feb. 1 Balance	90·00

Capital A/c   L 8

19..	£	19..	£
Jan. 31 Drawings	60·00	Jan. 1 Opening Balance	12 830·50
31 Balance	13 681·20	31 Net Profit	910·70
	£13 741·20		£13 741·20
		19..	£
		Feb. 1 Balance	13 681·20

Motor Vehicles A/c   L 9

19..	£
Jan. 1 Hague Motors Ltd.	850·00

Hague Motors Ltd. A/c   L 10

19..	£
Jan. 1 Motor Vehicles	850·00

Mercantile Bank Loan A/c   L 11

19..	£
Jan. 7 Bank	1 000·00

J. Denys A/c   L 12

19..	£
Jan. 6 Purchases	100·00

Purchases A/c   L 13

19..	£	19..	£
Jan. 2 Bank	175·00	Jan. 31 Trading A/c	529·50
24 Cash	14·50		
31 Sundry Creditors	340·00		
	£529·50		£529·50

Sales A/c   L 14

19..	£	19..	£
Jan. 31 Trading A/c	1 141·50	Jan. 10 Cash	480·00
		19 Cash	236·50
		31 Sundry Debtors	425·00
	£1 141·50		£1 141·50

Purchases-Returns A/c   L 15

19..	£	19..	£
Jan. 31 Trading A/c	150·00	Jan. 3 Sundry Creditors	150·00

Discount-Allowed A/c   L 16

19..	£	19..	£
Jan. 31 Sundry Discounts	32·30	Jan. 31 Profit and Loss A/c	32·30

Stationery A/c			L 17
19..	£	19..	£
Jan. 5		Jan. 31 Profit and	
Cash	17·50	Loss A/c	17·50

Postage A/c			L 18
19..	£	19..	£
Jan. 5		Jan. 31 Profit and	
Cash	3·50	Loss A/c	3·50

Repairs A/c			L 19
19..	£	19..	£
Jan. 5		Jan. 31 Profit and	
Cash	4·25	Loss A/c	4·25

General Expenses A/c			L 20
19..	£	19..	£
Jan. 22		Jan. 31 Profit and	
Cash	1·25	Loss A/c	1·25

Salaries A/c			L 21
19..	£	19..	£
Jan. 29		Jan. 31 Profit and	
Bank	95·00	Loss A/c	95·00

Drawings A/c			L 22
19..	£	19..	£
Jan. 31 Bank	60·00	Jan. 31 Capital A/c	60·00

Discount Received A/c			L 23
19..	£	19..	£
Jan. 31 Profit and		Jan. 31 Sundry	
Loss A/c	77·50	Discount	77·50

Trial Balance (as at January 31st 19..)

	Dr.	Cr.
	£	£
Cash	150·50	
Bank	1 945·70	
Stock	1 525·00	
Land and Buildings	7 500·00	
Furniture and Fittings	850·00	
Plant and Machinery	2 250·00	
M. Wittenhagen	425·00	
G. Van Swieten		90·00
Capital		12 830·50
Motor Vehicles	850·00	
Hague Motors Ltd.		850·00
Mercantile Bank Loan		1 000·00
J. Denys		100·00
Purchases	529·50	
Sales		1 141·50
Purchases Returns		150·00
Discount Allowed	32·30	
Stationery	17·50	
Postage	3·50	
Repairs	4·25	
General Expenses	1·25	
Salaries	95·00	
Drawings	60·00	
Discount Received		77·50
	£16 239·50	16 239·50

Trading A/c (for month ending January 31st 19..)

19..		£	£	19..	£
Jan. 31	Opening Stock		1 525·00	Jan. 31 Sales	1 141·50
	Purchases	529·50			
	Less Returns	150·00			
			379·50		
			1 904·50		
	Less Closing Stock		1 750·00		
	Cost of Stock Sold		154·50		
	Gross Profit		987·00		
			£1 141·50		£1 141·50

Profit and Loss A/c (for month ending January 31st 19..)

19..		£	19..	£
Jan. 31	Discount Allowed	32·30	Jan. 31 Gross Profit	987·00
	Stationery	17·50	Discount Received	77·50
	Postage	3·50		1 064·50
	Repairs	4·25		
	General Expenses	1·25		
	Salaries	95·00		
		153·80		
	Net Profit	910·70		
		£1 064·50		£1 064·50

Balance Sheet (as at January 31st 19..)

	£	£		£	£
Fixed Assets			**Capital**		
Land and Buildings		7 500·00	At Start		12 830·50
Plant and Machinery		2 250·00	Net Profit	910·70	
Furniture and Fittings		850·00	*Less* Drawings	60·00	
Motor Vehicles		850·00			850·70
		11 450·00			13 681·20
Current Assets			**Long-term Liability**		
Stock	1 750·00		Mercantile Bank Loan A/c		1 000·00
Debtors	425·00		**Current Liability**		
Bank	1 945·70		Creditors		1 040·00
Cash	150·50				
		4 271·20			
		£15 721·20			£15 721·20

Limitations of the Trial Balance

Exercises Set 24: Limitations of the Trial Balance

(1) *(SPA page 182)*

The types of error not disclosed by the Trial Balance are as follows:

    (a) Original Errors.
    (b) Errors of Omission.
    (c) Errors of Commission.
    (d) Errors of Principle.
    (e) Compensating Errors.

You may give any two of the following examples, but of course everyone will think of different sets of circumstances.

(a) *Original Errors.* An invoice is made out in error for £1 000·00, instead of £100. The book-keeper does not detect this error in the original document, and it appears in the Purchases Day Book as £1 000·00. It is then posted to the Creditor's Account at this figure, and is also included in the monthly total of the Purchases Day Book which is debited to Purchases Account.

(b) *Errors of Omission.* The charlady flicks a credit note down the back of a filing cabinet with her duster. It is not found, and is omitted from the accounts altogether. (Eventually an over-payment is made to the creditor who sent the credit note, and he is kind enough to notify us, and send a duplicate credit note.)

(c) *Errors of Commission.* A junior accounts clerk enters a cheque paid by B. Rose into B. Rowe's Account. The Trial Balance appears to balance, but this error is concealed.

(d) *Errors of Principle.* A machine purchased on July 5th is entered into the Purchases Day Book as an ordinary purchase, instead of being journalized as the purchase of an asset. The Trial Balance agrees, but the Purchases Account balance is too large, and the Machinery Account balance is too small.

(e) *Compensating Errors.* An arithmetical error of £10·00 in the Sales Account is balanced up by a similar slip in A. Debtor's Account.

(2) *(SPA page 183)*

This statement means that 'at a first look' (*prima facie*) the book is correct, but a more careful study later might reveal one of the errors outlined in Question 1 above.

(3) *(SPA page 183)*

The procedures to be followed in the event of a Trial Balance failing to agree are as follows:

(a) Add up the Trial Balance again in case a slip has been made. If this does not prove to be the case then (*b*) Deduct the smaller side from the larger. The difference on the books may be recalled by one of the accounts clerks as an item he remembers dealing with. This item should be checked to see that the double entry was correct. If the error is not cleared up try this:

(*c*) Halve the difference on the books. This could be an account entered in the wrong column, i.e. debited in the Trial Balance instead of being credited. If this does not solve the problem

(*d*) Take out Control Accounts on the debtors' and creditors' ledgers. This is an advanced piece of work (see *SPA page 403*).

(*e*) If the Control Accounts do not discover the error, check all entries in the General Ledger (the Nominal and Real Accounts) including the Cash Book and Petty-cash Book.

(*f*) If these checks do not reveal the error then open up a Suspense Account, giving it a balance on the debit or credit side—according to which is needed—of the amount of the 'difference on books'. This will make the Trial Balance agree, and of course eventually a complaint or something else will throw up the original error and it can then be corrected.

(4) (*SPA page 183*)

If an item is entered in the wrong column of a Trial Balance, it will make the column it is in bigger by the amount of the item, and the column it should be in smaller by the amount of the item. The two sides will differ by *twice* the amount of the item.

In the example to be used we might have, for example, the following figures:

Trial Balance (as at December 31st 19..)

	Dr. £	Cr. £
All other items	20 739·52	20 754·50
Discount Allowed		14·98
	£20 739·52	20 769·48

Deducting the smaller side from the larger we find as follows:

£
20 769·48
—20 739·52

Difference on books   £29·96

Dividing the 'difference on books' by 2 we find that the answer is £14·98.

Is there an item on the wrong side of the Trial Balance of this amount? Clearly there is: Discount Allowed is a loss and should be in the debit column. Transferring it we have:

Trial Balance (as at December 31st 19..)

	Dr. £	Cr. £
All other items	20 739·52	20 754·50
Discount Allowed	14·98	
	£20 754·50	20 754·50

The Trial Balance agrees and *prima facie* the book-keeping has been careful and accurate.

(5) Books of R. Taylor (*SPA page 183*)

(*a*) This is an error of commission, and the Journal entry to correct it is as follows:

19..				£	£
Sept.	30	D. Park A/c Dr.	L 127	18·00	
		P. Dark A/c	L 69		18·00
		Being correction of error whereby a payment from a debtor, P. Dark, was incorrectly credited to D. Park			

(*b*) When Taylor spends money on personal items unconnected with the business these should be debited not to Office Expenses Account but to Drawings Account. They represent sums drawn out of the business for personal use.

19..				£	£
Sept.	30	Drawings A/c Dr.	L 121	40·00	
		Office Expenses A/c	L 77		40·00
		Being correction of an error whereby sums paid for personal expenses of the proprietor were debited to Office Expenses A/c			

(*c*) This is an error of principle. The sale of an asset is not 'Sales' in the normal meaning of that word and should not have been credited in Sales Account. Instead it should have been credited in the asset account, to remove the furniture from the books.

19..				£	£
Sept.	30	Sales A/c Dr.	L 54	10·00	
		Furniture and Fittings A/c	L 36		10·00
		Being correction of an error where sales of furniture were treated as ordinary sales and credited to Sales A/c			

(6) Books of A. Trader (*SPA page 183*)

(*a*) Montgomery must be a creditor, since A. Trader is paying him money. The £28·00 should have been debited in his account, but instead it was debited in D. Montmorency's account. The Journal entry is therefore:

19..				£	£
May	31	D. Montgomery A/c Dr.	L 121	28·00	
		D. Montmorency A/c	L 79		28·00
		Being correction of posting in which Montmorency was debited instead of Montgomery			

(*b*) The purchase of furniture is not an 'expense', even though furniture costs money. It is the purchase of an asset, which is only a change of one asset, cash, into another asset, furniture. This is not a loss of the business, and it is an error of principle to debit the expenditure in the Office Expenses Account. The Journal entry is as follows:

19..				£	£
May	31	Office Furniture A/c Dr.	L 8	65·00	
		Office Expenses A/c	L 27		65·00
		Being correction of error in which the purchase of furniture was treated as an expense of the business			

(*c*) Discount Allowed should always be debited. Remember—the total of the discount columns are the only two items on the Cash Book which do not change sides when posted to the ledger accounts. In this case A. Trader only uses one Discount Account, so that Discount Allowed should be debited and Discount Received credited in this account. Since the Discount Allowed has been entered on the wrong side, it will cause an error of *twice* its amount. To correct this error a single-sided Journal entry of £20·00 is required.

19..				£	£
May	31	Discount A/c Dr.	L 20	20·00	
		No credit entry required			—
		This unusual journal entry corrects an error in which Discount Allowed of £10·00 was credited instead of being debited			

(7) Books of M. Bines (*SPA page 183*)

(*a*) This is an error of principle. The machinery is an asset, not a purchase of goods for resale. Machinery Account should have been debited, not Purchases Account. The Journal entry is therefore:

19..				£	£
June	30	Machinery A/c Dr.	L 5	1 600·00	
		Purchases A/c	L 12		1 600·00
		Being correction of error of principle, in which a purchase of an asset was debited to Purchases A/c			

(*b*) Rosner having disallowed the discount expects to be paid the money, and must be restored as a creditor on his account. The Discount-Received Account, one of the profits of the business, must be reduced by £7·50 since this profit has been refused; the creditor does not concede that Bines is entitled to discount.

19..				£	£
June	30	Discount-Received A/c Dr.	L 21	7·50	
		A. Rosner A/c	L 76		7·50
		Being credit restored to Rosner who refuses to allow discount claimed earlier this month			

(c) This is an error of commission. The Fixtures and Fittings Account has been reduced in value when in fact it is the machinery that has depreciated. The Journal entry must restore the Fixtures and Fittings to the proper value, and credit Machinery Account.

19.. June	30	Fixtures and Fittings A/c Dr. Machinery A/c Being correction of error in which Fixtures and Fittings were depreciated instead of Machinery	L 63 L 72	£ 80·00	£ 80·00

(8) (*SPA page 183*)

(a) A simple error of commission. We need to debit Furniture and Fittings Account and credit Furnishing Co. Ltd., to clear the incorrect entry.

19.. July	5	Furniture and Fittings A/c Dr. Furnishing Co. Ltd. A/c Being correction of error in which a purchase of furniture was debited to the wrong account	L 7 L 142	£ 120·00	£ 120·00

(b) When an asset is sold the book value of the asset must always be written off the asset account, even if the asset is sold for less than the book value. In this case the Motor Vehicles Account has been left with £45·00 on the debit side. There is no asset of this value; the lorry has gone to R. Gould and Co. We must regard this as a loss on sale of vehicles.

19.. Aug.	8	Sale of Motor Vehicles A/c Dr. Motor Vehicles A/c Being loss on motor vehicle sold on August 4th to R. Gould and Co.	L 36 L 9	£ 45·00	£ 45·00

(c) This is an error of omission. The invoice for the purchase of the machine has been mislaid, and the supplier is naturally annoyed. To placate him for the delay *six months' interest* is to be paid on the sum overdue.

19.. July	12	Machinery A/c Dr. Interest Paid A/c Dr. Bank A/c Being payment of an overdue account to Lucas Engineering Ltd., with interest at 5 per cent per annum. Document mislaid in January	L 7 L 43 CB 9	£ 2 000·00 50·00	£ 2 050·00

(9) Books of R. Whistler (*SPA page 184*)

(a) A Suspense Account is an account opened on the last day of any month if it is found that a Trial Balance will not agree. If routine checks will not discover the error, an entry 'Difference on Books' is made on the appropriate side of a Suspense Account. Eventually, as the errors are discovered, this account will be cleared by Journal entries.

(b) The cheque paid to R. Lawson should have been debited in his account He is a supplier who has now been paid. Since this entry was not made the 'credit' side of the Trial Balance was £45·00 too much, and this was why a Suspense Account was necessary. The following Journal entry corrects the error.

19.. May	17	R. Lawson A/c Dr. Suspense A/c Being correction of error causing the Suspense A/c; failure to post a cheque paid to R. Lawson to his account	L 94 L 177	£ 45·00	£ 45·00

		Suspense A/c			L 177
19.. Apr. 30 Difference on Books	J 6	£ 45·00	19.. May 17 R. Lawson	J 7	£ 45·00
		£45·00			£45·00

(10) Books of R. Hull (*SPA page 184*)

These two errors are easily corrected. Discount-Allowed Account must be debited (a loss of the business). R. Day must be credited (credit the giver of goods, or services or, as in this case, money). The Journal entries and Suspense Account are as follows:

19.. Sept.	15	Discount-Allowed A/c Dr. Suspense A/c Being correction of error in which the total of Discount Allowed was not posted to its account on August 31st	L 37 L 121	£ 8·50	£ 8·50
Sept.	25	Suspense A/c Dr. R. Day Being correction of error in which a payment by Day was not credited to his account	L 121 L 74	51·00	51·00

		Suspense A/c			L 121
19.. Sept. 25 R. Day		£ 51·00	19.. Aug. 31 Difference on Books Sept. 15 Discount Allowed		£ 42·50 8·50
		£51·00			£51·00

(11) Books of R. T. Crafty (*SPA page 184*)

Notes:

(a) The difference on books is £263·05 and must be entered on the credit side of the Suspense Account.

(b) The Purchases Account has been debited with £270·00 too much. It must be credited with that amount, which means a debit to Suspense Account.

(c) The Discount-Received Account has not been credited with enough; it needs a further £2·05. This means a debit to Suspense Account.

(d) Light and Heat Account has been under-debited by £9·00. This must be corrected, and the same figure will therefore be credited to Suspense Account.

(e) This entry does not affect the Suspense Account. It is an original error, which would not show up in the Trial Balance and hence would not cause a Suspense Account entry.

	Suspense A/c		L 159
19..	£	19..	£
Oct. 5 Purchases	270·00	Sept. 30 Difference on Books	263·05
11 Discount Received	2·05	Oct. 19 Light and Heat	9·00
	£272·05		£272·05

(12) Books of R. Lyons (SPA page 184)

	Suspense A/c		L 182
19..	£	19..	£
Nov. 7 T. White	81·69	Oct. 31 Difference on Books	93·30
11 Commission Received	69·35	Nov. 19 Discount A/c	57·74
	£151·04		£151·04

Notes:

(a) The difference on books must be credited in Suspense Account.

(b) T. White must be credited with £81·69 and the double entry is therefore a debit in Suspense Account.

(c) Commission-Received Account is correct, it is only the extraction of this total to the Trial Balance that is incorrect. This was not only the wrong amount, it was also put in the wrong column. This means that instead of a credit item of £38·50 there was a debit item of £30·85. The total effect on the 'difference on books' was therefore £69·35. To remove this we must debit Suspense Account by £69·35. There will be no 'second part' to this entry.

(d) The entry on November 17th is an error of commission. It does not affect the Trial Balance, and therefore does not affect the Suspense Account.

(e) The Discount Account has been credited instead of debited. The error of £28·87 is therefore corrected by debiting with *twice* that amount, i.e. £57·74. If Discount Account is debited with £57·74 then Suspense Account must be credited.

Unit Nineteen
Simultaneous Records

Exercises Set 25: Simultaneous Records

(1) *(SPA page 193)*

'Simultaneous records' is a term applied to any system of accounting where two or more records are prepared at the same time. Usually a document, a ledger entry and a day book entry are made at the same time. The document is placed on top of the ledger page, which is placed on top of the day book page. What is written on the document is also written simultaneously on the pages below it, either with carbon or NCR (no carbon required) methods.

Good examples are:

(*a*) Simultaneous sales records: the statement, the ledger and the Sales Day Book are prepared at the same time.

(*b*) Simultaneous wages records: the pay slip, the employee's day record and the weekly payroll are prepared together.

(2) *(SPA page 193)*

The advantages of a simultaneous records system are:

(*a*) Entries on all the records are made at the same time, so that errors in posting from one book to another cannot be made. If the original entry is correct the other entries will be correct.

(*b*) There is a considerable saving in time.

(*c*) Since all such systems are loose-leaf systems, the difficulties associated with bound books are avoided.

(*d*) The firms devising such schemes of book-keeping devise control checks which ensure that mistakes are reduced to an absolute minimum.

(3) *SPA page 193)*

(*a*) Code numbers are part of the PAYE system and enable the employer to deduct the correct tax without personally inquiring into the allowances available to an employee. The new PAYE system introduced in April 1973 means that a man's code number is simply his tax-free pay for the year, minus the last figure. Thus a man with tax-free pay of £955 would have code 95.

(*b*) Form P45. This is a form made out by an employer when an employee leaves his firm. It enables a new employer to know the tax code and past earnings of the employee, so that he can at once deduct tax at the correct figure from the employee's pay packet.

(*c*) Gross pay is the total pay earned. It may include basic pay, overtime, bonuses, etc. Taxable pay is that part of gross pay on which tax must be paid.

Taxable pay is calculated from the Inland Revenue tax tables, which give the tax-free pay for each week of the year for each code number. When this tax-free pay is deducted from gross pay it gives taxable pay. Net pay is the final sum payable to an employee. It is found by deducting from gross pay all statutory and voluntary deductions.

(d) Form P60. This is a form issued by the employer at the end of the year, showing the total pay earned, the total tax deducted, etc., for the whole year.

Unit Twenty
Bank Reconciliation Statements

Exercises Set 26: Bank Reconciliation Statements

(1) Books of R. Lawrence (*SPA page 199*)

Cash Book (Bank columns only)

19..		£	19..		£
Mar. 31	Balance	209·21	Mar. 31	Bank Interest	15·40
			31	Balance	193·81
		£209·21			£209·21
19..		£			
Mar. 31	Balance	193·81			

Bank Reconciliation Statement (as at March 31st 19..)

	£
Balance as per Cash Book	193·81
Deduct Cheques not yet cleared	126·55
	67·26
Add Cheques drawn but not yet presented	187·10
Balance as per Bank Statement	£254·36

(2) Books of B. Grant (*SPA page 199*)

Cash Book (Bank columns only)

19..		£	19..		£
Apr. 30	Balance	404·24	Apr. 30	Commission Paid	1·45
			30	Subscriptions Paid	5·25
			30	R. Sterling	39·79
			30	Balance	357·75
		£404·24			£404·24

Bank Reconciliation Statement (as at April 30th 19..)

		£
Balance as per Cash Book		357·75
Add back cheques not yet presented		
D. Jones	25·30	
T. Fortescue	42·45	
		67·75
Balance as per Bank Statement		£425·50

(3) Books of C. Roper (*SPA page 199*)

Cash Book (Bank columns only)

19..	£	19..	£
Mar. 31 Balance	485·00	Mar. 31 Bank Charges	8·25
31 Dividend Received	18·50	31 Balance	495·25
	£503·50		£503·50
19..	£		
Apr. 1 Balance	495·25		

Bank Reconciliation Statement (as at March 31st 19..)

	£
Balance as per Cash Book	495·25
Add back cheques not yet presented	142·00
	637·25
Deduct Cheques not yet cleared	137·50
Balance as per Bank Statement	£499·75

(4) Books of L. Roberts (*SPA page 200*)

Cash Book (Bank columns only)

19..	£	19..	£
June 30 Balance	362·43	June 30 Correction of Error (Jones)	45·00
30 H. Neale	42·60	30 Bank Charges	4·30
		30 Balance	355·73
	£405·03		£405·03
19..	£		
July 1 Balance	355·73		

Bank Reconciliation Statement (as at June 30th 19..)

		£
Balance as per Cash Book		355·73
Deduct Cheques not yet cleared		35·45
		320·28
Add Cheques not yet presented		
Harvey	72·60	
Roach	5·55	
Rudolfo	4·72	
		82·87
Balance as per Bank Statement		£403·15

(5) Books of A. Reader (*SPA page 200*)

(a)
Balance as per Cash Book	= £350·00
Add back Cheques drawn and not yet presented	= £135·00
Balance as per Bank Statement	= £485·00

(b)
Balance as per Bank Statement	= £450·00
Add back Standing order to arrive at Cash Book balance	= £20·00
Balance as per Cash Book	= £470·00

(c) Balance as per Bank Statement   = £700·00
  Deduct Cheques drawn but not yet presented   = £140·00

  Balance as per Cash Book   = £560·00

(d) Balance as per Bank Statement   = £780·00
  Deduct Cheque not yet entered in Cash Book   = £150·00

  Balance as per Cash Book   = £630·00

(6) Books of D. Stevenson (*SPA page 201*)

Cash Book (Bank columns only)

19..			£	19..			£
July 1 Balance		B/d	589·15	July 1 Bank Charges			5·25
1 Brown, Credit Transfer			10·00	1 Balance		c/d	593·90
			£599·15				£599·15
19..			£				
July 1 Balance		B/d	593·90				

Bank Reconciliation Statement (as at July 1st 19..)

	£	£
Balance as per Cash Book		593·90
Deduct Cheques not yet cleared		
Smithers	22·10	
Jones	15·15	
		37·25
		556·65
Add Cheques not yet presented		
Morris	10·12	
White	41·13	
		51·25
Balance as per Bank Statement		£607·90

(7) Books of A. Trader (*SPA page 201*)

Cash Book (Bank columns only)

19..			£	19..			£
Feb. 28 Balance		B/d	1 017·12	Feb. 28 Trade Association			10·50
28 Boxer			5·75	28 Bank Charges			4·22
28 Striker			16·60	28 Balance		c/d	1 024·75
			£1 039·47				£1 039·47
19..			£				
Mar. 1 Balance		B/d	1 024·75				

Bank Reconciliation Statement (as at February 28th 19..)

		£
Balance as per Cash Book		1 024·75

Add back cheques not yet presented

	£	
Green	115·10	
Riley	237·50	
Stokes	38·00	
		390·60
		1 415·35
Deduct Cheques not yet cleared		185·15
Balance as per Bank Statement		£1 230·20

(8) Books of R. Green (*SPA page 202*)

Cash Book (Bank columns only)

19..			£	19..			£
March 31	Balance	B/d	1 318·52	March 31	Trade Protection Society		10·50
31	Blanche		4·42	31	Bank Charges		4·46
31	Peters		103·08	31	Balance	c/d	1 411·06
			£1 426·02				£1 426·02

19..			£
Apr. 1	Balance	B/d	1 411·06

Bank Reconciliation Statement (as at March 31st 19..)

		£
Balance as per Cash Book		1 411·06

Add back cheques not yet presented

	£	
Abbot	111·74	
Moser	83·88	
Raven	201·95	
		397·57
		1 808·63
Deduct Amounts paid in but not yet credited	538·22	
Balance as per Bank Statement		£1 270·41

(9) Books of E. Hemingway (*SPA page 202*)

Cash Book (Bank columns only)

19..			£	19..			£
Jan. 31	Balance	B/d	1 192·13	Jan. 31	Bank Charges		5·55
31	Interest Received		12·15	31	Balance	c/d	1 198·73
			£1 204·28				£1 204·28

19..			£
Feb. 1	Balance	B/d	1 198·73

Bank Reconciliation Statement (as at January 31st 19..)

		£
Balance as per Cash Book		1 198·73

Add back cheque drawn but not yet presented

	£	
T. Burton	7·12	
		1 205·85
Deduct Cheque paid in and not yet cleared	114·05	
Balance as per Bank Statement		£1 091·80

(10) Books of M. Lowe (*SPA page 203*)

    (*i*) The following items need to be entered in the Cash Book:
        (*a*) The credit transfer from R. Johnson (£168·50 to be debited).
        (*b*) The sundries figure of £186·50, omitted in error (to be debited).
        (*c*) The dividend from the Bank of England (£25·00 to be debited).
        (*d*) The charges (£8·50 to be credited).

(*ii*)

Bank Reconciliation Statement (as at January 31st 19· ·)

		£
Balance as per Bank Statement		1 089·30
Deduct Cheques not yet presented		
	£	
A. Nicholls	42·50	
B. Lamb	1·55	
C. Forrester	108·20	
	152·25	
and Automatic Debit Transfer	10·50	
		162·75
		926·55
Add Items paid in but not yet credited		150·55
Balance as per Cash Book		£1 077·10

Unit Twenty-One

Capital and Revenue Expenditure and Receipts

Exercises Set 27: Capital and Revenue Expenditure

(1) *(SPA page 211)*

Capital expenditure is expenditure on durable assets, which are purchased for use in the business. They permanently increase the profit-making capacity of the business.

Revenue expenditure is expenditure on items which only temporarily increase the profit-making capacity of the business, their usefulness being short-lived. This type of purchase may be of three kinds:

(*a*) Purchase of goods for resale.

(*b*) Purchase of consumable items, e.g. postage stamps.

(*c*) Purchase of services.

The importance of the distinction is that revenue items are used in the calculation of the profits, their cost having been incurred solely for the purposes of earning the profit during the current trading period. Capital items may not be charged as losses against the profits of the period under consideration, except so far as depreciation has occurred in the period.

(2) *(SPA page 211)*

A capital receipt is any receipt which is not a revenue receipt. Examples are:

(*a*) New contributions of capital by the proprietor(s).

(*b*) Loans and mortgages arranged during the period under review.

(*c*) Tax refunds or any other income which has previously been subject to tax and is not therefore to be brought into account when calculating the profits of the current trading period.

A revenue receipt is any receipt which should properly be included in the calculation of the profits of the business for the trading period under review at present. It may be one of three types of receipt:

(*a*) Receipts for goods sold.

(*b*) Receipts for services rendered, e.g. work done.

(*c*) Any miscellaneous receipts, such as rent received, commission received, etc., but not receipts of a capital nature.

The letter to the Tax Inspector must make the point that the increased value of the business is partly due to extra capital invested, and is not entirely the result of profitable activities.

(3) *(SPA page 212)*

(*a*) See Question 1.

(b) Capital expenditure: (i) Machinery   (ii) Motor Vehicle
    Revenue expenditure: (i) Rent   (ii) Motor Vehicle Expenses

(c) (i) It would not be necessary to write this off as a loss. When the stock of
        crockery is counted it will be less than it would otherwise have been,
        because the breakages occurred. The loss is therefore taken as
        decreased stock.

    (ii) The repairs would be charged to Repairs Account and written off as a
         loss at the end of the year.

(4) (*SPA page 212*)

(a) Revenue expenditure, but it might be apportioned as a loss over, say,
    three years.
(b) Capital expenditure. It is the purchase of an asset.
(c) Capital expenditure. It creates an asset of a lasting nature.
(d) Revenue expenditure. These are stocks for re-sale.
(e) Capital expenditure. It is an asset of the club.

(5) (*SPA page 212*) See Question 1.

(a) An extension to the factory is a capital asset. The wages of workmen
employed on the extension must be regarded as capital expenditure.

(b) The cost of rebuilding a wall will be a repair, and consequently revenue
expenditure.

(6) (*SPA page 212*)

(a) Capital expenditure. It is an asset of the club.
(b) Revenue expenditure. It is a consumable.
(c) Revenue expenditure. Membership only lasts one year usually.
(d) Capital expenditure. These are permanent fittings.
(e) Revenue expenditure. It is consumable.
(f) Capital expenditure. They are assets.
(g) Capital expenditure. Motor vehicles are assets.
(h) Revenue expenditure. Crockery is breakable.
(i) Revenue expenditure. Bar stocks are goods for re-sale.
(j) Revenue expenditure. Tickets are consumable.

(7) (*SPA page 213*)

(a) Warehouse wages are revenue expenses. Trading Account.
(b) These wages should be capitalized as an increase in the value of the
    warehouse. This will appear on the Balance Sheet.
(c) Capital expenditure. Balance Sheet item (increase in Warehouse value).
(d) Capital expenditure. Balance Sheet.
(e) Revenue expenditure. Stock for re-sale.

(8) Books of Linden Manufacturing Organization (*SPA page 213*)

(a) Capital expenditure. It will be an asset.
(b) Revenue expenditure. It is consumable.
(c) Capital expenditure. It is an asset.
(d) Capital expenditure. It is an asset.
(e) Revenue expenditure. It is a consumable item.
(f) Revenue expenditure. It is a loss.
(g) Revenue expenditure. It is a loss.
(h) Revenue expenditure. It is consumable.
(i) Revenue expenditure. It is a loss.
(j) Capital expenditure. It is an asset.

(9) Books of A. Decorator (*SPA page 213*)

It is a stock item, and stock losses are taken into account when we count the stock. The missing items are not present and therefore cannot be included in the closing stock figure.

(10) Books of A. Motor Manufacturer (*SPA page 213*)

19..				£	£
July	30	Machinery A/c Dr.	L 7	17 330·00	
		Power Tools Ltd. A/c	L 12		16 000·00
		Leigh Building Co. A/c	L 13		450·00
		Wages A/c	L 27		880·00
		Being capitalization of machinery purchased and installed by own staff			

(11) Books of Plastics Ltd. (*SPA page 214*)

19..				£	£
July	14	Premises A/c Dr.	L 1	2 000·00	
		Wages A/c	L 5		580·00
		Building Materials A/c	L 7		650·00
		Appreciation of Buildings A/c	L 9		770·00
		Being capitalization of revenue expenses incurred in extending premises			

(12) (*SPA page 214*)

(a) (i) Premises, cutlery, china.
   (ii) Wages, petrol for re-sale, office stationery.
(b)

19..				£	£
Aug.	31	Decorations in Suspense A/c Dr.	L 17	1 000·00	
		Wages A/c			600·00
		Purchases A/c			400·00
		Being revenue expenditure capitalized to be written off over five years			

Unit Twenty-Two
More about Depreciation

Exercises Set 28: More about Depreciation

(1) Books of Mills Ltd. (*SPA page 222*)

Machinery A/c   L 75

			£				£
Year 1				Year 1			
Jan. 1	Bank	CB 5	1 500	Dec. 31	Depreciation	L 27	130
				31	Balance	c/d	1 370
			£1 500				£1 500
Year 2			£	Year 2			£
Jan. 1	Balance	B/d	1 370	Dec. 31	Depreciation	L 27	130
				31	Balance	c/d	1 240
			£1 370				£1 370
Year 3			£				
Jan. 1		B/d	1 240				

(2) Books of Thompson Ltd. (*SPA page 223*)

Machinery A/c   L 81

			£				£
Year 1				Year 1			
Jan. 1	Bank	CB 7	2 800	Dec. 31	Depreciation	L 43	300
				31	Balance ..	c/d	2 500
			£2 800				£2 800
Year 2			£	Year 2			£
Jan. 1	Balance	B/d	2 500	Dec. 31	Depreciation	L 43	300
				31	Balance	c/d	2 200
			£2 500				£2 500
Year 3			£	Year 3			£
Jan. 1	Balance	B/d	2 200	Dec. 31	Depreciation	L 43	300
				31	Balance	c/d	1 900
			£2 200				£2 200
Year 4			£				
Jan. 1	Balance	B/d	1 900				

(3) Books of T. Brown (*SPA pages 223*)

(a)

			Machinery A/c					L 87
Year 1			£	Year 1				£
Jan. 1	Bank	CB 11	3 000	Dec. 31	Depreciation	L 29		300
				31	Balance	c/d		2 700
			£3 000					£3 000
Year 2			£	Year 2				£
Jan. 1	Balance	B/d	2 700	Dec. 31	Depreciation	L 29		330
July 1	Bank	CB 142	600	31	Balance	c/d		2 970
			£3 300					£3 300
Year 3			£	Year 3				£
Jan. 1	Balance	B/d	2 970	Dec. 31	Depreciation	L 29		360
				31	Balance	c/d		2 610
			£2 970					£2 970
Year 4								
Jan. 1	Balance	B/d	2 610					

(b)

Balance Sheet (for year ending December 31st 19..)

	£	£
Fixed Assets		
Machinery (at cost)	3 600·00	
Less Depreciation	990·00	
		2 610·00

(4) Books of Marshall Bros. (*SPA page 223*)

			Furniture and Fittings A/c					L 42
Year 1			£	Year 1				£
Jan. 1	Cash	CB 5	1 200	Dec. 31	Depreciation	L 26		60
				31	Balance	c/d		1 140
			£1 200					£1 200
Year 2			£	Year 2				£
Jan. 1	Balance	B/d	1 140	Dec. 31	Depreciation	L 26		72
Apr. 1	Cash	CB 27	400	31	Balance	c/d		1 468
			£1 540					£1 540
Year 3			£					
Jan. 1	Balance	B/d	1 468					

(5) Books of Peter Walker (*SPA page 223*)

Machinery A/c   L 25

			£				£
Year 1				Year 1			
Jan. 1	Bank	J 1	1 800·00	Dec. 31	Depreciation	L 48	450·00
				31	Balance	c/d	1 350·00
			£1 800·00				£1 800·00
Year 2			£	Year 2			£
Jan. 1	Balance	B/d	1 350·00	Dec. 31	Depreciation	L 48	337·50
				31	Balance	c/d	1 012·50
			£1 350·00				£1 350·00
Year 3			£				
Jan. 1	Balance	B/d	1 012·50				

(6) Books of John Mainway (*SPA page 223*)

Motor Lorries A/c   L 7

			£				£
Year 1				Year 1			
Jan. 1	Bank	J 1	2 000	Dec. 31	Depreciation	L 17	400
				31	Balance	c/d	1 600
			£2 000				£2 000
Year 2			£	Year 2			£
Jan. 1	Balance	B/d	1 600	Dec. 31	Depreciation	L 17	600
July 1	Bank	J 42	2 000	31	Balance	c/d	3 000
			£3 600				£3 600
Year 3			£	Year 3			£
Jan. 1	Balance	B/d	3 000	Dec. 31	Depreciation	L 17	900
Oct. 1	Bank	J 68	2 000	31	Balance	c/d	4 100
			£5 000				£5 000
Year 4			£	Year 4			£
Jan. 1	Balance	B/d	4 100	Dec. 31	Depreciation	L 17	1 200
				31	Balance	c/d	2 900
			£4 100				£4 100
Year 5			£				
Jan. 1	Balance	B/d	2 900				

Depreciation calculations:

Year 1 $\frac{1}{5}$th of £2 000 = £400

Year 2 $\frac{1}{5}$th of £2 000 + $\frac{1}{10}$th of £2 000 ($\frac{1}{2}$ year only) = £600

Year 3 $\frac{1}{5}$th of £4 000 + $\frac{1}{20}$th of £2 000 ($\frac{1}{4}$ year only) = £900

Year 4 $\frac{1}{5}$th of £6 000 = £1 200

(7) Books of Tom Smith (*SPA page 223*)

Motor Lorries A/c   L 27

19..	(Year 1)		£	19..	(Year 4)		£
Jan. 1	Bank	CB 5	9 600	Jan. 1	Bank and Provision for		
19..	(Year 4)				Depreciation		2 400
Jan. 1	Bank	CB 177	2 700	Dec. 31	Balance	c/d	9 900
			£12 300				£12 300
19..	(Year 5)		£				
Jan. 1	Balance	B/d	9 900				

Note: No action needs to be taken on this account in years 2 and 3.

Provision for Depreciation on Motor Lorries A/c   L 28

19..	(Year 4)		£	19..	(Year 1)		£
Jan. 1	Motor Lorry A/c	J 56	1 440	Dec. 31	Depreciation	J 5	1 920
Dec. 31	Balance	c/d	6 300	19..	(Year 2)		
				Dec. 31	Depreciation	J 27	1 920
				19..	(Year 3)		
				Dec. 31	Depreciation	J 54	1 920
				19..	(Year 4)		
				Dec. 31	Depreciation	J 73	1 980
			£7 740				£7 740
				19..	(Year 5)		£
				Jan. 1	Balance		6 300

Notes: At any given moment the value of the motor lorries in hand is their book value (as stated in the Motor Lorries Account) *less* the total depreciation written off to date (as stated in the Provision for Depreciation Account).

When a motor lorry is sold we must take the following actions:

(*a*) Remove the original cost from the Motor Lorry Account.

(*b*) Remove from the Provision For Depreciation Account that part of the depreciation which has been written off this particular vehicle (in this case three years' depreciation at £480 per year).

(*c*) Adjust for any discrepancy on the realized price of the old vehicle. In this case the journal entry would have shown this adjustment as follows:

19..				£	£
Jan. 1	Bank A/c	Dr.		1 500	
	Provision for Depreciation A/c	Dr.		1 440	
	Motor Lorries A/c				2 400
	Sale of Motor Lorry A/c				540
	Being profit on sale of motor lorry at a price in excess of book value				

(*d*) The profit on sale of £540 would be taken to the Profit and Loss Account at the end of the year.

(8) Books of A. Trader (*SPA page 224*)

Statement of Depreciation for year.

Motor Vans at start: 1 year's depreciation at 20% on £1 240.00 = £248

New Van purchased March 1st = 10 months at 20% per annum
  on £630.00 = £105

New Van purchased September 1st = 4 months at 20% per
  annum on £720.00 = £ 48

£401

				Delivery-Vans A/c				L 47
19..			£	19..				£
Jan. 1	Balance	B/d	1 240·00	Dec. 31	Depreciation			401·00
Mar. 1	Cash	CB 27	630·00	31	Balance	c/d		2 189·00
Sept. 1	Van Sales Ltd	J 17	720·00					
			£2 590·00					£2 590·00
19..			£					
Jan. 1	Balance	B/d	2 189·00					

(9) Books of Marketing Ltd. (*SPA page 224*)

19..		(Year 3)		£	£
Dec.	31	Depreciation A/c Dr.		506	
		Machinery A/c			506
		Being depreciation on machinery calculated as follows:			
		Value of Machine No. 1 at start = £2 430			
		£3 000 — 10% = 2 700 (Year 1)			
		£2 700·00 — 10% = £2 430 (Year 2)			
		Value of Machine No. 2 at start = £2 280			
		£2 400 — 10% for ½ year = £2 280			
		New machine on Oct. 1st = £1 400			
		∴ Depreciation =			
		£243 + £228 + 2½% of £1 400 =			
		£471 + £35 = £506			

(10) Books of A. Manufacturer (*SPA page 224*)

Depreciation Calculations:

£

Machine No. 1 $\dfrac{12}{100} \times £600$ = 72

Machine No. 2 $\dfrac{12}{100} \times £400$ = 48

Machine No. 3 $\dfrac{1}{2} \times \dfrac{12}{100} \times £500$ = 30

Machine No. 4 $\dfrac{11}{12} \times \dfrac{12}{100} \times £700$ = 77

Machine No. 5 $\dfrac{3}{4} \times \dfrac{12}{100} \times £800$ = 72

Machine No. 6 $\dfrac{5}{12} \times \dfrac{12}{100} \times £1\,000$ = 50

Machine No. 7 $\dfrac{1}{12} \times \dfrac{12}{100} \times £1\,200$ = 12

Total = £361

Disposal of Machine No. 3 A/c

19..		£	19..			£
Jan. 1	Value at Cost	500	Jan. 1		Depreciation to Date	135
			July 1		Depreciation to Date	30
				1	Proceeds of Sale	300
				1	Loss on Sale	35
		£500				£500

Unit Twenty-Three
Columnar Books

Exercises Set 29: Columnar Books

(1) (*SPA page 228*)

Date		Details	Furni-ture	Soft Furnish-ings	Elec-trical Goods	Carpets	F	Details	Total
19..			£	£	£	£		£	£
May	1	R. T. Brown							
		Coffee Tables	157·50					157·50	
		Cushions		27·00				27·00	
		Sideboard	38·50					38·50	
							L 3		223·00
	4	M. Bloom and Sons							
		Bedroom suites	585·00					585·00	
		Carpeting				284·50		284·50	
		Floor underlay				62·50		62·50	
							L 27		932·00
	11	Palace Electric Co. Ltd.							
		Fireplaces			128·50			128·50	
		Overmantels	27·00					27·00	
		Bathroom switches			14·25			14·25	
							L 46		169·75
			£808·00	27·00	142·75	347·00			£1 324·75
			L 5	L 5	L 5	L 5			L 5

(2) (*SPA page 228*)

Date		Details	A–K	L–Z		Discount	Cash	Bank
19..			£	£		£	£	£
Dec.	1	R. Lomax		150·00	L 52	7·50		142·50
	1	R. Baxter	100·00		L 15	5·00		95·00
	2	S. Sharpe		50·00	L 89	2·50		47·50
	3	C. Chowdhary	110·00		L 16	5·50		104·50
	3	M. Leonard		120·00	L 70	6·00		114·00
			£210·00	320·00		26·50		503·50
			L 72	L 73				

(3) (*SPA page 230*)

Date	Details	Cigar-ettes etc.	Confec-tionery	Gifts	F	Details	Total
		£	£	£		£	£
19.. Dec. 1	R. Tyler and Co.						
	200 packets of 50 'gold'	100·00				100·00	
	5 presentation lighters			26·25		26·25	
					L 47		126·25
4	M. Light Ltd.						
	24 jars assorted sweets		18·00		L 36		18·00
	Richards and Wyatt						
	100 packets of 50 'gold'	50·00				50·00	
	200 Havana cigars	50·00				50·00	
	20 presentation chocolates		22·00			22·00	
	1 gold cigarette case			32·50		32·50	
					L 41		154·50
		£200·00	40·00	58·75			£298·75
		L 66	L 66	L 66			L 66

(4) Books of G. Jenkins (*SPA page 230*)

Date	Details	Roses	Trees	Shrubs	Bulbs	F	Details	Total
		£	£	£	£		£	£
19.. June 13	B. Lobley							
	100 rose bushes	22·00					22·00	
	100 shrubs			28·80			28·80	
	10 sacks bulk narcissi				15·00		15·00	
						L 72		65·80
18	R. Brown							
	6 boxes crocuses				4·50		4·50	
	12 roses (standards)	9·25					9·25	
	3 boxes iris bulbs				2·25		2·25	
						L 29		16·00
27	B. Grant							
	100 trees (cypresses)		17·50				17·50	
	2 000 rose bushes	400·00					400·00	
	2 000 shrubs			500·00			500·00	
						L 46		917·50
30	G. Wakeman							
	6 boxes crocus bulbs				4·50		4·50	
	100 shrubs			28·80			28·80	
	100 rose bushes	22·00					22·00	
						L 92		55·30
		£453·25	17·50	557·60	26·25			£1 054·60
		L 5	L 5	L 5	L 5			L 5

(5) Books of Pop Musical Co. (*SPA page 230*)

Date	Details	Sheet Music and Records £	Record Players £	Hi-Fi Equipment £	Musical Instruments £	F	Details £	Total £
19.. Apr. 1	Musical Instruments Co. Ltd. 6 guitars @ £8·50 each				51·00	L 42		51·00
11	R. T. Lamb (Electrical) Ltd. 12 record players @ £15·25		183·00				183·00	
	Batteries to fit		25·50			L 38	25·50	208·50
19	Recording Ltd. 200 L.P. discs @ £1·00 each	200·00					200·00	
	4 violins @ £3·75 each				15·00	L 74	15·00	215·00
25	A. Dealer 2 saxophones @ £29·00				58·00	L 22		58·00
30	R.K. Radios 10 Hi-Fi panels @ £5·75 each			57·50		L 70		57·50
		£200·00	208·50	57·50	124·00			£590·00
		L 12	L 12	L 12	L 12			L 12

Unit Twenty-Four
The Bank Cash Book

Exercises Set 30: The Bank Cash Book

(1) Books of A. Trader (SPA page 233)

19..	Particulars		£	£	£	19..	Particulars		£	£	£
May 27	Balance	B/d			872·80	May 28	J. Battle and Co. Ltd.	L 6			290·13
28	Sales	L 17		45·80		30	W. Thorley and Co. Ltd.	L 34			195·00
	B. Bath	L 5	2·50	60·00		31	Petty Cash	PCB 17			26·15
	L. Poole	L 12		97·50			Drawings	L 102			50·00
30	Sales	L 17		39·00	203·30		Motor Vehicle Expenses	L 56			17·11
31	Sales	L 17		41·50	44·15		Balance	c/d			622·36
	H. Winton	L 38			80·50						
			£2·50		1 200·75				£—		1 200·75
19.. June 1	Balance	B/d	L 72		£ 614·36						

(2) Books of George Vyner (SPA page 233)

19..	Particulars		£	£	£	19..	Particulars		£	£	£
May 3	Balance	B/d			375·40	May 4	H. Moore and Sons	L 27			172·11
4	Sales	L 5		31·17		4	W. Blake and Co.	L 10	5·00		95·00
	J. Hart	L 17		18·10		5	Light and Heat	L 31			19·10
	G. Farley	L 16	2·50	47·50		6	Drawings	L 42		20·00	
5	Sales	L 5		48·00	96·77		Petty Cash	PCB 4		8·66	28·66
6	Sales	L 5		42·45	51·17	6	Balance	c/d			298·92
	R. Nelson	L 29			90·45						
			£2·50		613·79				£5·00		613·79
19.. May 7	Balance	B/d	L 7		£ 298·92				L 8		

(3) Books of D. Lobley (SPA page 234)

19.. May			£	£	£
27	Balance	B/d			893·00
28	Sales	L 14		49·00	
	A. Plum	L 73	3·00	50·00	
	B. Berry	L 10		97·00	
29	Sales	L 14		40·00	196·00
30	Sales	L 14		35·00	48·00
	C. Flower	L 29			75·00
			£3·00		1 212·00
19.. June 1	Balance	B/d L 15			593·00

19.. May			£	£	£
28	Orchard and Co. Ltd.	L 68			327·00
29	Hedges and Co.	L 44	5·00	29·00	195·00
30	Petty Cash	PCB 7		50·00	79·00
	Drawings	L 95			18·00
31	Motor Vehicle Expenses	L 27			593·00
31	Balance	c/d			
			£5·00		1 212·00
		L 16			

(4) Books of A. Heathcliff (SPA page 234)

19.. July			£	£	£
4	Balance	B/d			676·50
5	Sales	L 9		135·50	
	R. Loosely	L 52	2·50	60·00	
	L. Driver	L 27		97·50	
7	Sales	L 9		39·00	293·00
8	Sales	L 9		41·50	57·50
	R. Windsor	L 81			80·50
			£2·50		1 107·50
19.. July 9	Balance	B/d L 12			562·25

19.. July			£	£	£
5	J. Ranch and Co. Ltd.	L 61			256·00
7	W. Thorpe and Co.	L 71	5·00		195·00
	Petty Cash	PCB 5			26·75
8	Drawings	L 90			50·00
	Motor Vehicle Expenses	L 55			17·50
	Balance	c/d			562·25
			£5·00		1 107·50
		L 13			

(5) Books of M. Tyler (*SPA page 235*)

19.. June			£	£	£		19.. June			£	£	£
8	Balance	B/d			893·00		9	Trihard and Co. Ltd.	L 72	5·00		287·00
9	Sales	L 5		48·00			10	Bloom and Co.	L 11			185·00
9	R. Thomas	L 71		150·00			11	Petty Cash	PCB 7		39·00	
9	B. Brown	L 12	2·00	98·00	296·00			Drawings	L 85		50·00	89·00
10	Sales	L 5			40·00			Motor Vehicle Expenses	L 52			28·00
11	Sales	L 5		40·00				Balance	c/d			725·00
	R. Maitland	L 51		45·00	85·00							
			£2·00 L 17		1 314·00					£5·00 L 18		1 314·00
19.. June												
12	Balance	B/d			725·00							

Unit Twenty-Five
Stock Valuation

Exercises Set 31: The Valuation of Closing Stock

(1) (*SPA page 239*)

Valuation of item on stock sheets:

		£
20 discoloured items (valued at current selling price)	=	20·00
180 at cost price £1·50 each	=	270·00
100 at cost price £1·70 each	=	170·00
120 at cost price £2·00 each	=	240·00
Total value		£700·00

(2) Books of Badbuyers Ltd. (*SPA page 239*)

Valuation of item:

		£
4 damaged items (at current selling price)	=	80·00
16 items at cost price £39·50	=	632·00
64 items at cost price £45·50	=	2 912·00
		£3 624·00

(3) Books of Peter Lawson (*SPA page 239*)

(*a*) Stock is valued at cost price or current selling price, whichever is the lower.
(*b*) Calculations of stock in hand:

Original Stock		4 000 pairs
Purchases January	2 500	
February	2 500	
		5 000 pairs
		9 000 pairs
Less Sales January	1 800	
February	3 000	
		4 800 pairs
		4 200 pairs

Of these we have the following stocks

100 pairs (January 1 stock)
2 500 pairs (February stock)

2 600

∴ Balance is stock bought in January = 1 600 pairs

4 200 pairs

Valuation of Stock:

		£
100 pairs purchased prior to January 1st at £2·00 each	=	200·00
1 600 pairs purchased in January at £2·30 each	=	3 680·00
2 500 pairs purchased in February at £2·20 each	=	5 500·00
4 200 pairs at a total value of		£9 380·00

(4) Books of John Richards (*SPA page 239*)

(*a*) Stock is valued at cost price or current selling price whichever is the lower.

(*b*) As current selling price is above all Richards's cost prices the stock must be valued at cost price.

		£
40 tons @ £28·50	=	1 140·00
60 tons @ £29·50	=	1 770·00
100 tons @ £27·00	=	2 700·00
Total value		£5 610·00

(5) (*SPA page 240*)

Stock calculations:

Good items:		Damaged items:	
Original Stock	8 000	Purchases	2 000
Purchases	14 000	*Less* Sales	1 400
	22 000	Final Stock	600 (Cost price
Less Sales	14 000		£0·12 each)
Final Stock	8 000 (Cost price		
	£0·17 each)		

Current selling prices:

Good items £0·26 each.   Damaged items £0·10 each.

∴ Stock valuation is as follows:

		£
Good items (valued at cost price £0·17 each) 8 000 × £0·17	=	1 360·00
Damaged items (valued at current selling price = £0·10 each)		
600 × £0·10	=	60·00
Total value		£1 420·00

(6) (*SPA page 240*)

(*a*) Stocks in hand:

	A	B	C
Stocks at Start	186	94	100
Manufactured in year	2 350	1 800	1 500
	2 536	1 894	1 600
Less Sales	2 500	1 600	1 550
Closing Stock	36	294	50
Valuation per item: (cost price)	£2·50	£1·50	£0·50

∴ Stock value is as follows:

		£
Item A (36 × £2·50)	=	90·00
Item B (294 × £1·50)	=	441·00
Item C (50 × £0·50)	=	25·00
Total value		£556·00

(*b*) Calculation of trading profit:

Opening Stocks:

		£
Item A (186 × £2·50)	=	465·00
Item B (94 × £1·50)	=	141·00
Item C (100 × £0·50)	=	50·00
Total value		£656·00

Cost of Goods Manufactured:

		£
Item A (2 350 × £2·50)	=	5 875·00
Item B (1 800 × £1·50)	=	2 700·00
Item C (1 500 × £0·50)	=	750·00
Total cost		£9 325·00

Sales:

		£
Item A (2 500 × £15·25)	=	38 125·00
Item B (1 600 × £3·20)	=	5 120·00
Item C (1 550 × £0·95)	=	1 472·50
Total takings		£44 717·50

Trading Account (for year ended December 31st 19..)

19..		£	19..		£
Dec. 31	Opening Stock	656·00	Dec. 31	Sales	44 717·50
	Cost of Manufactured Goods				
	(regarded as being purchased				
	from factory)	9 325·00			
		9 981·00			
	Less Closing Stock	556·00			
	Cost of Stock Sold	9 425·00			
	Gross Profit	35 292·50			
		£44 717·50			£44 717·50

Trading Profit for year was £35 292·50

Exercises Set 32: Stock-taking Problems

(1) Books of R. and T. Traders (*SPA page 242*)

Calculation of Stock at December 31st 19 ..:

		£
Stock at cost on January 2nd		3 180
Deduct Goods delivered on January 1st and 2nd	£340	
And goods returned by customer	£32	
Less Profit Margin		
($\frac{1}{3}$ on Cost Price = $\frac{1}{4}$ off Selling Price)	8	
		24
		364
		2 816
Add Back sales on January 1st and 2nd		
Cash	88	
Credit	108	
	196	
Less Profit Margin	49	
		147
Correct stock valuation at December 31st		£2 963

(2) **Books of A. Trader** (*SPA page 242*)

Calculation of stock value at June 30th 19 .. :

			£
Stock value at cost on July 4th			7 250·00
Deduct Purchases on July 1st–3rd		£460·00	
Deduct Stock sold on June 30th	£120·00		
Less Profit Margin 25%	30·00		
		90·00	
(*Note*: In this case the margin is given			550·00
as a percentage of 'sales' not 'cost.')			
			6 700·00
Add Back sales on July 1st–4th	£725·00		
Less Profit Margin 25%	181·25		
			543·75
Correct stock value at June 30th 19..			£7 243·75

(3) **Books of R. Marshall** (*SPA page 243*)

Calculation of stock value at December 31st 19..:

			£
Value of stock at December 27th			12 725·00
Add Purchases		1 055·00	
and Returns by customer	60·00		
Less Profit Margin			
(50% on cost = ⅓ off selling)	20·00		
		40·00	
		1 095·00	
			13 820·00
Deduct Sales:			
Cash	895·00		
Credit	585·00		
	1 480·00		
Less Profit Margin	493·33		
		986·67	
and Returns to suppliers		48·00	
Drawings in kind		12·00	
Stock contaminated by paraffin		128·00	
			1 174·67
			£12 645·33

∴ Stock valuation to nearest £1 = £12 645

(4) Books of J. Cook and Son (*SPA page 243*)

Calculation of stock lost in burglary on September 30th 19..:

		£
Stock at cost on July 1st 19..		7 840
Purchases July—September		15 600
		23 440
Deduct Sales at Cost Price:		
Sales	18 400	
Less Profit Margin (25%)	4 600	
		13 800
		9 640
Less Stock remaining after burglary		2 420
Value of stock stolen		£7 220

(5) Books of R. Green (*SPA page 243*)

Stock valuation at December 31st 19..

		£
Opening Stock		1 600
Purchases		8 400
		10 000
Deduct Sales at Cost Price:		
Sales at Selling Price	£11 600	
Less Gross Profit	2 900	
		8 700
Value of closing stock		£1 300

(6) Books of R. Butler (*SPA page 243*)

Calculation of stock value at September 30th 19..

			£
Stock at September 1st 19..			1 300
Add Purchases		£15 000	
and Sales Returns	£800		
Less Profit Margin (20%)	160		
	———	640	
		———	15 640
			16 940
Deduct			
Sales		20 000	
Stock taken by Butler		400	
		———	
		20 400	
Less Profit Margin (20%)		4 080	
		———	16 320
Value of stock on September 30th 19..			£ 620

(7) Books of A. Draper (*SPA page 244*)

			£
Value of stock on December 30th 19..			7 280
Add Purchases		£240	
And Sales Returns	£300		
Less Profit Margin (⅕th)	50		
	———	£250	
		———	490
			7 770
Deduct Sales:			
Cash		£180	
Credit		420	
		———	
		600	
Less Profit Margin (⅕th)		100	
		———	500
Stock value on December 31st 19..			£7 270

(8) Books of R. Mortimer (*SPA page 244*)

			£
Stock at cost on May 27th 19..			6 650
Add Purchases		£530	
And Sales Returns	£16		
Less Profit Margin (¼ on Cost			
Price = ¼ off Selling Price)	4		
	──	12	
		──	542
			7 192
Deduct Sales:			
Cash		£156	
Credit		152	
		──	
		308	
Less Profit Margin (¼)		77	
		──	231
Value of stock on May 31st 19..			£6 961

(9) Books of P. Larkins (*SPA page 244*)

			£
Stock at cost on December 27th 19..			5 320
Add Purchases		£424	
And Sales Returns	£12		
Less Profit Margin (¼)	3		
	──	9	
		──	433
			5 753
Deduct Sales:			
Credit		£124	
Cash		120	
		──	
		244	
Less Profit Margin (¼)		61	
		──	183
Stock value on December 31st 19..			£5 570

Adjustments in Final Accounts

Exercises Set 33: Payments in Advance and Accrued Expenses

(1) Books of J. Cakebread (*SPA page 251*)

Rent Paid A/c		L 27	
19..	£	19..	£
Dec. 31 Sundry Cash Payments		Dec. 31 Profit and Loss A/c	1 000
	750		
31 Balance	250		
	£1 000		£1 000
		19..	£
		Jan. 1 Balance	250

Rates A/c		L 28	
19..	£	19..	£
Dec. 31 Sundry Cash Payments		Dec. 31 Profit and Loss A/c	375
	500	31 Balance	125
	£500		£500
19..	£		
Jan. 1 Balance	125		

Wages A/c		L 29	
19..	£	19..	£
Dec. 31 Sundry Cash	36 000	Dec. 31 Trading A/c	36 500
31 Balance	500		
	£36 500		£36 500
		19..	£
		Jan. 1 Balance	500

Interest on Loan A/c		L 30	
19..	£	19..	£
Dec. 31 Sundry Cash	100	Dec. 31 Profit and Loss A/c	200
31 Balance	100		
	£200		£200
		19..	£
		Jan. 1 Balance	100

Insurance A/c		L 31	
19..	£	19..	£
Dec. 31 Sundry Cash	120	Dec. 31 Profit and Loss A/c	90
		31 Balance	30
	£120		£120
19..	£		
Jan. 1 Balance	30		

(2) Books of Goodsell (*SPA page 251*)

Rent-Payable A/c		L 21	
19..	£	19..	£
Mar. 25 Bank	425	Dec. 31 Profit and Loss A/c	1 700
June 24 Bank	425		
Sept. 29 Bank	425		
Dec. 31 Balance	425		
	£1 700		£1 700
		19..	£
		Jan. 1 Balance	425

Rent-Receivable A/c		L 22	
19..	£	19..	£
Dec. 31 Profit and Loss A/c	125	Aug. 2 Bank	75
31 Balance	25	Nov. 1 Bank	75
	£150		£150
		19..	£
		Jan. 1 Balance	25

(3) Books of P. Mugleston (*SPA page 251*)

Electricity A/c   L 47

19..			£	19..				£
Feb. 8	Cash	CB 5	38·00	Jan. 1	Balance		B/d	20·00
May 13	Cash	CB 12	36·00	Dec. 31	Profit and Loss A/c	L 194		128·80
Aug. 11	Cash	CB 17	27·00					
Nov. 12	Cash	CB 24	31·00					
Dec. 31	Balance	c/d	16·80					
			£148·80					£148·80
				19..				£
				Jan. 1	Balance		B/d	16·80

(4) Books of D. Bird (*SPA page 252*)

Rent and Rates A/c   L 52

19..			£	19..				£
Jan. 1	Balance	B/d	22	Jan. 1	Balance		B/d	150
Mar. 27	Bank	CB 5	300	Dec. 31	Profit and Loss A/c	L 194		719
Apr. 4	Bank	CB 7	44	31	Balance		c/d	23
Sept. 29	Bank	CB 13	320					
Oct. 8	Bank	CB 16	46					
Dec. 31	Balance	c/d	160					
			£892					£892
19..			£	19..				£
Jan. 1	Balance	B/d	23	Jan. 1	Balance		B/d	160

(5) Books of A. Retailer (*SPA page 252*)

Rent A/c   L 38

19..			£	19..			£
Dec. 31	Profit and Loss A/c	L 187	312	19..			£
				Mar. 25	Bank	CB 5	78
				June 30	Bank	CB 17	78
				Sept. 29	Bank	CB 23	78
				Dec. 31	Balance	c/d	78
			£312				£312
19..			£				
Jan. 1	Balance	B/d	78				

(6) Books of Unworthy Wholesaling Co. Ltd. (*SPA page 252*)

Wages A/c   L 94

19..			£	19..				£
Jan. 1/Dec. 31	Bank	CB 6	360 000	Jan. 1	Balance		B/d	7 000
				Dec. 31	Warehouse			
Dec. 31	Balance	c/d	6 500		Maintenance	L 68		12 000
				31	Trading A/c	L 177		347 500
			£366 500					£366 500
				19..				£
				Jan. 1	Balance		B/d	6 500

(7) **Books of H. Hollow** (*SPA page 252*)

Trading A/c (for year ending March 31st 19..)   L 168

19..		£	£	19..		£
Mar. 31	Opening Stock		1 320·00	Mar. 31	Sales	18 294·75
	Purchases	5 246·00			Less Sales Returns	124·00
	Add Carriage In	160·00				
					Net Turnover	18 170·75
		5 406·00				
	Less Purchases Returns	196·75				
			5 209·25			
			6 529·25			
	Less Closing Stock		1 800·00			
	Cost of Stock Sold		4 729·25			
	Factory Wages	1 624·00				
	Add Wages Due	48·50				
			1 672·50			
	Cost of Sales		6 401·75			
	Gross Profit		11 769·00			
			£18 170·75			£18 170·75

Profit and Loss A/c (for year ending March 31st 19..)

19..		£	19..			£
Mar. 31	Office Salaries	2 735·25	Mar. 31	Gross Profit		11 769·00
	Office Light and Heat	38·00		Commission		
	Office Expenses	28·25		Received	594·00	
	Advertising	164·00		Add Commission		
	Discount Allowed	27·00		Due	26·00	
	Carriage Outwards	28·50				620·00
				Discount Received		36·75
		3 021·00				
	Net Profit	9 404·75				
		£12 425·75				£12 425·75
						12 425·75

Balance Sheet (as at March 31st 19..)

	£	£		£	£
Fixed Assets:			Capital:		
Premises		4 000·00	At Start		5 000·00
Plant and Machinery		1 270·00	Add Net Profit	9 404·75	
Office Furniture		866·50	Less Drawings	4 600·00	4 804·75
Motor Vehicles		850·00			
					9 804·75
		6 986·50			
Current Assets:			Long-term Liability:		
Stock	1 800·00		Loan (M. Long)		4 406·00
Debtors	686·50		Current Liabilities:		
Bank	6 975·00		Creditors	2 339·75	
Cash	125·00		Wages Due	48·50	
Commission Due	26·00				2 388·25
		9 612·50			
		£16 599·00			£16 599·00

(8) Books of R. Green (*SPA page 253*)

Stationery A/c   L 47

19..		£	19..			£
Jan. 1	Balance (Stock)	18	Jan. 1	Balance (due to supplier)		15
28	Bank	43	Mar. 31	Profit and Loss A/c		96
Feb. 26	Bank	17	31	Balance (Stock in Hand)		32
Mar. 29	Bank	57				
31	Balance	8				
		£143				£143
19..		£	19..			£
Apr. 1	Balance (Stock)	32	Apr. 1	Balance (due to supplier)		8

(9) Books of P. Green (*SPA page 253*)

Rent-Received A/c   L 21

19..			£	19..			£
June 30	Profit and Loss A/c		210	Jan. 1	Cash	CB 4	35
				Feb. 3	Cash	CB 7	35
				Mar. 2	Cash	CB 10	35
				Apr. 9	Cash	CB 14	35
				May 14	Cash	CB 18	35
				June 30	Balance	c/d	35
			£210				£210
19..			£				
June 30	Balance	B/d	35				

(10) Books of F. Grosvenor (*SPA page 254*)

Trading A/c (for year ending December 31st 19..)

19..		£	£	19..		£
Dec. 31	Opening Stock		1 250	Dec. 31	Sales	46 650
	Purchases	24 750			*Less* Sales Returns	150
	Add Carriage In	250				
		25 000			Net Turnover	46 500
	Less Purchases Returns	650				
			24 350			
	Total Stock Available		25 600			
	Less Closing Stock		1 000			
	Cost of Stock Sold		24 600			
	Wages	2 500				
	Add Wages Due	50				
			2 550			
	Cost of Sales		27 150			
	Gross Profit		19 350			
			£46 500			£46 500

Profit and Loss A/c (for year ending December 31st 19..)

19..		£	£	19..		£
Dec. 31	Postage		385	Dec. 31	Gross Profit	19 350
	Printing and Stationery		525		Rent Received	355
	Carriage Out		190		Bad Debt Recovered	25
	Office Salaries		3 100		Discount Received	20
	Rent and Rates	800				
	Less Rates in Advance	20				19 750
			780			
	Insurance		250			
	Discount Allowed		150			
	Advertising		3 300			
	Distribution Expenses		6 700			
			15 380			
	Net Profit		4 370			
			£19 750			£19 750

Balance Sheet (as at December 31st 19..)

	£	£		£	£
Fixed Assets:			Capital (F. Grosvenor):		
Premises		5 500	At Start		4 735
Machinery and Plant		3 250	Add Profit	4 370	
Furniture and Fittings		800	Less Drawings	1 000	
Motor Vehicles		1 500			3 370
					8 105
		11 050			
Current Assets:			Long-term Liability:		
Closing Stock	1 000		Loan (P. Carr)		4 000
Debtors	4 250		Current Liabilities:		
Cash at Bank	1 560		Creditors	5 750	
Cash in Hand	25		Wages Due	50	
Rates in Advance	20				5 800
		6 855			
		£17 905			£17 905

Exercises Set 34: Bad Debts and Provision for Bad Debts

(1) (*SPA page 258*)

Provision for Bad Debts A/c   L 127

19..			£	19..			£
Dec. 31	Bad Debts		130·00	Jan. 1	Balance		140·00
31	Balance	c/d	133·50	Dec. 31	Profit and Loss A/c		123·50
			£263·50				£263·50
				19..			£
				Jan. 1	Balance	B/d	133·50

Profit and Loss A/c   L 128

19		£	
Dec. 31	Provision for Bad Debts	123·50	

Balance Sheet (as at December 31st 19..)

19..	£	£
Current Assets		
Debtors	2 670·00	
Less Provision	133·50	
		2 536·50

(2) (*SPA page 258*)

Statement of Charge to Profit and Loss A/c for year ended December 31st 19..

		£
Original Provision at January 1st (5 % of £24 240·00)	=	1 212·00
Deduct Bad Debts		132·00
		1 080·00
Add Sum Recovered		24·00
Balance of Provision for Bad Debts A/c	=	£1 104·00

		£
New Provision required (5 % of £26 360·00)	=	1 318·00
Balance already available (see above)	=	1 104·00
Charge to Profit and Loss A/c	=	£ 214·00

(3) (*SPA page 259*)

Statement of Charge to Profit and Loss A/c for year ended March 31st 19..

		£
Original Provision at April 1st 19.. (5 % of £18 750)	=	937·50
Deduct Bad Debt		380·00
		557·50
Add Bad Debt Recovered		46·00
Balance on Provision from last year	=	603·50
New Provision required (5 % of £11 500)	=	575·00
Amount to be reclaimed from Provision and restored to Profit and Loss A/c	=	£ 28·50

(4) Books of N. Thorn (*SPA page 259*)

Provision for Bad and Doubtful Debts A/c — L 171

19..		£	19..		£
May 31	T. Tomkins	26	Jan. 1	Balance	225
31	S. Carter	145	Oct. 1	Bad Debts Recovered	6
July 31	P. Lane	40	Nov. 17	Bad Debts Recovered	30
Nov. 30	N. Lucas	57	Dec. 31	Profit and Loss A/c	275
Dec. 31	Balance	268			
		£536			£536
			19..		£
			Jan. 1	Balance	268

(5) Books of J. Wilson (*SPA page 259*)

Bad Debts A/c — L 27

19..	£	19..		£
Jan.–Dec. Bad Debts	350	Jan.–Dec.	Bad Debts Recovered	72
		Dec. 31	Provision for Bad Debts A/c	278
	£350			£350

Provision for Bad Debts A/c — L 28

19..		£	19..		£
Dec. 31	Bad Debts	278	Jan. 1	Balance	440
31	Balance	650	Dec. 31	Profit and Loss A/c	488
		£928			£928
			19..		£
			Jan. 1	Balance	650

Profit and Loss A/c (for year ending December 31st 19..) — L 129

19..		£
Dec. 31	New Provision for Bad Debts	488

Balance Sheet (as at December 31st 19..)

	£	£
Current Assets		
Debtors	6 500	
Less Provision	650	
		5 850

(6) Books of Roberts and Brown Ltd. (*SPA page 259*)

Bad Debts Provision A/c — L 126

19..			£	19..			£
Dec. 31	Bad Debts A/c		176	Jan. 1	Balance		126·60
31	Balance	c/d	140	Dec. 31	Profit and Loss A/c		189·40
			£316				£316·00
				19..			£
				Jan. 1	Balance	B/d	140·00

Bad Debts A/c   L 127

19..		£	19..		£
Dec. 31	Peterson	150	Dec. 31	Provision for Bad Debts	176
31	Johannsen	26			
		£176			£176

Profit and Loss A/c   L 189

19..		£
Dec. 31	Bad Debts Provision	189·40

(7) Books of C. Bolton (*SPA page 260*)

Provision for Bad Debts A/c   L 121

19..		£	19..		£
Dec. 31	Bad Debts	350	Jan. 1	Balance	425
31	Balance	900	Dec. 31	Profit and Loss A/c	825
		£1 250			£1 250
			19..		£
			Jan. 1	Balance	900

Bad Debts A/c   L 122

19..		£	19..		£
Jan.–Dec.	Bad Debtors	500	Jan.–Dec.	Bad Debt Recovered	150
			Dec. 31	Provision for Bad Debts A/c	350
		£500			£500

Profit and Loss A/c   L 189

19..		£
Dec. 31	Provision for Bad Debts	825

Balance Sheet (as at December 31st 19..)

	£	£
Current Assets		
Debtors	9 000	
Less Provision	900	
		8 100

(8) Books of M. Rooselar (*SPA page 260*)

Trading A/c (for year ending December 31st 19..)

19..		£	£	19..		£
Dec. 31	Opening Stock		1 950	Dec. 31	Sales	34 000
	Purchases	25 000			*Less* Returns	86
	Less Returns	36				
			24 964		Net Turnover	33 914
			26 914			
	Less Closing Stock		3 000			
	Cost of Stock Sold		23 914			
	Gross Profit		10 000			
			£33 914			£33 914

Profit and Loss A/c (for year ending December 31st 19..)

19..		£	19..		
Dec. 31	Carriage Out	26	Dec. 31	Gross Profit	10 000
	Sundry Expenses	300		Discount Received	125
	Salaries	2 350			
	Discount Allowed	26			10 125
	Light and Heat	190			
	Commission Paid	760			
	Rent and Rates	242			
	Bad Debts	50			
	Provision for Bad Debts	200			
		4 144			
	Net Profit	5 981			
		£10 125			£10 125

Balance Sheet (as at December 31st 19..)

	£	£		£	£
Fixed Assets			Capital		
Land and Buildings		3 500	At Start		6 377
Plant and Machinery		1 500	*Add* Net Profit	5 981	
Office Furniture		1 850	*Less* Drawings	2 000	
		6 850			3 981
Current Assets					10 358
Stock	3 000				
Debtors	1 484				
Less Provision	200				
		1 284			
Bank		2 875	Current Liabilities		
Cash		25	Creditors		3 676
		7 184			
		£14 034			£14 034

(9) Books of Gerard Eliasson (*SPA page 261*)

Trading A/c (for year ending December 31st 19..)

19..		£	£	19..		£
Dec. 31	Opening Stock		780	Dec. 31	Sales	13 612
	Purchases	8 248			*Less* Returns	112
	Less Returns Out	48				
			8 200		Net Turnover	13 500
			8 980			
	Less Closing Stock		1 250			
			7 730			
	Wages		450			
			8 180			
	Gross Profit		5 320			
			£13 500			£13 500

Profit and Loss A/c (for year ending December 31st 19..)

19..		£	19..		£
Dec. 31	Salaries	580	Dec. 31	Gross Profit	5 320
	Light and Heat	420		Commission Received	650
	Telephone Expenses	120		Rent Received	100
	Insurance	250			
	Interest on Loan	150			6 070
	Bad Debts	150			
	Provision for Bad Debts	310			
	Provision for Discount	140			
		2 120			
	Net Profit	3 950			
		£6 070			£6 070

Balance Sheet (as at December 31st 19..)

	£	£	£		£	£
Fixed Assets				Capital		
Land and Buildings			4 000	At Start		2 812
Plant and Machinery			1 400	*Add* Net Profit	3 950	
Motor Vehicles			250	*Less* Drawings	1 000	
						2 950
			5 650			5 762
Current Assets						
Stock		1 250				
Debtors	3 100					
Less Provision						
for Bad Debts	310					
		2 790				
Less Provision				Long-term Liabilities		
for Discounts	140			Loan (Southern Bank)		2 000
		2 650				
Bank		2 465		Current Liabilities		
Cash		27		Creditors		4 280
			6 392			
			£12 042			£12 042

Exercises Set 35: Difficult Final Accounts Exercises

(1) Books of J. March (*SPA page 266*)

Trading A/c (for year ending December 31st 19..)

19..		£	£	19..		£
Dec. 31	Opening Stock		2 036	Dec. 31	Sales	73 572
	Purchases	68 496			*Less* Returns	67
	Less Returns	403				
			68 093			73 505
			70 129			
	Less Closing Stock		9 645			
			60 484			
	Wages	2 848				
	Add Wages Due	34				
			2 882			
			63 366			
	Gross Profit		10 139			
			£73 505			£73 505

Profit and Loss A/c (for year ending December 31st 19..)

19..		£	19..		£
Dec. 31	Advertising	138	Dec. 31	Gross Profit	10 139
	Insurance	203			
	Bad Debts	37			
	Telephone Expenses	45			
	Rates and Water	112			
	Light and Heat	102			
	Postage	149			
	Depreciation Lease	500			
	Depreciation Motor Vehicle	300			
	Depreciation Furniture and Fittings	111			
	Provision for Bad Debts	230			
	Net Profit	8 212			
		£10 139			£10 139

Balance Sheet (for year ending December 31st 19..)

	£	£	£		£	£
Fixed Assets				Capital		
Leasehold Premises	5 000			At Start		17 800
Less Depreciation	500			Add Net Profit	8 212	
		4500		Less Drawings	1 000	
Furniture and Fittings	1 110					7 212
Less Depreciation	111					25 012
		999				
Motor Vans	938					
Less Depreciation	300					
		638				
		6 137				
Current Assets				Current Liabilities		
Stock		9 645		Creditors	9 570	
Debtors	14 898·00			Wages Due	34	
Less Provision	230·00					9 604
		14 668				
Bank		3 803				
Cash in Hand		363				
		28 479				
		£34 616				£34 616

(2) Books of R. Smart (SPA page 266)

Light and Heat A/c　　　　　　　　　　　　　　　　L 27

19..		£	19..		£
Jan. 1	Balance (fuel oil)	42·50	Jan. 1	Balance (electricity due)	62·50
16	Bank (electricity)	62·50	Dec. 31	Profit and Loss A/c	422·80
Mar. 31	Bank (fuel oil)	96·50	31	Balance (fuel oil)	51·40
Apr. 20	Bank (electricity)	55·75			
July 18	Bank (electricity)	45·25			
Sept. 30	Bank (fuel oil)	100·20			
Oct. 16	Bank (repairs)	0·90			
17	Bank (electricity)	52·50			
Dec. 31	Balance (electricity due)	80·60			
		£536·70			£536·70
19..		£	19..		£
Jan. 1	Balance (fuel oil)	51·40	Jan. 1	Balance (electricity due)	80·60

(3) Books of Saul, a trader *(SPA page 267)*

Trading A/c (for year ending December 31st 19..)

19..		£	19..		£
Dec. 31	Opening Stock	11 400	Dec. 31	Sales	105 200
	Purchases	78 600			
		90 000			
	Less Closing Stock	15 800			
		74 200			
	Gross Profit	31 000			
		£105 200			£105 200

Profit and Loss A/c (for year ending December 31st 19..)

19..		£	£	19..		£
Dec. 31	Light and Heat	178		Dec. 31	Gross Profit	31 000
	Add Amount Due	28			Discount Received	1 764
			206			32 764
	General Expenses		3 602			
	Discount Allowed		2 228			
	Rates and Insurance	192				
	Less Amount in Advance	50				
			142			
	Wages and Salaries		14 970			
	Bad Debts		860			
	Provision for Bad Debts		140			
	Depreciation:					
	Motor Vehicles	160				
	Furniture	134				
			294			
			22 442			
	Net Profit		10 322			
			£32 764			£32 764

Balance Sheet (as at December 31st 19..)

		£	£			£	£
Fixed Assets				Capital			
Goodwill		1 200		At Start			25 000
Less Amount Written Off		300		*Add* Net Profit		10 322	
			900	*Less* Drawings		5 880	
Freehold Land and Buildings			9 000			4 442	
Furniture and Fittings		1 340		*Less* Goodwill Written			
Less Depreciation		134		Off		300	
			1 206				4 142
			11 106				29 142
Current Assets				Current Liabilities			
Stock		15 800		Creditors		7 650	
Debtors	9 500			Light and Heat Due		28	
Less Provision	460						7 678
		9 040					
Bank		824					
Rates in Advance		50					
			25 714				
			£36 820				£36 820

(4) Books of S. Smith (*SPA page 268*)

Trading A/c (for year ending December 31st 19..)

19..		£	£	19..		£
Dec. 31	Opening Stock		2 720	Dec. 31	Sales	50 261
	Purchases	33 436			*Less* Returns Inwards	240
	Add Carriage In	546				
					Net Turnover	50 021
		33 982				
	Less Purchases					
	Returns	120				
			33 862			
			36 582			
	Less Closing Stock		4 270			
	Cost of Stock Sold		32 312			
	Gross Profit		17 709			
			£50 021			£50 021

Profit and Loss A/c (for year ending December 31st 19..)

19..		£	£	19..		£
Dec. 31	Bad Debts Provision		98	Dec. 31	Gross Profits	17 709
	Rent and Rates	626			Discount Received	59
	Less Rates in Advance	100				
			526		Net Turnover	17 768
	Salaries	5 226				
	Add Amount Due	426				
			5 652			
	General Expenses		920			
	Bank Interest etc.		56			
	Carriage Out		720			
	Discount Allowed		65			
	Bad Debts		240			
	Depreciation					
	Motor Vehicles	500				
	Furniture and					
	Fittings	200				
			700			
			8 977			
	Net Profit		8 791			
			£17 768			£17 768

Balance Sheet (as at December 31st 19..)

	£	£		£	£
Fixed Assets			**Capital**		
Freehold Buildings		10 300	At Start		10 059
Fixtures and Fittings	4 000		Net Profit	8 791	
Less Depreciation	400		*Less* Drawings	2 459	
		3 600			6 332
Motor Vans	2 000				16 391
Less Depreciation	1 000				
		1 000			
		14 900			
Current Assets			**Current Liabilities**		
Stock	4 270		Creditors	6 735	
Debtors	7 009		Bank Overdraft	2 522	
Less Provision	260		Wages and Salaries Due	426	
		6 749			9 683
Petty Cash		55			
Rates in Advance		100			
		11 174			
		£26 074			£26 074

(5) Books of Wormley, a trader (*SPA page 269*)

Trading A/c (for year ending December 31st 19..)

19..		£	19..		£
Dec. 31	Opening Stock	8 726	Dec. 31	Sales	45 622
	Purchases	36 291			
		45 017			
	Less Closing Stock	9 428			
		35 589			
	Gross Profit	10 033			
		£45 622			£45 622

Profit and Loss A/c (for year ending December 31st 19..)

19..		£	£	19..		£
Dec. 31	Rent and Rates	800		Dec. 31	Gross Profit	10 033
	Less Amount in Advance	60				
			740			
	Salaries		3 969			
	General Expenses	1 062				
	Add Amount Due	166				
			1 228			
	Provision for Bad Debts		253			
	Depreciation					
	Furniture	105				
	Motor Vehicles	425				
			530			
	Loss on Motor Vehicle		250			
			6 970			
	Net Profit		3 063			
			£10 033			£10 033

Balance Sheet (as at December 31st 19..)

	£	£			£
Fixed Assets			**Capital**		
Furniture and Equipment			At Start		11 219
At Cost	2 100		Net Profit	3 063	
Less Depreciation	565		*Less* Drawings	1 788	
		1 535			1 275
Motor Vans					12 494
At Cost	1 900				
Less Depreciation	805				
		1 095			
		2 630			
Current Assets			**Current Liabilities**		
Stock		9 428	Creditors	3 164	
Debtors	4 289		Motor Vehicle Creditor	650	
Less Provision	241		General Expenses Due	166	
	4 048				3 980
Bank	308				
Rates in Advance	60				
		13 844			
		£16 474			£16 474

Notes:

(*a*) In this exercise the Provision for Bad Debts charge to Profit and Loss Account was calculated as follows:

Provision for Bad Debts A/c

19..			£	19..			£
Dec. 31	Bad Debts		281	Jan. 1	Balance		269
31	Balance	c/d	241	Dec. 31	Profit and Loss A/c		253
			£522				£522
				19..			£
				Jan. 1	Balance		241

(*b*) Motor Vehicle calculations are as follows:

  (i) Cost figure:

	£
Motor Vehicles originally cost	1 700
Deduct Vehicle owned for only one year	800
Original cost of other vehicles	900
Add Cost of new vehicle	1 000
New cost figure	£1 900

  (ii) Loss on vehicle sold:

	£
Original cost	800
One year's depreciation	200
	600
Realized value	350
Loss	£250

(iii) Value of vehicles at close of year:

		£
Original cost of other vehicles		900
Deduct Depreciation to January 1st		580
		320
Deduct 25% Depreciation		225
		95
Add New vehicle		1 000
		£1 095

(6) Books of M. Smith (*SPA page 270*)

(a) Profit and Loss Account entries:

Profit and Loss A/c (for year ending December 31st 19..)

19..		£	19..		£
Dec. 31	Depreciation	400	Dec. 31 Rent Received		150
31	Rates	180	31 Bad Debts Provision Recovered		10

(b) Balance Sheet entries:

Balance Sheet (as at December 31st 19..)

	£	£		£
Fixed Assets				
Furniture and Fittings	3 000			
Less Depreciation	400			
		2 600		
Current Assets			Current Liabilities	
Debtors	4 800		Rates Due	45
Less Provision	240			
		4 560		
Rent Receivable		10		
		4 570		

(c) Ledger Account entries, showing the final balances

Rent Received A/c   L 17

19..			£	19..				£
Dec. 31	Profit and Loss A/c		150	Jan.	1	Balance		20
				Jan.-Dec.	Bank			120
				Dec. 31	Balance		c/d	10
			£150					£150
19..			£					
Jan. 1	Balance	B/d	10					

Shop Furniture and Fittings A/c   L 29

19..			£	19..				£
Jan. 1	Balance		2 400	Dec. 31	Depreciation			400
Jan.-Dec.	Bank		600	31	Balance		c/d	2 600
			£3 000					£3 000
19..			£					
Jan. 1	Balance	B/d	2 600					

Provision for Bad Debts A/c   L 37

19..		£	19..		£
Dec. 31	Profit and Loss A/c	10	Jan. 1	Balance	250
31	Balance	240			
		£250			£250
			19..		£
			Jan. 1	Balance	240

Rates A/c   L 52

19..		£	19..		£
Jan. 1	Balance	45	Dec. 31	Profit and Loss A/c	180
Jan.-Dec.	Bank	90			
Dec. 31	Balance	45			
		£180			£180
			19..		£
			Jan. 1	Balance	45

(7) Books of C. Violet (*SPA page 271*)

Trading A/c (for year ending September 30th 19..)

19..		£	£	19..		£
Sept. 30	Stock at Start		3 972	Sept. 30	Sales	48 699
	Purchases	43 694			*Less* Sales Returns	195
	Add Carriage In	286				
		43 980			Net Turnover	48 504
	Less Purchases					
	Returns	987				
			42 993			
			46 965			
	Less Closing Stock		4 196			
	Cost of Stock Sold		42 769			
	Gross Profit		5 735			
			£48 504			£48 504

Profit and Loss A/c (for year ending September 30th 19..)

19..		£	£	19..		£
Sept. 30	Bad Debts		106	Sept. 30 Gross Profit		5 735
	Carriage Out		59			
	General Expenses		211			
	Insurance	130				
	Less Amount in Advance	30				
			100			
	Light and Heat		118			
	Rent	360				
	Add Rent Due	120				
			480			
	Salaries		1 762			
	Upkeep of Premises	50				
	Add Amount Due	28				
			78			
	Van Expenses		397			
	Provision for Bad Debts		12			
	Provision for Discounts		135			
	Depreciation					
	Motor Vehicles	144				
	Equipment	100				
			244			
			3 702			
	Net Profit		2 033			
			£5 735			£5 735

Balance Sheet (as at September 30th 19..)

	£	£	£		£	£
Fixed Assets				Capital		
Equipment at Cost		550		At Start		4 496
Less Depreciation		100		Net Profit	2 033	
			450	*Less* Drawings	1 200	
Motor Van at Cost		720				833
Less Depreciation		288				5 329
			432			
			882			
Current Assets				Current Liabilities		
Stock			4 196	Creditors	1 693	
Debtors	2 838			Bank Overdraft	567	
Less Provision for				Rent Due	120	
Bad Debts	138			Repairs Due	28	
						2 408
	2 700					
Less Provision for						
Discounts	135					
		2 565				
Cash in Hand		64				
Insurance in Advance		30				
			6 855			
			£7 737			£7 737

Unit Twenty-Seven
Partnership Accounts

Exercises Set 36: Partnership Appropriation Accounts

(1) Books of Sybrandt and Cornelis (*SPA page 278*)

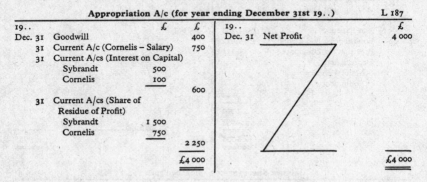

Appropriation A/c (for year ending December 31st 19..)

19..		£	£	19..		£
Dec. 31	Goodwill		400	Dec. 31	Net Profit	4 000
31	Current A/c (Cornelis – Salary)		750			
31	Current A/cs (Interest on Capital)					
	Sybrandt	500				
	Cornelis	100				
			600			
31	Current A/cs (Share of Residue of Profit)					
	Sybrandt	1 500				
	Cornelis	750				
			2 250			
			£4 000			£4 000

(2) Books of Wheel and Barrow (*SPA page 278*)

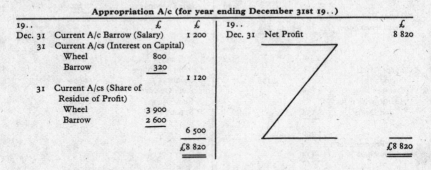

Appropriation A/c (for year ending December 31st 19..)

19..		£	£	19..		£
Dec. 31	Current A/c Barrow (Salary)		1 200	Dec. 31	Net Profit	8 820
31	Current A/cs (Interest on Capital)					
	Wheel	800				
	Barrow	320				
			1 120			
31	Current A/cs (Share of Residue of Profit)					
	Wheel	3 900				
	Barrow	2 600				
			6 500			
			£8 820			£8 820

(3) Books of Able, Baker and Charles (*SPA page 279*)

Appropriation A/c (for year ending December 31st 19..)

19..		£	£	19..		£
Dec. 31	Current A/cs (Salaries)			Dec. 31	Net Profit	4 500
	Able	600				
	Baker	600				
			1 200			
31	Current A/cs (Interest on Capital)					
	Able	500				
	Baker	400				
	Charles	300				
			1 200			
31	Current A/cs (Share of Residue of Profit)					
	Able	1 050				
	Baker	700				
	Charles	350				
			2 100			
			£4 500			£4 500

(4) Books of Hawtrey and Grigg (*SPA page 279*)

Appropriation A/c (for half-year ending December 31st 19..)

19..		£	£	19..		£
Dec. 31	Current A/c Grigg (Salary)		750	Dec. 31	Net Profit	3 650
31	Current A/cs (Interest on Capital)					
	Hawtrey	320				
	Grigg	80				
			400			
31	Current A/cs (Share of Residue)					
	Hawtrey	1 875				
	Grigg	625				
			2 500			
			£3 650			£3 650

(5) Books of Melville and Ahab (*SPA page 279*)

Appropriation A/c (for 9 months ending December 31st 19..)

19..		£	£	19..		£
Dec. 31	Current A/c Ahab (Salary)		487·50	Dec. 31	Net Profit	2 799·00
31	Current A/cs (Interest on Capital)					
	Melville	180·00				
	Ahab	45·00				
			225·00			
31	Current A/cs (Share of Residue of Profit)					
	Melville	1 391·00				
	Ahab	695·50				
			2 086·50			
			£2 799·00			£2 799·00

Exercises Set 37: Current Accounts of Partners

(1) Books of Salt and Pepper (*SPA page 282*)

			Current A/c (Pepper)				L 12
19..			£	19..			£
Dec. 31	Drawings		1 040·00	Jan. 1	Balance	B/d	180·00
31	Sales		78·00	Dec. 31	Salary		750·00
31	Balance	c/d	904·50	31	Interest on Capital		60·00
				31	Share of Residue		1 032·50
			£2 022·50				£2 022·50
				19..			£
				Jan. 1	Balance	B/d	904·50

Calculations for the above required the preparation of an Appropriation Account. Here it is, for your information.

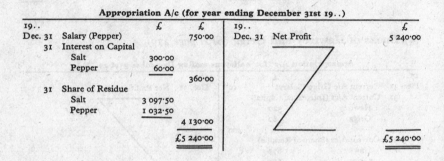

				Appropriation A/c (for year ending December 31st 19..)			
19..		£	£	19..			£
Dec. 31	Salary (Pepper)		750·00	Dec. 31	Net Profit		5 240·00
31	Interest on Capital						
	Salt	300·00					
	Pepper	60·00					
			360·00				
31	Share of Residue						
	Salt	3 097·50					
	Pepper	1 032·50					
			4 130·00				
			£5 240·00				£5 240·00

(2) Books of Jackson (*SPA page 282*)

	Capital A/c (Jackson)		L 2
	19..		£
	Jan. 1	Balance	3 000
	May 1	Bank	600
	Dec. 31	Current A/c	1 400

Note : There is no real need to tidy up this account and bring down the balance, but it does help clarify affairs to do so.

		Current A/c (Jackson)				L 3
19..		£	19..			£
Dec. 31	Drawings	1 600	Jan. 1	Balance		450
31	Capital	1 400	Dec. 31	Salary		800
31	Balance	520	31	Interest on Capital		170
			31	Share of Residue		2 100
		£3 520				£3 520
			19..			£
			Jan. 1	Balance		520

(3) Books of Wilson and Brown (*SPA page 282*)

Current A/c (Wilson)   L 5

19..			£	19..			£
Dec. 31	Drawings		2 000	Jan. 1	Balance		420
31	Balance	c/d	1 370	Dec. 31	Interest on Capital		400
				31	Share of Residue		2 550
			£3 370				£3 370
				19..			£
				Dec. 31	Balance	B/d	1 370

Current A/c (Brown)

19..			£	19..			£
Dec. 31	Drawings		1 800	Jan. 1	Balance		350
31	Balance	c/d	1 000	Dec. 31	Salary		400
				31	Commission		100
				31	Interest on Capital		250
				31	Share of Residue		1 700
			£2 800				£2 800
				19..			£
				Jan. 1	Balance	B/d	1 000

Note: In order to prepare these Current Accounts it is necessary to draw up the Appropriation Account. Here it is, for your information.

Calculations:

Appropriation A/c (for year ending December 31st 19..)

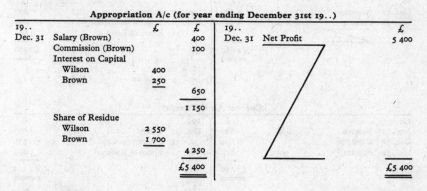

19..		£	£	19..		£
Dec. 31	Salary (Brown)		400	Dec. 31	Net Profit	5 400
	Commission (Brown)		100			
	Interest on Capital					
	Wilson	400				
	Brown	250				
			650			
			1 150			
	Share of Residue					
	Wilson	2 550				
	Brown	1 700				
			4 250			
			£5 400			£5 400

(4) (*SPA page 283*)

(*a*) The Capital Account in partnerships is usually fixed, that is, it remains at the original capital contribution, and is only varied if some permanent change in capital arrangements is agreed between the partners. The Current Account has to be introduced therefore to record the fluctuating part of the net worth of the business, that is, the extent to which profits are 'ploughed back' into the business.

(b) No, it is not true. Although Capital Accounts nearly always do have credit balances, a succession of bad years with low profits may mean that the capital is consumed and eventually a debit balance on capital may appear. This is called a Deficit on Capital Account. Clearly creditors may refuse to grant further credit in this sort of situation and the firm is likely to cease trading.

(c) A Current Account shows a debit balance whenever the sums drawn out exceed the profits, interest, etc., earned. A partner whose drawings exceed his earnings in this way is living on his capital to the extent of the debit balance on his Current Account.

(5) Books of Smith and Edwards (*SPA page 283*)

Appropriation A/c Smith and Edwards (for year ending December 31st 19..)

19..		£	£	19..		£
Dec. 31	Salary (Edwards)		1 000	Dec. 31	Net Profit	7 400
	Interest on Capital					
	Smith	650				
	Edwards	350				
			1 000			
	Share of Residue					
	Smith	3 600				
	Edwards	1 800				
			5 400			
			£7 400			£7 400

Current A/c (Smith)

19..			£	19..			£
Dec. 31	Drawings		3 500	Jan. 1	Balance	B/d	400
31	Balance	c/d	1 150	Dec. 31	Interest on Capital		650
				31	Share of Residue		3 600
			£4 650				£4 650
				19..			£
				Jan. 1	Balance	B/d	1 150

Current A/c (Edwards)

19..			£	19..			£
Jan. 1	Balance	B/d	350	Dec. 31	Salary		1 000
Dec. 31	Drawings		2 000	31	Interest on Capital		350
31	Balance	c/d	800	31	Share of Residue		1 800
			£3 150				£3 150
				19..			£
				Jan. 1	Balance	B/d	800

Exercises Set 38: Final Accounts of Partnerships

(1) Books of Lester and Payne (*SPA page 284*)

Appropriation A/c (for year ending December 31st 19..)

19..		£	£	19..			£
Dec. 31	Loan Interest (Lester)		36	Dec. 31	Net Profit		4 012
	Salary (Payne)		600				
	Share of Residue						
	Lester	2 532					
	Payne	844					
			3 376				
			£4 012				£4 012

Current A/c (Lester)

19..			£	19..			£
Dec. 31	Drawings		1 210	Jan. 1	Balance	B/d	208
	Balance	c/d	1 566	Dec. 31	Loan Interest		36
				31	Share of Residue		2 532
			£2 776				£2 776
				19..			£
				Jan. 1	Balance	B/d	1 566

Current A/c (Payne)

19..			£	19..			£
Dec. 31	Drawings		920	Jan. 1	Balance	B/d	122
	Balance	c/d	646	Dec. 31	Salary		600
					Share of Residue		844
			£1 566				£1 566
				19..			£
				Jan. 1	Balance	B/d	646

Balance Sheet (as at December 31st 19..)

	£	£		£	£
Fixed Assets			Capital		
Furniture and Equipment	2 200		Lester	2 000	
Less Depreciation	320		Payne	1 500	
		1 880			3 500
Motor Van	600				
Less Depreciation	110				
		490			
		2 370	Current A/cs		
Current Assets			Lester	1 566	
Stock	2 840		Payne	646	
Debtors	938				2 212
Less Provision	70		Long-term Liability		
	868		Loan (Lester)		600
Bank	630		Current Liabilities		
Cash	35		Creditors	416	
Insurance Pre-paid	25		Rent Due	40	
		4 398			456
		£6 768			£6 768

(2) (*SPA page 285*)

Where there is no agreement between the partners, the Partnership Act of 1890 will be used to decide how profits are to be shared. This Act specifies that no partner may have a salary for his work, nor interest on the capital contributed. Profits and losses must be shared equally. Therefore, unless Bull can prevail upon Cow to accept this or some other arrangement, the suggestions he has made will have to be abandoned and he must be content with half the profits. If this was a dispute that had arisen after several years of business he might be able to show that his ideas had in fact been used in earlier years to develop the business. In other words he could prove agreement to these arrangements by his course of conduct over the years. This is not possible here as it appears to be the first year of the business.

(3) Books of Baker and Grocer (*SPA page 285*)

Appropriation A/c (for year ending December 31st 19..)

19..		£	£	19..		£
Dec. 31	Interest on Capital			Dec. 31	Net Profit	3 600
	Baker	350				
	Grocer	250				
			600			
	Share of Residue					
	Baker	1 500				
	Grocer	1 500				
			3 000			
			£3 600			£3 600

Current A/c (Baker)

19..			£	19..			£
Dec. 31	Drawings		1 400	Jan. 1	Balance	B/d	275
	Balance		725	Dec. 31	Interest on Capital		350
					Share of Residue		1 500
			£2 125				£2 125
				19..			£
				Jan. 1	Balance	B/d	725

Current A/c (Grocer)

19..			£	19..		£
Jan. 1	Balance	B/d	125	Dec. 31	Interest on Capital	250
Dec. 31	Drawings		1 700		Share of Residue	1 500
					Balance	75
			£1 825			£1 825
19..			£			
Jan. 1	Balance		75			

Balance Sheet (as at December 31st 19..)

	£	£		£	£
Fixed Assets			Capital		
Premises		8 000	Baker		7 000
Vans (at Cost)	2 500		Grocer		5 000
Less Depreciation	500				
		2 000			12 000
Fittings (at Cost)	1 000				
Less Depreciation	100				
		900			
		10 900			
Current Assets			Current A/c		
Stock	1 700		Baker		725
Debtors	30		Current Liabilities		
Current A/c (Grocer)	75		Creditors	450	
Bank	400		Rates Due	50	
Cash	60				500
Insurance	60				
		2 325			
		£13 225			£13 225

(4) Books of G. Wilson and W. Gibbs (*SPA page 286*)

Appropriation A/c (for six months ending December 31st 19..)

19..			£	£	19..		£
Dec. 31	Salary (Gibbs)			350	Dec. 31	Net Profit	1 485
	Interest on Capital						
	Wilson		250				
	Gibbs		45				
				295			
	Share of Residue						
	Wilson		560				
	Gibbs		280				
				840			
				£1 485			£1 485

Current A/c (W. Gibbs)

19..			£	19..			£
Aug.-Dec.	Drawings		1 100	July 1	Capital		500
Dec. 31	Balance	c/d	75	Dec. 31	Salary		350
				31	Interest on Capital		45
				31	Share of Residue		280
			£1 175				£1 175
				19..			
				Jan. 1	Balance	B/d	75

(5) Books of Ross and Glass (*SPA page 287*)

Trading A/c (for year ending December 31st 19..)

19		£	19..		£
Dec. 31	Opening Stock	2 476	Dec. 31	Sales	47 389
	Purchases	32 496			
		34 972			
	Less Closing Stock	2 984			
	Cost of Stock Sold	31 988			
	Gross Profit	15 401			
		£47 389			£47 389

Profit and Loss A/c (for year ending December 31st 19..)

19..		£	19..		£
Dec. 31	Rates and Insurance	1 450	Dec. 31	Gross Profit	15 401
	Wages	8 210		Discount Received	612
	Bad Debts	430			16 013
	Discount Allowed	838			
	General Expenses	897			
	Van Running Expenses	248			
	Provision for Bad Debts	80			
		12 153			
	Net Profit	3 860			
		£16 013			£16 013

Appropriation A/c (for year ending December 31st 19..)

19..		£	19..		£
Dec. 31	Share of Profit		Dec. 31	Net Profit	3 860
	Ross	1 930			
	Glass	1 930			
		£3 860			£3 860

Current A/c (Ross)

19..			£	19..			£
Dec. 31	Drawings		2 060	Dec. 31	Share of Profit		1 930
					Balance	c/d	130
			£2 060				£2 060
19..			£				
Jan. 1	Balance	B/d	130				

Current A/c (Glass)

19..			£	19..			£
Dec. 31	Drawings		1 980	Dec. 31	Share of Profit		1 930
					Balance	c/d	50
			£1 980				£1 980
19..			£				
Jan. 1	Balance	B/d	50				

Balance Sheet (as at December 31st 19..)

	£	£	£			£
Fixed Assets				Capital		
Buildings at Cost			6 000	Ross		8 507
Plant at Cost *Less* Depreciation			2 800	Glass		6 894
Motor Vans at Cost *Less* Depreciation			400			
						15 401
			9 200			
Current Assets						
Stock		2 984				
Debtors	3 938					
Less Provision	395					
		3 543				
Current Accounts				Current Liabilities		
Ross	130			Creditors		2 840
Glass	50					
		180				
Bank		2 334				
			9 041			
			£18 241			£18 241

(6) Books of Brown and Marshall (*SPA page 288*)

Balance Sheet (as at December 31st 19..)

	£	£	£		£	£
Fixed Assets				Capital		
Premises			8 000	Brown	10 000	
Machinery			3 200	Marshall	4 000	
Fixtures and Fittings		1 000				14 000
Less Depreciation		240				
			760			
Motor Vehicles		2 800				
Less Depreciation		700				
			2 100			
			14 060			
Current Assets				Current A/cs		
Stock		4 600		Brown	4 400	
Debtors	4 300			Marshall	2 200	
Less Provision	700					6 600
		3 600				
Bank		1 640		Current Liabilities		
Cash		100		Creditors		3 400
			9 940			
			£24 000			£24 000

Calculations used:

Net Profit £9 600 divided 2:1

∴ Brown £6 400

∴ Marshall £3 200

Drawings £3 000 divided 2:1

∴ Brown £2 000

∴ Marshall £1 000

Current Account balances as follows:

Brown   £6 400 − £2 000 = £4 400
Marshall £3 200 − £1 000 = £2 200

(7) Books of Bennett and Clark (SPA page 289)

Profit and Loss A/c (for year ending December 31st 19..)

19..		£	£	19..		£
Dec. 31	Salaries		785	Dec. 31	Gross Profit	8 660
	Light and Heat		490		Discount Received	200
	Rates		435			
	Bad Debts		515			8 860
	Discount Allowed		240			
	Carriage Out		610			
	Vehicle Expenses		725			
	Building Repairs		250			
	Loan Interest	70				
	Add Amount Due	70				
			140			
	Advertising	600				
	Less Amount in Advance	200				
			400			
	Depreciation		400			
			4 990			
	Net Profit		3 870			
			£8 860			£8 860

Appropriation A/c (for year ending December 31st 19..)

19..		£	£	19..		£
Dec. 31	Salary (Clark)		500	Dec. 31	Net Profit	3 870
	Interest on Capital					
	Bennett	595				
	Clark	500				
			1 095			
			1 595			
	Share of Residue:					
	Bennett	1 365				
	Clark	910				
			2 275			
			£3 870			£3 870

Current A/c (Bennett)

19..			£	19..			£
Dec. 31	Drawings		1 500	Jan. 1	Balance	B/d	175
	Balance	c/d	635	Dec. 31	Interest on Capital		595
					Share of Profit		1 365
			£2 135				£2 135
				19..			£
				Jan. 1	Balance	B/d	635

Current A/c (Clark)

19..			£	19..		£
Jan. 1	Balance	B/d	105	Dec. 31	Salary	500
Dec. 31	Drawings		1 395		Interest on Capital	500
	Balance		410		Share of Profit	910
			£1 910			£1 910
				19..		£
				Jan. 1	Balance	410

Balance Sheet (as at December 31st 19..)

	£	£	£			£	£
Fixed Assets				Capital			
Goodwill			2 100	Bennett			12 800
Land and Buildings			9 500	Clark			10 000
Motor Vehicles		4 000					22 800
Less Depreciation		400					
			3 600	Current A/cs			
			15 200	Bennett		635	
Current Assets				Clark		410	
Stock		6 995					1 045
Debtors	5 120			Long-Term Liability			
Less Provision	640			Bank Loan			2 000
		4 480		Current Liabilities			
Bank		1 125		Creditors		2 250	
Cash		165		Loan Interest Due		70	
Advertising in Advance		200					2 320
			12 965				
			£28 165				£28 165

(8) (*SPA page 290*)

(*a*) The cost of installing a new machine would be capitalized as part of the value of the machine and would therefore appear as an asset, 'Machinery Account', under the sub-heading 'Fixed Assets' on the Balance Sheet.

(*b*) The credit balance of an account in the sales ledger would indicate a debtor who was temporarily a creditor—presumably because he had returned goods for which he had already paid. This item would appear as a reduction in the total Debtors' figure on the assets side of the Balance Sheet; but some businessmen might regard it as an increase to the total creditors figure on the liabilities side.

(*c*) A loan to a partner would appear as an Asset-Loan to Partner, on the assets side of the Balance Sheet. It would depend on the terms of the loan whether it appeared as a Current Asset or a Fixed Asset.

(*d*) The interest would appear as a credit entry on the Profit and Loss Account and also as a debit entry on the Current Account of the partner. It would not need to appear on the Balance Sheet as 'Interest Due' since it would no longer be due, the debit in the Current Account having effectively made the partner 'pay' it.

(*e*) Shares of the sum written off Goodwill would appear in the partners'

Current Accounts on the debit side. Alternatively they could be debited in the Appropriation Account, which has the effect of removing this from the profits before they are shared up between the partners.

(*f*) This is similar to (*b*) above—a creditor this time who is temporarily a debtor. The item would appear either as a deduction of the total creditors' figure on the Balance Sheet, or it could be treated as an increase in the debtors' figure.

(*g*) This would appear in two places: as a deduction from the total stock available in the Trading Account, and as a balance of Stock in Hand on the 'Current Assets' part of the Balance Sheet.

(9) **Books of Knowle and Sentry** (*SPA page 290*)

Trading A/c (for year ending December 31st 19..)

19..	£	19..	£
Dec. 31 Stock at Start	6 144	Dec. 31 Sales	57 690
Purchases	44 720	*Add* Drawings in Kind	190
	50 864	Net Turnover	57 880
Less Closing Stock	8 451		
Cost of Stock Sold	42 413		
Gross Profit	15 467		
	£57 880		£57 880

Profit and Loss A/c (for year ending December 31st 19..)

19..		£	£	19..	£
Dec. 31	Repairs	763		Dec. 31 Gross Profit	15 467
	Less Improvements	480		Discount Received	801
			283		16 268
	General Expenses		1 494		
	Car Expenses	297			
	Add Amount Paid Privately	79			
			376		
	Wages and Salaries	8 416			
	Add Amount Due	249			
			8 665		
	Discount Allowed		1 038		
	Rates and Insurance	236			
	Less Amount in Advance	56			
			180		
	Bad Debts		347		
	Provision for Bad Debts		36		
			12 419		
	Net Profit		3 849		
			£16 268		£16 268

Appropriation A/c (for year ending December 31st 19..)

19.. Dec. 31	Share of Profit	£	£	19.. Dec. 31	Net Profit	£
	Knowle	2 566				3 849
	Sentry	1 283				
			3 849			
			£3 849			£3 849

Current A/c (Knowle)

19.. Dec. 31	Drawings		£	19.. Dec. 31	Share of Profit		£
	Sales		2 420				2 566
			190		Balance	c/d	44
			£2 610				£2 610
19.. Jan. 1	Balance	B/d	£ 44				

Current A/c (Sentry)

19.. Dec. 31	Drawings		£ 1 790	19.. Dec. 31	Car Expenses		£ 79
					Share of Profit		1 283
					Balance	c/d	428
			£1 790				£1 790
19.. Jan. 1	Balance	B/d	£ 428				

Balance Sheet (as at December 31st 19..)

	£	£	£		£	£
Fixed Assets				Capital		
Land and Buildings		8 500		Knowle		12 509
Add Improvements		480		Sentry		8 791
			8 980			21 300
Fixtures and Fittings		1 380				
Motor Cars		900				
			11 260			
Current Assets				Current Liabilities		
Stock		8 451		Creditors	3 987	
Current A/cs				Wages and Salaries Due	249	
Knowle	44					4 236
Sentry	428					
		472				
Debtors	5 178					
Less Provision	164					
		5 014				
Bank		283				
Rates in Advance		56				
			14 276			
			£25 536			£25 536

(10) Books of Richard and Stanley Bridges (*SPA page 291*)

Journal Proper

19..					£	£
Dec.	31	Profit and Loss A/c Dr.	L 194	200	
		Lease A/c	L 5		200
		Being amortization of lease for one year at this date			
Dec.	31	Current Account (Stanley) Dr.	L 86	27	
		Current Account (Richard)	L 87		27
		Being removal of excess entitlement from Stanley's account, and its transfer to Richard's account			

The calculations for the second entry above are as follows (interest not allocated:

$$£$$

Richard 6% of £4 500 = 270
Stanley 6% of £2 250 = 135
                          ——
                          £405

This £405 had already been shared between the partners 3:2 instead of as shown above.

∴ of the £405 Richard received £243
            Stanley received £162

∴ Stanley must give up £27 to Richard as shown in the Journal entry above.

(11) Books of Rathlin and Lambay (*SPA page 292*)

Trading A/c (for year ending December 31st 19..)

19..		£	19..		£
Dec. 31	Opening Stock	21 000	Dec. 31	Sales	206 000
	Purchases	152 000			
		173 000			
	Less Closing Stock	23 500			
		149 500			
	Gross Profit	56 500			
		£206 000			£206 000

Profit and Loss A/c (for year ending December 31st 19..)

19..		£	£	19..		£	£
Dec. 31	Wages and Salaries	25 454		Dec. 31	Gross Profit		56 500
	Add Amount Due	304			Discount Received		1 630
			25 758		Rents Received	156	
	Rates	300			*Less* Amount in		
	Less Amount in Advance	60			Advance	12	
			240				144
	General Expenses		9 832				58 274
	Discount Allowed		4 154				
	Depreciation		170				
			40 154				
	Net Profit		18 120				
			£58 274				£58 274

Appropriation A/c (for year ending December 31st 19..)

19..		£	£	19..		£
Dec. 31	Interest on Capital			Dec. 31	Net Profit	18 120
	Rathlin	1 400			Interest on Drawings	280
	Lambay	700				
			2 100			
	Share of Residue					
	Rathlin	9 780				
	Lambay	6 520				
			16 300			
			£18 400			£18 400

Current A/c (Rathlin)

19..			£	19..			£
Dec. 31	Drawings		6 800	Dec. 31	Interest on Capital		1 400
	Interest on Drawings		170		Share of Residue		9 780
	Balance	c/d	4 210				
			£11 180				£11 180
				19..			£
				Dec. 31	Balance	B/d	4 210

Current A/c (Lambay)

19..			£	19..			£
Dec. 31	Drawings		4 400	Dec. 31	Interest on Capital		700
	Interest on Drawings		110		Share of Residue		6 520
	Balance	c/d	2 710				
			£7 220				£7 220
				19..			£
				Dec. 31	Balance	B/d	2 710

Balance Sheet (as at December 31st 19..)

	£	£		£	£
Fixed Assets			Capital		
Freehold Property		18 500	Rathlin		28 000
Fixtures and Fittings	1 700		Lambay		14 000
Less Depreciation	510				
		1 190			42 000
		19 690	Current A/cs		
			Rathlin	4 210	
Current Assets			Lambay	2 710	
Stock	23 500				6 920
Debtors	16 328		Current Liabilities		
Bank	2 408		Creditors	12 750	
Rates in Advance	60		Wages Due	304	
		42 296	Rent Received in		
			Advance	12	
					13 066
		£61 986			£61 986

(12) Books of Bristol and Avon (*SPA page 293*)

Trading A/c (for year ending December 31st 19..)

19..		£	£	19..		£
Dec. 31	Opening Stock		6 332	Dec. 31	Sales	24 232
	Purchases	10 402			Less Returns	362
	Less Returns	302				
			10 100		Net Turnover	23 870
	Total Stock Available		16 432			
	Less Closing Stock		4 429			
	Cost of Stock Sold		12 003			
	Warehouse Wages		3 200			
	Warehouse Light and Heat		429			
	Warehouse Rates		186			
	Cost of Sales		15 818			
	Gross Profit		8 052			
			£23 870			£23 870

Profit and Loss A/c (for year ending December 31st 19..)

19..		£	£	19..			£
Dec. 31	Salaries		1 800	Dec. 31	Gross Profit		8 052
	Bad Debts		75		Discount Received		418
	Stationery		166		Bad Debts Provision		
	Advertising		377		reclaimed		15
	Light and Heat		143				
	Rates		62				8 485
	Postage and Telephones		130				
	Insurance	60					
	Less Amount in Advance	10					
			50				
	Discount Allowed		246				
	Motor Vehicle Expenses		394				
	Sundry Expenses		54				
	Depreciation						
	Fixtures and Fittings	164					
	Motor Vehicles	280					
			444				
			3 941				
	Net Profit		4 544				
			£8 485				£8 485

Appropriation A/c (for year ending December 31st 19..)

19..		£	£	19..		£
Dec. 31	Share of Profit			Dec. 31	Gross Profit	4 544
	Bristol	3 408				
	Avon	1 136				
			4 544			
			£4 544			£4 544

Current A/c (Bristol)

19..			£	19..				£
Dec. 31	Drawings		1 950	Jan. 1	Balance		B/d	1 105
	Balance	c/d	2 563	Dec. 31	Share of Profit			3 408
			£4 513					£4 513
				19..				£
				Jan. 1	Balance		B/d	2 563

Current A/c (Avon)

19..			£	19..				£
Dec. 31	Drawings		1 250	Jan. 1	Balance		B/d	863
	Balance	c/d	749	Dec. 31	Share of Profit			1 136
			£1 999					£1 999
				19..				£
				Jan. 1	Balance		B/d	749

Balance Sheet (as at December 31st 19..)

	£	£	£			£	£
Fixed Assets				Capital			
Freehold Premises			8 500	Bristol			12 000
Furniture and Equipment		1 640		Avon			4 000
Less Depreciation		164					
			1 476				16 000
Motor Vehicles		1 400					
Less Depreciation		280					
			1 120				
			11 096				
Current Assets				Current Accounts			
Stock			4 429	Bristol		2 563	
Debtors	5 500			Avon		749	
Less Provision	110						3 312
			5 390	Current Liabilities			
Bank			1 744	Creditors			3 400
Cash			43				
Insurance in Advance			10				
			11 616				
			£22 712				£22 712

(13) Books of Bush and Mill (SPA page 294)

Trading A/c (for year ending December 31st 19..)

19..		£	19..		£
Dec. 31	Opening Stock	4 288	Dec. 31	Sales	22 718
	Purchases	15 226			
	Total Stock Available	19 514			
	Less Closing Stock	5 263			
	Cost of Stock Sold	14 251			
	Gross Profit	8 467			
		£22 718			£22 718

Profit and Loss A/c (for year ending December 31st 19..)

19..		£	£	19..		£
Dec. 31	Discount Allowed		418	Dec. 31	Gross Profit	8 467
	Motor Vehicle Expenses		326		Discount Received	249
	Rent and Rates	940				8 716
	Add Rent Due	200				
		1 140				
	Less Rates in Advance	80				
			1 060			
	Salaries		2 461			
	Light and Heat	322				
	Add Amount Due	39				
			361			
	Bad Debts		298			
	General Expenses		649			
	Depreciation		600			
	Bad Debts Provision		50			
	Bank Charges		28			
			6 251			
	Net Profit		2 465			
			£8 716			£8 716

Appropriation A/c (for year ending December 31st 19..)

19..		£	19..		£
Dec. 31	Share of Profit		Dec. 31	Net Profit	2 465
	Bush	1 479			
	Mill	986			
		£2 465			£2 465

Current A/c (Bush)

19..			£	19..			£
Dec. 31	Drawings		1 800	Dec. 31	Share of Profit		1 479
				31	Balance	c/d	321
			£1 800				£ 1800
19..			£				
Jan. 1	Balance	B/d	321				

Current A/c (Mill)

19..			£	19..			£
Dec. 31	Drawings		1 420	Dec. 31	Share of Profit		986
				31	Balance	c/d	434
			£1 420				£1 420
19..			£				
Jan. 1	Balance	B/d	434				

Balance Sheet (as at December 31st 19..)

	£	£	£			£	£
Fixed Assets				Capital			
Freehold Buildings			6 700	Bush			8 823
Motor Vehicles		3 000		Mill			6 132
Less Depreciation		1 100					
			1 900				14 955
			8 600				
Current Assets							
Stock		5 263					
Current Accounts				Current Liabilities			
Bush	321			Creditors		1 869	
Mill	434			Rent Due		200	
		755		Light and Heat Due		39	
Debtors	2 401						2 108
Less Provision	500						
		1 901					
Bank	492						
Less Charges	28						
		464					
Rates in Advance		80					
			8 463				
			£17 063				£17 063

(14) Books of Ross and Cromarty (*SPA page 295*)

Trading A/c (for year ending March 31st 19..)

19..		£	£	19..		£
Mar. 31	Opening Stock		4 969	Mar. 31	Sales	81 213
	Purchases	70 835			*Less* Returns	581
	Add Carriage In	1 638				
					Net Turnover	80 632
		72 473				
	Less Returns	915				
			71 558			
	Total Stock Available		76 527			
	Less Closing Stock		5 395			
	Cost of Stock Sold		71 132			
	Gross Profit		9 500			
			£80 632			£80 632

Profit and Loss A/c (for year ending March 31st 19..)

19..		£	£	19..		£
Mar. 31	Salaries		3 251	Mar. 31	Gross Profit	9 500
	Rent and Rates	660			Discount Received	185
	Add Amount Due	60				
			720			9 685
	Insurance	136				
	Less Amount in Advance	49				
			87			
	General Expenses		804			
	Discount Allowed		165			
	Bad Debts		121			
	Depreciation		38			
	Provision for Bad Debts		99			
			5 285			
	Net Profit		4 400			
			£9 685			£9 685

Appropriation A/c (for year ending March 31st 19..)

19..		£	£	19..		£
Mar. 31	Interest on Capital			Mar. 31	Net Profit	4 400
	Ross	350				
	Cromarty	150				
			500			
	Share of Profit					
	Ross	2 600				
	Cromarty	1 300				
			3 900			
			£4 400			£4 400

Current A/c (Ross)

19..			£	19..			£
Mar. 31	Drawings		2 040	Mar. 31	Interest on Capital		350
	Balance	c/d	910		Share of Profit		2 600
			£2 950				£2 950
				19..			£
				Apr. 1	Balance	B/d	910

Current A/c (Cromarty)

19..			£	19..			£
Mar. 31	Drawings		020	Mar. 31	Interest on Capital		150
	Balance	c/d	430		Share of Profit		1 300
			£1 450				£1 450
				19..			£
				Apr. 1	Balance	B/d	430

Balance Sheet (as at March 31st 19..)

	£	£	£		£	£
Fixed Assets				Capital		
Furniture and Fittings			760	Ross		7 000
Less Depreciation			340	Cromarty		3 000
			420			10 000
Current Assets				Current Account		
Stock		5 395		Ross	910	
Debtors	6 179			Cromarty	430	
Less Provision	179					1 340
		6 000		Current Liabilities		
Bank		3 272		Creditors	3 736	
Insurance in Advance		49		Rent Due	60	
			14 716			3 796
			£15 136			£15 136

(15) Books of Copeland and Bangor (*SPA page 296*)

Trading and Profit and Loss A/c (for year ending December 31st 19..)

19..		£	£	19..		£
Dec. 31	Opening Stock		23 641	Dec. 31	Sales	237 864
	Purchases		179 465			
			203 106			
	Less Closing Stock		24 780			
	Cost of Stock Sold		178 326			
	Gross Profit		59 538			
			£237 864			£237 864

19..		£	£	19..		£
Dec. 31	Salaries	26 192		Dec. 31	Gross Profit	59 538
	Add Amount Due	514			Discount Received	2 146
			26 706			61 684
	Rates	500				
	Less Amount in Advance	120				
			380			
	Discount Allowed		4 264			
	General Expenses		10 261			
	Bad Debts		478			
	Depreciation: Furniture		250			
			42 339			
	Net Profit		19 345			
			£61 684			£61 684

Appropriation A/c (for year ending December 31st 19..)

19..		£	£	19..		£	£
Dec. 31	Interest on Capital			Dec. 31	Net Profit		19 345
	Copeland	1 325			Interest on Drawings		
	Bangor	710			Copeland	204	
			2 035		Bangor	162	
	Share of Profit						366
	Copeland	11 784					
	Bangor	5 892					
			17 676				
			£19 711				£19 711

Current A/c (Copeland)

19..			£	19..			£
Dec. 31	Drawings		6 450	Dec. 31	Interest on Capital		1 325
	Interest on Drawings		204		Share of Residue		11 784
	Balance	c/d	6 455				
			£13 109				£13 109
				19..			£
				Jan. 1	Balance	B/d	6 455

Current A/c (Bangor)

19..			£	19..			£
Dec. 31	Drawings		4 200	Dec. 31	Interest on Capital		710
	Interest on Drawings		162		Share of Residue		5 892
	Balance	c/d	2 240				
			£6 602				£6 602
				19..			£
				Jan. 1	Balance	B/d	2 240

Balance Sheet (as at December 31st 19..)

	£	£			£	£
Fixed Assets			Capital			
Freehold Property		17 500	Copeland			26 500
Furniture and Equipmen	2 500		Bangor			14 200
Less Depreciation	1 100					40 700
		1 400				
			Current A/c			
		18 900	Copeland		6 455	
Current Assets			Bangor		2 240	
Stock	24 780					8 695
Debtors	16 564		Current Liabilities			
Bank	2 694		Creditors		13 149	
Rates in Advance	120		Salaries Due		514	
		44 158				13 663
		£63 058				£63 058

Non-profit-making Organizations

Exercises Set 39: Simple Receipts and Payments Accounts

(1) Newtown Football Club (*SPA page 301*)

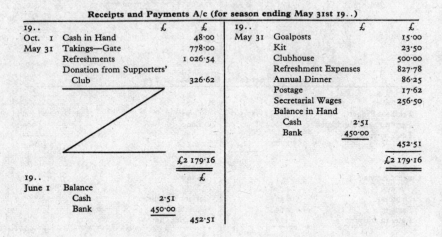

	Receipts and Payments A/c (for season ending May 31st 19..)							
19..		£	£	19..			£	£
Oct. 1	Cash in Hand		48·00	May 31	Goalposts			15·00
May 31	Takings—Gate		778·00		Kit			23·50
	Refreshments		1 026·54		Clubhouse			500·00
	Donation from Supporters'				Refreshment Expenses			827·78
	Club		326·62		Annual Dinner			86·25
					Postage			17·62
					Secretarial Wages			256·50
					Balance in Hand			
					Cash	2·51		
					Bank	450·00		
								452·51
			£2 179·16					£2 179·16
19..			£					
June 1	Balance							
	Cash	2·51						
	Bank	450·00						
		452·51						

(2) Jolly Wanderers Rambling Club (*SPA page 301*)

	Receipts and Payments A/c (for year ending December 31st 19..)							
19..		£	£	19..			£	£
Jan. 1	Balances			Dec. 31	Purchases—Bar			3 600·00
	Cash	57·50			Wages			713·00
	Bank	120·00			Furniture			25·00
			177·50		Rent and Rates			290·00
Dec. 31	Bar Takings		5 085·00		Repairs			120·00
	Subscriptions Received		955·00		General Expenses			401·00
	Dividends		105·00		Balances			
					Cash	55·00		
					Bank	1 118·50		
								1 173·50
			£6 322·50					£6 322·50
19..			£					
Jan. 1	Balances							
	Cash	55·00						
	Bank	1 118·50						
		1 173·50						

(3) **Roman Camp Archaeological Society** (*SPA page 302*)

Receipts and Payments A/c (for season ending October 31st 19..)

19..		£	19..		£
Nov. 1	Balance	27·50	Oct. 31	Equipment	45·40
Oct. 31	Subscriptions Received	276·00		Material	16·00
	Sales of Finds	132·75		Printing	47·20
	Earnings	585·50		Donation to Museum	100·00
				Wages	285·00
				Transport	84·50
				Balance	443·65
		£1 021·75			£1 021·75

19..		£
Nov. 1	Balance	443·65

(4) **Robert Burns Society** (*SPA page 302*)

Receipts and Payments A/c (for year ending December 31st 19..)

19..		£	19..		£
Jan. 1	Balance	175·50	Dec. 31	Transport	25·50
Dec. 31	Subscriptions	148·05		Refreshments	31·50
				Musicians	33·00
				Wages	48·00
				Stationery	7·50
				Postage	12·25
				Repairs	17·55
				Entrance Fees to Festivals	147·50
				Balance	0·75
		£323·55			£323·55

19..		£
Jan. 1	Balance	0·75

(5) **Kingswood Community Association** (*SPA page 302*)

(a) ### Receipts and Payments A/c (for year ending December 31st 19..)

19..		£	19..		£
Jan. 1	Balance	33·81	Dec. 31	Use of Hall	60·00
Dec. 31	Subscriptions Received	275·35		Refreshments	128·30
	Donations	20·00		Party	37·35
	Bazaar Takings	73·35		Outing	28·25
				Honorarium	20·00
				Balance	128·61
		£402·51			£402·51

19..		£
Jan. 1	Balance	128·61

(b) It would be best to open a bank account with a local bank, where the majority of this money could be deposited.

Exercises Set 40: Final Accounts of Non-profit-making Organizations

(1) Books of the Snowdonia Young Climbers' Club (*SPA page 309*)

Income and Expenditure A/c (for season ending October 31st 19..)

19..		£	19..		£
Oct. 31	Magazines	10·25	Oct. 31	Subscriptions	240·00
	Ropes and Gear	80·25		Refreshment Profits	25·00
	Camping Fees	25·00		Charges to Visiting Parents	65·50
	Printing and Stationery	15·00			330·50
	Travelling Expenses				
	(accident victim)	12·50			
	Ambulance Charges	3·15			
	Donation to Mountain Rescue				
	Service	20·00			
	Surplus	164·35			
		£330·50			£330·50

(2) Books of the Forsyth Tennis Club (*SPA page 309*)

Receipts and Payments A/c (for year ending December 31st 19..)

19..		£	19..		£
Jan. 1	Balance	300	Dec. 31	Prizes	40
Dec. 31	Subscriptions	350	31	Postage	10
31	Fees	70		Light and Heat	30
				Rates	60
				Garden Roller	40
				Repairs	10
				Decorations	50
				Wages	250
				Balance	230
		£720			£720

19..		£
Jan. 1	Balance	230

Income and Expenditure A/c (for year ending December 31st 19..)

19..		£	£	19..		£	£
Dec. 31	Prizes		40	Dec. 31	Subscriptions	350	
	Postage		10		*Less* Arrears	5	
	Light and Heat		30			345	
	Rates	60			*Plus* Amount Due	15	
	Less Arrears	10					360
		50			Tournament Fees		70
	Less Amount in Advance	10					430
			40				
	Repairs		10				
	Decorations (one year)		10				
	Wages		250				
	Depreciation		20				
			410				
	Surplus		20				
			£430				£430

(3) Books of the Brownridge Town Band (*SPA page 310*)

Cash A/c (for year ending March 31st 19..)

19..		£	19..		£
Apr. 1	Balance in Hand	29	May 28	Guest Instrumentalists	2
3	Grant from Council	50	June 30	Performing Rights	2
May 28	Brownbank Park	10	July 8	Guest Instrumentalists	1
June 3	Tolverton Park	25	Oct. 23	Music	2
10	St. John's Fete	5	Feb. 17	Entrance Fee	2
24	Brownbank Park	10	20	Music	2
July 1	Little Barr Park	20	2ᵛ	Hire of Rehearsal Room	2
8	Brownbank Floral Show	30	Mar. 11	Hire of Coach	15
29	Little Barr Horse Show	20	31	Balance in Hand	261
Sept. 1	Tolverton Labour Club	5			
15	Brownbank Conservative Club	25			
Oct. 3	Grant from Council	50			
Mar. 11	Charge to Supporters	3			
11	Prize Money	7			
		£289			£289

19..		£
Apr. 1	Balance in Hand	261

Income and Expenditure A/c (for year ending March 31st 19..)

19..		£	19..		£
Mar. 31	Performance Expenses	9	Mar. 31	Grants from Council	100
	Competition Expenses	19		Fees Received	150
	Repairs to Instruments	2		Charges to Supporters	3
	New Uniforms	24		Prize Money	7
	Surplus for Year	206			
		£260			£260

(4) Books of the Good Companions Sports Club (*SPA page 311*)

Income and Expenditure A/c (for year ending December 31st 19..)

19..			£	19..		£
Dec. 31	Printing, Postage and Stationery		13	Dec. 31	Subscriptions	
	Periodicals		18		Current Year	272
	Competition Prizes		12		*Plus* Amount Due	18
	Sundry Expenses		20			
	Wages		78			290
	Rent		120		Profit on Refreshment	35
	Rates	49			Competition Fees	18
	Add Amount in Advance					
	at Start of Year	12				343
		61				
	Less Amount in Advance					
	at End of Year	13				
			48			
	Depreciation		16			
			325			
	Surplus		18			
			£343			£343

(5) Books of the Mid-Sussex Gun-dog Society (*SPA page 311*)

Income and Expenditure A/c (for year ending December 31st 19..)

19..		£	£	19..		£	£
Dec. 31	Bad Debts		15	Dec. 31	Subscriptions for		
.	Printing	80			Current Year	140	
	Add Amount Due	12			*Add* Subscriptions		
			92		Due	18	
	Stationery and Postage		23				158
	Hire of Training Ground		50		Field Trials Entrance Fees		144
	Trainer's Fees		30		Advertising Receipts		55
	General Expenses		15				
	Field Trials						357
	Judge's Fees	100			Deficiency		14
	Expenses	21					
			121				
	Depreciation		25				
			£371				£371

Balance Sheet (as at December 31st 19..)

		£	£			£	£
Fixed Assets				Accumulated Fund			
	Equipment	125			At Start		220
	Less Depreciation	25			*Less* Deficiency		14
		100					206
	Add New Equipment	18					
			118				
Current Assets				Current Liabilities			
	Subscriptions Due	18			Subscriptions in Advance	25	
	Bank Balance	107			Printing Bill Due	12	
			125				37
			£243				£243

(6) Tennis Club Accounts (*SPA page 312*)

Calculations for entries in Income and Expenditure Account.

		£
(*a*) Rent		
Rent paid during year		80
Deduct Rent owing at start of the year and presumably paid; part of the £80		18
		62
Add Amount due at end of year		28
Correct charge to Income and Expenditure Account for year		£90
(*b*) Subscriptions:		£
Subscriptions received during the year		340
Deduct Overdue subscriptions from previous year		10
		330
Deduct Subscriptions received in advance for next year		6
Correct income figure for subscriptions for current year		£324

(c) Rates:

	£
Rates paid during the year	19
Add Amount pre-paid at start of year	4
	23
Deduct Amount pre-paid for next year	3
Correct charge for rates for the current year	£20

(7) Accounts of a Social Club (*SPA page 312*)

Subscriptions A/c Year 2

Year 2		£	Year 2		£
Jan. 1	Subscriptions Due	69	Jan. 1	Subscriptions in Advance	43
Dec. 31	Subscriptions in Advance	29	Dec. 31	Subscriptions Received in Year	837
31	Transfer to Income and		31	Subscriptions Due	76
	Expenditure A/c	858			
		£956			£956
Year 3		£	Year 3		£
Jan. 1	Subscriptions Due	76	Jan. 1	Subscriptions in Advance	29

N.B. The point here is that the subscriptions due in each year at the start of the year must appear on the debit side of the account as they are an asset of the club. The subscriptions in advance on the first day of the year must appear on the credit side of the account because they are a liability (since the club owes members who have pre-paid a year's entertainment). In order to appear on the correct sides after being brought down, these items must appear on the opposite sides before being brought down. On the debit side the £29 reduces the amount of subscriptions to be transferred to Income and Expenditure Account, while on the credit side the subscriptions due (£76) increases the amount to be transferred.

(8) Accounts of the Daleshire Social Club (*SPA page 313*)

(a)

Subscription A/c

19..			£	19..			£
Dec. 31	Income and Expenditure A/c		200	Dec. 31	Subscriptions Received		214
	Subscriptions in Advance	c/d	18		Subscriptions Due	c/d	4
			£218				£218
19..			£	19..			£
Jan. 1	Subscriptions Due	B/d	4	Jan. 1	Subscriptions in Advance B/d		18

(b) The term used instead of Net Profit in a non-profit-making club is surplus (of income over expenditure).

(9) Accounts of the New Social Club (*SPA page 313*)

For the sake of clarity the whole five years of the Life Members' Subscription Account is shown here, but you would be perfectly correct if you were to show the final year only.

Life Members' Subscription A/c

Year 1			£	Year 1			£
Dec. 31	Income and Expenditure A/c		10·50	Jan. 1	Subscriptions		52·50
	Balance	c/d	42·00				
			£52·50				£52·50
Year 2			£	Year 2			£
Dec. 31	Income and Expenditure A/c		10·50	Jan. 1	Balance	B/d	42·00
	Balance	c/d	31·50				
			£42·00				£42·00
Year 3			£	Year 3			£
Dec. 31	Income and Expenditure A/c		10·50	Jan. 1	Balance	B/d	31·50
	Balance	c/d	21·00				
			£31·50				£31·50
Year 4			£	Year 4			£
Dec. 31	Income and Expenditure A/c		10·50	Jan. 1	Balance	B/d	21·00
	Balance	c/d	10·50				
			£21·00				£21·00
Year 5			£	Year 5			£
Dec. 31	Income and Expenditure A/c		10·50	Jan. 1	Balance	B/d	10·50

Ordinary Members' Subscription A/c

Year 5			£	Year 5			£
Jan. 1	Subscriptions Due		7·35	Dec. 31	Subscriptions Received		121·80
Γ 31	Income and Expenditure A/c		117·60		Subscriptions Due	c/d	3·15
			£124·95				£124·95
Year 6			£				
Jan. 1	Subscriptions Due	B/d	3·15				

(10) Books of the Greensward Cricket and Social Club (*SPA page 314*)

Refreshment Trading A/c (for year ending December 31st 19..)

19..		£	19..		£
Dec. 31	Purchases	185	Dec. 31	Sales	243
	Add Amounts Due	12			
		197			
	Less Closing Stock	16			
		181			
	Profit on Refreshments	62			
		£243			£243

Income and Expenditure A/c (for year ending December 31st 19..)

19..		£	£	19..		£
Dec. 31	Bad Debts		5	Dec. 31	Subscriptions Received	370
	Maintenance		42		*Add* Amounts Due	15
	Postage		76			—
	Insurance		18			385
	Sundry Expenses		48		Games Receipts	182
	Printing and Stationery		84		Profit on Refreshments	62
	Wages		208			—
	Depreciation					629
	Sports Equipment	54				
	Clubroom Equipment	42				
			96			
			577			
	Surplus		52			
			£629			£629

Balance Sheet (as at December 31st 19..)

	£	£		£
Fixed Assets			Accumulated Fund	
Clubhouse		2 000	At Start	2 136
Equipment	420		*Add* Surplus	52
Less Depreciation	42			—
		378		2 188
Sports Equipment	270		Long-term Liability Loan	
Less Depreciation	54		from a Member	500
		216		
		2 594		
Current Assets			Current Liability	
Stock	16		Creditors	12
Subscriptions Due	15			
Bank	62			
Cash	13			
		106		
		£2 700		£2 700

(11) Books of the Herring Bone Club (*SPA page 315*)

Bar Trading A/c (for year ending December 31st 19..)

19..		£	£	19..		£
Dec. 31	Opening Stock		861	Dec. 31	Bar Takings	22 184
	Purchases	17 146				
	Less Amount Due at					
	Start to Creditors	1 241				
		15 905				
	Add Amount Due to					
	Creditors at Close	1 266				
			17 171			
	Total Stock Available		18 032			
	Less Closing Stock		928			
	Cost of Stock Sold		17 104			
	Profit on Bar		5 080			
			£22 184			£22 184

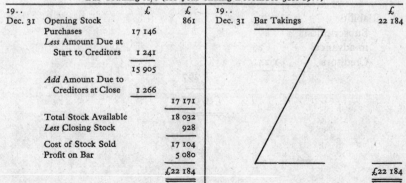

Income and Expenditure A/c (for year ending December 31st 19..)

19..		£	19..		£
Dec. 31	Depreciation	285	Dec. 31	Subscriptions	
	Cost of Social Events	722		In Advance at Start	26
	Wages	2 468		Current Year	1 864
	General Expenses	1 962			
	Repairs	1 400			1 890
				Receipts from Social Events	794
		6 837		Profit on Bar	5 080
	Surplus of Income over				7 764
	Expenditure	927			
		£7 764			£7 764

Balance Sheet (as at December 31st 19..)

	£	£			£	£
Fixed Assets			Accumulated Fund			
Buildings		15 000	At Start of Year			16 956
Furniture	1 600		(see below)			
Additions	2 500		Add Surplus			927
	4 100					17 883
Less Depreciation	285					
		3 815	Current Liabilities			
		18 815	Creditors		1 266	
Current Assets			Subscriptions in Advance		21	
Stock		928	Bank Overdraft		573	
						1 860
		£19 743				£19 743

Calculation of Accumulated Fund at start of year:

Assets owned:	£	£
Cash		762
Buildings		15 000
Furniture		1 600
Stocks		861
		£18 223

Liabilities:		
Subscriptions		
in advance	26	
Creditors	1 241	
		1 267
		£16 956

(12) Books of the XYZ Recreation Club (*SPA page 315*)

(*a*) A Receipts and Payments Account differs from an Income and Expenditure Account in the following ways:

(i) A Receipts and Payments Account is the analysed Cash Book of a club, not a 'Profit and Loss Account' of a club.

(ii) It contains all the receipts and payments during the year, irrespective of whether they were capital or revenue items. The Income and Expenditure Account is a 'revenue account' only.

(iii) It contains all the receipts and payments during the year, irrespective of which year they applied to. The Income and Expenditure Account only contains items relevant to the trading period named in the heading.

(iv) The result of taking out a Receipts and Payments Account is the discovery of the cash balance (or cash and bank balances). The result of drawing up an Income and Expenditure Account is the discovery of the surplus or deficiency on the club's activities for the year or season under review.

(*b*)

Receipts and Payments A/c (for year ending March 31st 19..)

19..		£	19..		£
Apr. 1	Cash at Start of Year	210	Mar. 31	Rent and Rates	160
Mar. 31	Subscriptions Received	196		Light and Heat	42
	Darts and Billiards	72		New Darts Boards	7
	Savings Bank Interest	5		Repairs to Billiard Table	9
				Sundry Expenses	12
				Balance	253
		£483			£483
19..		£			
Apr. 1	Balance	253			

Income and Expenditure A/c (for year ending March 31st 19..)

19..		£	£	19..		£	£
Mar. 31	Rent and Rates	160		Mar. 31	Subscriptions	196	
	Less Rent in Advance	10			*Less* Those for		
			150		Previous Year	8	
	Light and Heat	42				188	
	Add Amount Due	14			*Add* Subscriptions		
			56		Due	6	
	Repairs to Billiard Table		9				194
	Sundry Expenses		12		Darts and Billiards		72
	Depreciation		27		Savings Bank Interest		5
			254				271
	Surplus		17				
			£271				£271

Balance Sheet (for year ending March 31st 19..)

	£	£		£
Fixed Assets			Accumulated Fund	
Furniture and Equipment		370	At Start (*see below*)	588
New Dart Boards		7	*Add* Surplus	17
		377		605
Less Depreciation		27		
		350		
Current Assets			Current Liability	
Subscriptions Due	6		Light and Heat Due	14
Rent in Advance	10			
Cash in Hand	253			
		269		
		£619		£619

Calculation of Accumulated Fund at start:

	£
Cash in Hand at start	210
Furniture and Equipment	370
Subscriptions Due	8
	£588

Unit Twenty-Nine
Manufacturing Accounts

Exercises Set 41: Manufacturing Accounts

(1) Books of R. Rayner (*SPA page 323*)

Manufacturing A/c (for year ending December 31st 19..)
Prime-Cost Section

19..		£	£	19..		£
Dec. 31	*Raw Materials*			Dec. 31	Prime Cost of Goods	
	Opening Stock		7 250		Manufactured	24 850
	Purchases	18 250				
	Add Carriage In	550				
			18 800			
			26 050			
	Less Closing Stock		8 500			
	Cost of Raw Materials					
	Used		17 550			
	Wages		7 300			
			£24 850			£24 850

Cost of Manufactured Goods Section

19..		£	£	19..		£
Dec. 31	Prime Costs		24 850	Dec. 31	Cost of Manufactured Goods	
	Factory Expenses		4 700		(carried to Trading A/c)	28 405
			29 550			
	Work in Progress					
	(at Factory Cost)					
	Opening Stock	2 755				
	Less Closing Stock	3 900				
			−1 145			
			£28 405			£28 405

Trading A/c (for year ending December 31st 19..)

19..		£	19..		£
Dec. 31	Opening Stock of Finished		Dec. 31	Sales	49 500
	Goods	19 275			
	Cost of Manufactured Goods	28 405			
		47 680			
	Less Closing Stock	16 375			
	Cost of Stock Sold	31 305			
	Gross Profit (to Profit and				
	Loss A/c)	18 195			
		£49 500			£49 500

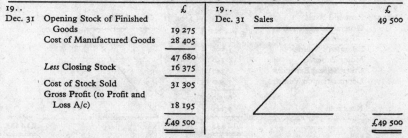

(2) Books of M. Lockhart Ltd. (*SPA page 324*)

Manufacturing A/c (for year ending December 31st 19..)
Prime-Cost Section

19..		£	19..		£
Dec. 31	*Raw Materials*		Dec. 31	Prime Cost	27 465
	Opening Stock	5 275			
	Purchases	13 850			
		19 125			
	Less Closing Stock	4 385			
	Cost of Raw Materials Used	14 740			
	Manufacturing Wages	12 725			
		£27 465			£27 465

Cost of Manufactured Goods Section

19..		£	£	19..		£
Dec. 31	Prime Cost		27 465	Dec. 31	Cost of Manufactured Goods	32 515
	Overheads					
	Factory Expenses	2 500				
	Factory Rent and Rates	1 500				
	Depreciation on Plant	500				
			4 500			
			31 965			
	Work in Progress					
	Opening Stock	3 800				
	Less Closing Stock	3 250				
			550			
			£32 515			£32 515

Trading A/c (for year ending December 31st 19..)

19..		£	19..		£
Dec. 31	Opening Stock of Finished Goods	17 350	Dec. 31	Sales	48 000
	Cost of Manufactured Goods	32 515			
		49 865			
	Less Closing Stock	16 000			
		33 865			
	Gross Profit	14 135			
		£48 000			£48 000

Profit and Loss A/c (for year ending December 31st 19..)

19..		£	19..		£
Dec. 31	Rent and Rates	500	Dec. 31	Gross Profit	14 135
	General Administration Expenses	3 250			
	Salesmen's Salaries	1 750			
	Motor Expenses	550			
	Other Selling Expenses	340			
	Depreciation on Vehicles	400			
		6 790			
	Net Profit	7 345			
		£14 135			£14 135

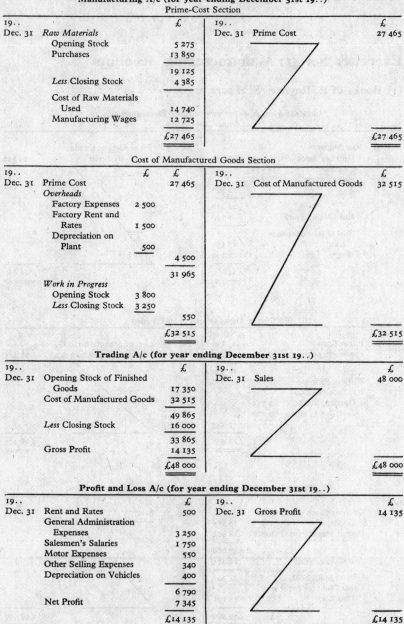

(3) Books of Robespierre Ltd. *(SPA page 324)*

Manufacturing A/c (for year ending December 31st 19..)
Prime-Cost Section

19.. Dec. 31		£	19.. Dec. 31		£
	Raw Materials			Prime Cost of Goods	
	Opening Stock	3 585		Manufactured	13 035
	Purchases	5 850			
		9 435			
	Less Closing Stock	3 400			
	Cost of Raw Materials Used	6 035			
	Manufacturing Wages	7 000			
		£13 035			£13 035

Cost of Manufactured Goods Section

19.. Dec. 31		£	£	19.. Dec. 31		£
	Prime Costs		13 035		Market Value of	
	Overheads				Manufactured Goods	20 000
	Factory Expenses	4 000				
	Rent and Rates	620				
	Depreciation Plant					
	and Machinery	800				
			5 420			
			18 455			
	Work in Progress					
	Opening Stock	2 725				
	Less Closing Stock	3 000				
			−275			
			18 180			
	Profit on Manufactures		1 820			
			£20 000			£20 000

Trading A/c (for year ending December 31st 19..)

19.. Dec. 31		£	19.. Dec. 31		£
	Stock of Manufactured Goods	12 725		Sales	27 000
	Market Value of Finished				
	Goods	20 000			
		32 725			
	Less Closing Stock of				
	Manufactured Goods	11 855			
	Cost of Goods Sold	20 870			
	Gross Profit	6 130			
		£27 000			£27 000

Profit and Loss A/c (for year ending December 31st 19..)

19..		£	19..		£
Dec. 31	Rent and Rates Office	280	Dec. 31	Profit on Manufactures	1 820
	General Administration			Gross Profit	6 130
	Expenses	2 200			
	Motor Expenses	480			7 950
	Salesman's Salaries	1 550			
	Other Selling Expenses	350			
	Depreciation Motor Vehicles	400			
		5 260			
	Net Profit	2 690			
		£7 950			£7 950

(4) Books of Sudbury Ltd. (*SPA page 325*)

Manufacturing A/c (for year ending December 31st 19..)
Prime-Cost Section

19..		£	19..		£
Dec. 31	*Raw Materials*		Dec. 31	Prime Cost	230 549
	Opening Stock	16 249			
	Purchases	144 252			
		160 501			
	Less Closing Stock	18 216			
		142 285			
	Manufacturing Wages	88 264			
		£230 549			£230 549

Cost of Manufactured Goods Section

19..		£	£	19..		£
Dec. 31	Prime Cost		230 549	Dec. 31	Cost of Manufactured	
	Overheads				Goods	270 783
	Factory Expenses	21 826				
	Rent and Rates	10 000				
	Depreciation of					
	Plant	9 000				
			40 826			
			271 375			
	Work in Progress					
	Opening Stock	22 706				
	Less Closing Stock	23 298				
			−592			
			£270 783			£270 783

Trading A/c (for year ending December 31st 19..)

19..		£	19..		£
Dec. 31	Stock of Manufactured Goods	19 241	Dec. 31	Sales	366 487
	Cost of Manufactured Goods	270 783			
		290 024			
	Less Closing Stock	17 485			
		272 539			
	Gross Profit	93 948			
		£366 487			£366 487

Profit and Loss A/c (for year ending December 31st 19..)

19..		£	19..		£
Dec. 31	Rent and Rates	4 500	Dec. 31	Gross Profit	93 948
	General Administration				
	Expenses	24 269			
	Salesmen's Salaries	7 836			
	Motor Expenses	4 367			
	Other Selling Expenses	7 602			
	Depreciation—Motor Vans	2 200			
		50 774			
	Net Profit	43 174			
		£93 948			£93 948

(5) Books of Rymer and Ross Ltd. (*SPA page 326*)

Manufacturing A/c (for year ending December 31st 19..)
Prime-Cost Section

19..		£	19..		£
Dec. 31	*Raw Materials*		Dec. 31	Prime Cost	25 954
	Opening Stock	3 854			
	Purchases	17 275			
		21 129			
	Less Closing Stock	3 600			
	Cost of Raw Materials Used	17 529			
	Manufacturing Wages	8 425			
		£25 954			£25 954

Cost of Manufactured Goods Section

19..		£	£	19..		£
Dec. 31	Prime Cost		25 954	Dec. 31	Market Value of	
	Overheads				Manufactured Goods	40 000
	Factory Expenses	1 100				
	Rent and Rates	750				
	Salary of Manager	2 850				
	Repairs	650				
	Depreciation on					
	Plant	600				
			5 950			
			31 904			
	Work in Progress					
	Opening Stock	1 816				
	Less Closing Stock	1 450				
			366			
			32 270			
	Manufacturing Profit		7 730			
			£40 000			£40 000

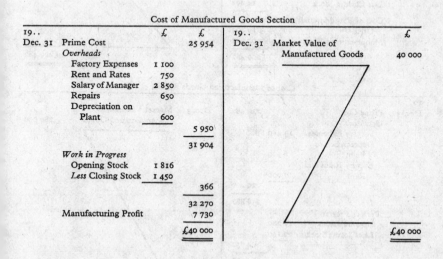

Trading A/c (for year ending December 31st 19..)

19..		£	19..		£
Dec. 31	Opening Stock of Finished Goods	12 724	Dec. 31	Sales	49 258
	Market Value of Goods Transferred	40 000			
		52 724			
	Less Closing Stock	10 500			
	Cost of Goods Sold	42 224			
	Repairs to Warehouse	880			
	Depreciation on Fittings	580			
		43 684			
	Gross Profit	5 574			
		£49 258			£49 258

Profit and Loss A/c (for year ending December 31st 19..)

			19..		£
			Dec. 31	Manufacturing Profit	7 730
				Gross Profit	5 574

(6) Books of Tradescantia Ltd. (*SPA page 326*)

Manufacturing A/c (for year ending December 31st 19..)
Prime-Cost Section

19..		£	19..		£
Dec. 31	*Raw Materials*		Dec. 31	Prime Cost	229 482
	Opening Stock	12 491			
	Purchases	128 294			
		140 785			
	Less Closing Stock	14 292			
	Cost of Raw Materials Used	126 493			
	Manufacturing Wages	102 989			
		£229 482			£229 482

Cost of Manufactured Goods Section

19..		£	£	19..		£
Dec. 31	Prime Cost		229 482	Dec. 31	Market Value of Manufactured Goods	280 000
	Overheads					
	Factory Expenses	13 480				
	Depreciation on Plant	8 920				
	Factory Rates and Rent	7 000				
			29 400			
			258 882			
	Work in Progress					
	Opening Stock	17 289				
	Less Closing Stock	22 140				
			−4 851			
			254 031			
	Manufacturing Profit		25 969			
			£280 000			£280 000

Trading A/c (for year ending December 31st 19..)

19..		£	19..		£
Dec. 31	Stock of Manufactured Goods	15 428	Dec. 31	Sales	322 243
	Market Value of Manufactured				
	Goods	280 000			
		295 428			
	Less Closing Stock	16 140			
	Cost of Stock Sold	279 288			
	Gross Profit	42 955			
		£322 243			£322 243

Profit and Loss A/c (for year ending December 31st 19..)

19..		£	19..		£
Dec. 31	Administrative Expenses	31 228	Dec. 31	Manufacturing Profit	25 969
	Salesmen's Salaries	6 298		Gross Profit	42 955
	Sundry Selling Expenses	8 449			68 924
	Carriage Out	4 200			
	Office Rent and Rates	2 980			
		53 155			
	Net Profit	15 769			
		£68 924			£68 924

(7) Books of Suffolk Ltd. (*SPA page 327*)

(a)

Manufacturing A/c (for year ending December 31st 19..)
Prime-Cost Section

19..		£	19..		£
Dec. 31	*Raw Materials*		Dec. 31	Prime Cost	442 550
	Opening Stock	32 330			
	Purchases	279 800			
		312 130			
	Less Closing Stock	36 480			
	Cost of Raw Materials				
	Used	275 650			
	Manufacturing Wages	166 900			
		£442 550			£442 550

Cost of Manufactured Goods Section

19..		£	£	19..		£
Dec. 31	Prime Cost		442 550	Dec. 31	Market Value of Goods	480 000
	Overheads				Manufacturing Loss	40 700
	Factory Expenses	42 550				520 700
	Factory Rent and					
	Rates	20 000				
	Depreciation—					
	Plant	16 850				
			79 400			
			521 950			
	Work in Progress					
	Opening Stock	25 500				
	Closing Stock	26 750				
			−1 250			
			£520 700			£520 700

Trading A/c (for year ending December 31st 19..)

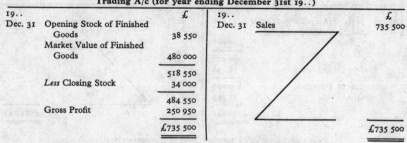

19..		£	19..		£
Dec. 31	Opening Stock of Finished Goods	38 550	Dec. 31	Sales	735 500
	Market Value of Finished Goods	480 000			
		518 550			
	Less Closing Stock	34 000			
		484 550			
	Gross Profit	250 950			
		£735 500			£735 500

Profit and Loss A/c (for year ending December 31st 19..)

19..		£	19..		£
Dec. 31	Office Rent and Rates	9 050	Dec. 31	Gross Profit	250 950
	General Administration Expenses	45 250			
	Salesmen's Salaries	14 924			
	Motor Expenses	8 725			
	Other Selling Expenses	15 717			
	Depreciation—Motor Vehicles	3 400			
	Manufacturing Loss	40 700			
		137 766			
	Net Profit	113 184			
		£250 950			£250 950

(b) *Reasons for accepting the offer :*

   (i) The manufacturer is offering to supply the goods for £20 700 less than the firm of Suffolk Ltd. can make them. Profits would therefore rise by this amount.

   (ii) Capital at present tied up in the business could be released for other purposes.

Reasons for refusing the offer :

   (i) Non-economic factors such as (a) unemployment for present staff undesirable; (b) loss of status as an important manufacturer in the area; (c) loss of interesting employment for owner (if he is directly involved, e.g. if it is a private company).

   (ii) No guarantee that the arrangement is permanent. If the supplier finds other uses for his capacity he may cut off supplies, or raise prices, in the future.

Unit Thirty
Incomplete Records

Exercises Set 42: Simple Incomplete Records

(1) Books of John Brown (*SPA page 331*)

Statement of Affairs (as at January 1st 19..)

	£		£
Assets	15 000	Capital	7 000
		Current Liabilities	
		Creditors	8 000
	£15 000		£15 000

Statement of Affairs (as at December 31st 19..)

	£		£
Assets	21 000	Capital	12 000
		Current Liabilities	
		Creditors	9 000
	£21 000		£21 000

Calculation of profit:

Increase in Net worth = Capital at close − Capital at start
= £12 000 − £7 000
= £5 000

	£
Adjustments: Increase in Net Worth	5 000
(a) *Deduct* Extra capital contributed in the year (since this has partly caused the increase in Net Worth)	2 000
	3 000
(b) *Add* Drawings £20 × 52 weeks =	1 040
Net Profit for year £	4 040

(2) Books of H. Cook (*SPA page 331*)

Statement of Affairs (as at January 1st 19..)

	£	£		£
Fixed Assets			Capital	
Motor Vehicles		1 200	Net Worth	4 620
Current Assets			Current Liabilities	
Stock	2 100		Creditors	960
Debtors	1 300			
Bank	900			
Rates in Advance	80			
		4 380		
		£5 580		£5 580

Statement of Affairs (as at December 31st 19..)

	£		£
Fixed Assets		Capital	5 720
Motor Vehicles	1 000	Net Worth	
Current Assets		Current Liabilities	
Stock	2 240	Creditors	1 000
Debtors	1 040		
Bank	2 344		
Rates in Advance	96		
	5 720		
	£6 720		£6 720

Calculation of Profit for the year:

Increase in Net Worth		= £5 720 − £4 620
		= £1 100
Add Drawings		1 200
		£2 300
Deduct Legacy (which was partly the cause of the increase in Net Worth)		400
Net Profit		£1 900

(3) Books of John Smith (*SPA page 331*)

Statement of Affairs (as at January 1st 19..)

	£	£		£
Fixed Assets			Capital	23 766
Land and Buildings		15 000	Long-term Liability	
Plant and Machinery		4 500	Loan	3 000
Furniture and Fittings		800		
		20 300		
Current Assets			Current Liabilities	
Stock	3 750		Creditors	2 918
Debtors	4 186			
Bank	1 273			
Cash	175			
		9 384		
		£29 684		£29 684

(a) The Statement of Affairs above shows Smith's capital at January 1st to be £23 766.

(b) Net Profit: Before calculating this we need to do a Statement of Affairs as at December 31st 19 . . .

Statement of Affairs (as at December 31st 19..)

	£	£		£	£
Fixed Assets			Capital		24 432
Land and Buildings		15 000	Long term Liability		
Plant and Machinery		5 000	Loan		3 000
Furniture and Fittings		700			
		20 700			
Current Assets			Current Liabilities		
Stock	4 100		Creditors	2 184	
Debtors	5 319		Bank Overdraft	628	
Cash	125				2 812
		9 544			
		£30 244			£30 244

Calculation of Profit:

$$\text{Increase in Net Worth} = £24\,432 - £23\,766$$
$$= 666$$
$$Add \text{ Drawings } £200 \times 12 = 2\,400$$
$$£\,3\,066$$

(c) Statement of Affairs showing the Capital Account in detail.

Statement of Affairs (as at December 31st 19..)

	£	£		£	£	£
Fixed Assets			Capital			
Land and Buildings		15 000	At Start		23 766	
Plant and Machinery		5 000	Add Profit	3 066		
Furniture and Fittings		700	Less Drawings	2 400		
		20 700			666	
						24 432
			Long-term Liability			
			Loan			3 000
Current Assets			Current Liabilities			
Stock	4 100		Creditors	2 184		
Debtors	5 319		Bank Overdraft	628		
Cash	125					2 812
		9 544				
		£30 244				£30 244

(4) Books of M. Law (SPA page 332)

Statement of Affairs (as at July 1st 19..)

	£	£		£
Fixed Assets		3 250	Capital	
Current Assets			Net Worth	6 340
Stock	1 860		Current Liabilities	
Debtors	620		Creditors	490
Bank	1 100			
		3 580		
		£6 830		£6 830

Statement of Affairs (as at June 30th 19..)

	£	£		£
Fixed Assets		3 000	Capital	7 470
Current Assets			Current Liabilities	
Stock	2 140		Creditors	350
Debtors	950			
Bank	1 730			
		4 820		
		£7 820		£7 820

Calculation of Profit:

Increase in Net Worth $= £7\ 470 - £6\ 340$

$= £1\ 130$

Add Drawings	£800	
and Drawings in kind		
(goods taken home)	£125	
		£ 925
Profit for year		£2 055

(5) Books of C. Cropper (*SPA page 332*)

Statement of Affairs (as at October 1st 19..)

	£	£		£
Fixed Assets		600	Capital	
Current Assets			Net Worth	1 295
Stock	300		Current Liabilities	
Debtors	120		Van Repairs Due	75
Bank	350			
		770		
		£1 370		£1 370

Statement of Affairs (as at December 31st 19..)

	£	£		£
Fixed Assets			Capital	
Motor Van		500	Net Worth	891
Current Assets			Current Liabilities	
Stock	628		Creditors	1 009
Debtors	488			
Bank	264			
Van Licence, etc.	20			
		1 400		
		£1 900		£1 900

Calculation of Profit or Loss:

	£
Decrease in Net Worth	= 1 295
	− 891
Apparent loss	404
Add back drawings (which had they not been drawn would have reduced the apparent loss)	104
Loss for quarterly period October–December	£ 300

(6) Books of T. Newman (*SPA page 332*)

Statement of Affairs (as at January 1st 19..)

	£		£
Current Assets		Capital	3 000
Bank	4 000	Long-term Liability	
		Loan (V. Trusting)	1 000
	£4 000		£4 000

Statement of Affairs (as at December 31st 19..)

	£	£		£	£
Fixed Assets			Capital		3 350
Furniture and Fittings		1 200	Long-term Liability		
Motor Vehicles		900	Loan (V. Trusting)		1 000
		2 100			
Current Assets			Current Liabilities		
Stock	1 700		Creditors	1 240	
Debtors	540		Interest on Loan	50	
Bank	1 300				1 290
		3 540			
		£5 640			£5 640

Calculation of Profit:

	£
Increase in Net Worth	= 3 350
	− 3 000
	350
Add Drawings (£16 × 52)	= 832
Profit for year	£1 182

(7) Books of I. Gamble (*SPA page 332*)

Statement of Affairs (as at July 1st 19..)

	£		£
Bank	1 300	Capital	1 300
	£1 300		£1 300

Statement of Affairs (as at December 31st 19..)

	£	£		£
Fixed Assets			Capital	570
Motor Vehicle		380		
Current Assets			Current Liabilities	
Stock	416		Creditors	640
Debtors	230			
Bank	158			
Cash	26			
		830		
		£1 210		£1 210

Result of Trading for the six-month period:

		£
Decline in Net Worth	=	1 300
	–	570
Apparent Loss		730
Deduct Personal Drawings		
(Had this not been drawn he		
would have made a smaller		
apparent loss.)		710
Net Loss for Year	£	20

Exercises Set 43: Building up a Set of Final Accounts from Incomplete Records

(1) Books of C. Monger (*SPA page 337*)

(a)

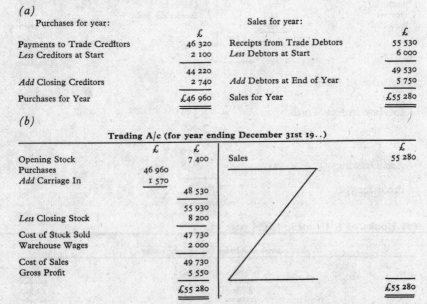

Purchases for year:		£	Sales for year:		£
Payments to Trade Creditors		46 320	Receipts from Trade Debtors		55 530
Less Creditors at Start		2 100	*Less* Debtors at Start		6 000
		44 220			49 530
Add Closing Creditors		2 740	*Add* Debtors at End of Year		5 750
Purchases for Year		£46 960	Sales for Year		£55 280

(b)

Trading A/c (for year ending December 31st 19..)

	£	£		£
Opening Stock		7 400	Sales	55 280
Purchases	46 960			
Add Carriage In	1 570			
		48 530		
		55 930		
Less Closing Stock		8 200		
Cost of Stock Sold		47 730		
Warehouse Wages		2 000		
Cost of Sales		49 730		
Gross Profit		5 550		
		£55 280		£55 280

(2) Books of F.K. (*SPA page 337*)

Calculations:

Purchases for Year		£		Sales for Year		£
To Creditors		11 740		Cash Sales		14 200
Add Creditors at Close of Year		1 210		*Add* sums from takings not banked		
				but used for other purposes		
Purchases for Year		£12 950		Light and Heat	105	
				Sundry Expenses	65	
				Drawings	1 500	
				Cash in Hand	130	
						1 800
				Sales for Year		£16 000

Bank A/c

19..	£	19..	£
Capital	400	Rates	360
Cash Sales	14 200	Shop Fittings	300
		Rent	975
		Delivery Van	800
		Trade Creditors	11 740
		Insurance	40
		Balance	385
	£14 600		£14 600

19..		£
Jan. 1	Balance	385

Trading A/c (for year ending December 31st 19..)

19..		£	19..		£
Dec. 31	Purchases	12 950	Dec. 31	Sales	16 000
	Less Closing Stock	1 150			
	Cost of Stock Sold	11 800			
	Gross Profit	4 200			
		£16 000			£16 000

Profit and Loss A/c (for year ending December 31st 19..)

19..		£	£	19..		£
Dec. 31	Rates	360		Dec. 31	Gross Profit	4 200
	Add Rates Due	120				
			480			
	Rent	975				
	Less Rent in Advance	75				
			900			
	Insurance		40			
	Light and Heat	105				
	Add Light and Heat					
	Due	35				
			140			
	Sundry Expenses		65			
	Depreciation					
	Fittings	15				
	Motor Vehicles	160				
			175			
			1 800			
	Net Profit		2 400			
			£4 200			£4 200

Balance Sheet (as at December 31st 19..)

	£	£		£	£
Fixed Assets			Capital		
Shop Fittings	300		At Start		400
Less Depreciation	15		*Add* Net Profit	2 400	
		285	*Less* Drawings	1 500	
Delivery Van	800				900
Less Depreciation	160				
		640			1 300
		925			
Current Assets			Current Liabilities		
Stock	1 150		Creditors	1 210	
Bank	385		Rates Due	120	
Cash	130		Electricity Due	35	
Rent in Advance	75				1 365
		1 740			
		£2 665			£2 665

(3) Books of F. L. Winter·(*SPA page 338*)

Calculations:

Purchases Figure	£	*Sales Figure*	£	£
Payments to Trade Creditors	5 988	Cash Sales		6 943
Deduct Creditors at Start	1 240	*Less* Returns		3
	4 748			6 940
Add Creditors at Close	1 570	*Add* sums received from		
		Trade Debtors	1 236	
Purchases for year	£6 318	*Less* Debtors at Start	194	
			1 042	
		Add Debtors at Close	136	
				1 178
		Sales for Year		£8 118

Cash Book

19..	£	19..	£
Cash Balance	541	Payments to Trade Creditors	5 988
Cash Sales	6 943	Drawings	700
Receipts from Debtors	1 236	Rent, Rates and Insurance	540
		Light and Heat	42
		Motor Van Expenses	226
		Repairs and Renewals	17
		New Shop Fittings	50
		Refunds to Customers	3
		General Expenses	84
		Balance	1 070
	£8 720		£8 720
19..	£		
Balance	1 070		

Statement of Affairs (as at January 1st 19..)

	£	£		£
Fixed Assets			Capital	1 334
Furniture and Fittings		250		
Motor Vehicles		600		
		850		
Current Assets			Current Liabilities	
Stock	989		Creditors	1 240
Debtors	194			
Cash in Hand and at Bank	541			
		1 724		
		£2 574		£2 574

Trading and Profit and Loss A/c (for year ending December 31st 19..)

19..		£	£	19..		£
Dec. 31	Opening Stock		989	Dec. 31	Sales	8 118
	Purchases		6 318			
			7 307			
	Less Closing Stock		910			
	Cost of Stock Sold		6 397			
	Gross Profit		1 721			
			£8 118			£8 118
Dec. 31	Rent, Rates and			Dec. 31	Gross Profit	1 721
	Insurance	540				
	Less Rates in Advance	30				
			510			
	Light and Heat	42				
	Add Amount Due	11				
			53			
	Motor Expenses		226			
	Repairs and Renewals		17			
	General Expenses		84			
	Depreciation					
	Furniture	30				
	Motor Vehicles	120				
			150			
			1 040			
	Net Profit		681			
			£1 721			£1 721

Balance Sheet (as at December 31st 19..)

	£	£			£
Fixed Assets			Capital		
Furniture and Fittings	250		At Start		1 334
Add Additions	50		*Add* Net Profit	681	
			Less Drawings	700	
	300				−19
Less Depreciation	30				1 315
		270			
Motor Vehicles	600				
Less Depreciation	120				
		480			
		750			
Current Assets			Current Liabilities		
Stock	910		Creditors	1 570	
Debtors	136		Light and Heat Due	11	
Cash at Bank	1 070				1 581
Rates in Advance	30				
		2 146			
		£2 896			£2 896

(4) Books of G. Smith (*SPA page 339*)

Cash Book

19..	£	19..	£
Capital	3 000	Motor Van	1 000
Receipts for Work Done	4 000	Purchases	1 750
		Motor Vehicle Expenses	270
		Insurance	20
		Equipment	1 300
		Drawings	1 000
		Building Society (Drawings)	400
		Rent	100
		Balance	1 160
	£7 000		£7 000
19..	£		
Balance	1 160		

Statement of Affairs (as at January 1st 19..)

	£		£
Bank	3 000	Capital	3 000
	£3 000		£3 000

Trading and Profit and Loss A/c (for year ending December 31st 19..)

19..		£	£	19..		£
Dec. 31	Purchases	1 750		Dec. 31	Receipts for Work Done	4 000
	Less Closing Stock	250			Add Debts Due for Payment	150
	Cost of Stock Used	1 500				4 150
	Gross Profit	2 650				
			£4 150			£4 150

19..			£	19..		£
Dec. 31	Motor Vehicle Expenses		270	Dec. 31	Gross Profit	2 650
	Insurance		20			
	Rent		100			
	Depreciation					
	Motor Vehicles	200				
	Equipment	130				
			330			
			720			
	Net Profit		1 930			
			£2 650			£2 650

Balance Sheet (for year ending December 31st 19..)

	£	£		£	£
Fixed Assets			Capital		
Equipment	1 300		At Start		3 000
Less Depreciation	130		Add Net Profit	1 930	
		1 170	Less Drawings	1 400	
Motor Vehicles	1 000				530
Less Depreciation	200				3 530
		800			
		1 970			
Current Assets					
Stock	250				
Debtors	150				
Cash at Bank	1 160				
		1 560			
		£3 530			£3 530

(5) Books of W. Davis (*SPA page 339*)

Cash Book

19..			£	19..			£
Opening Balances				Purchases			7 400
Cash			20	Drawings			1 500
Bank			500	Light and Heat			200
Takings (Sales)			10 000	Cleaning			30
				Wages			500
				Furniture			200
				Cash in Hand Balance	c/d		30
				Bank Balance	c/d		660
			£10 520				£10 520
19..			£				
Jan. 1	Balances	B/d	30				
	Balances	B/d	660				

Trading and Profit and Loss A/c (for year ending December 31st 19..)

19..		£	19..		£
Dec. 31	Opening Stock	150	Dec. 31	Sales	10 000
	Purchases	7 400			
		7 550			
	Less Closing Stock	150			
		7 400			
	Gross Profit	2 600			
		£10 000			£10 000

19..		£	£	19..		£
Dec. 31	Light and Heat	200		Dec. 31	Gross Profit	2 600
	Less Amount treated					
	as Drawings	100				
			100			
	Cleaning		30			
	Wages		500			
			630			
	Net Profit		1 970			
			£2 600			£2 600

Balance Sheet (as at December 31st 19..)

		£	£			£	£
Fixed Assets				Capital			
Premises			3 000	At Start			4 670
Furniture		1 000		Net Profit		1 970	
Add Additions		200		*Less* Drawings	1 500		
			1 200	*Add* Light and			
			4 200	Heat	100		
						1 600	
Current Assets							370
Stock		150					5 040
Bank		660					
Cash		30					
			840				
			£5 040				£5 040

(6) Books of R. T. (*SPA page 340*)

Bank Account

19..		£	19..		£
Dec. 31	Opening Capital	500	Dec. 31	Rates	420
	Cash Sales	15 700		Shop Fittings	400
				Rent	866
				Delivery Van	700
				Creditors	12 340
				Insurance	50
				Balance	1 424
		£16 200			£16 200
19..		£			
Jan. 1	Balance	1 424			

Purchases Figure	£	Sales Figure	£
Amounts Paid to Creditors	12 340	Cash Sales Paid In	15 700
Add Amounts Due	1 670	*Add* Amounts used in other ways	
	£14 010	Light and Heat	124
		Sundry Expenses	72
		Drawings	1 600
		Cash in Hand	165
		Sales for Year	£17 661

Trading A/c (for year ending December 31st 19..)

19..		£	19..		£
Dec. 31	Purchases	14 010	Dec. 31	Sales	17 661
	Less Closing Stock	1 280			
	Cost of Stock Sold	12 730			
	Gross Profit	4 931			
		£17 661			£17 661

Profit and Loss A/c (for year ending December 31st 19..)

19..		£	£	19..		£
Dec. 31	Rates	420		Dec. 31	Gross Profit	4 931
	Add Rates Due	150				
			570			
	Rent	866				
	Less Amount in Advance	66				
			800			
	Insurance		50			
	Light and Heat	124				
	Add Electricity Due	42				
			166			
	Sundry Expenses		72			
	Depreciation					
	Fittings	20				
	Motor Vehicles	140				
			160			
			1 818			
	Net Profit		3 113			
			£4 931			£4 931

Balance Sheet (as at December 31st 19..)

	£	£		£	£
Fixed Assets			Capital		
Shop Fittings	400		At Start		500
Less Depreciation	20		Net Profit	3 113	
		380	*Less* Drawings	1 600	
Delivery Van	700				1 513
Less Depreciation	140				2 013
		560			
		940			
Current Assets			Current Liabilities		
Stock	1 280		Creditors	1 670	
Bank	1 424		Rates Due	150	
Cash	165		Electricity Due	42	
Rent in Advance	66				1 862
		2 935			
		£3 875			£3 875

The Accounts of Companies

Exercises Set 44: Company Final Accounts

(1) Books of Shubunkin Ltd. (*SPA page 356*)

Appropriation A/c (for year ending December 31st 19..)

19..		£	19..		£
Dec. 31	General Reserve	12 000	Dec. 31	Balance	3 300
	Dividend	8 000		Net Profit	20 070
		20 000			
	Balance	3 370			
		£23 370			£23 370
			19..		£
			Jan. 1	Balance	3 370

Balance Sheet (as at December 31st 19..)

Fixed Assets	At Cost	Less Depreciation			Ordinary Shareholders' Interest in the Co.		Authorized	Issued
Freehold					Ordinary Shares of £1			
Property	70 000	—	70 000		fully paid		80 000	80 000
Furniture and								
Fittings	4 000	1 200	2 800					
			72 800		Reserves			
Current Assets					Capital:			
Stock in Trade		28 950			Share Premium A/c	10 000		
Debtors	15 000				Revenue:			
Less Provision	400				General			
		14 600			Reserve	12 000		
Bank		27 200			Balance on Appro-			
Rates in Advance		50			priation A/c	3 370	15 370	
			70 800					25 370
Less Current Liabilities								105 370
Dividend Due	8 000				Debentures (6%)			20 000
Creditors	9 280							
Debenture Interest								
Due	600							
Wages and Salaries								
Due	350							
		18 230						
Net Working Capital			52 570					
			£125 370					£125 370

(2) Books of Rostrevor Ltd. (*SPA page 357*)

Appropriation A/c (for year ending December 31st 19..)

19..		£	19..		£
Dec. 31	General Reserve	5 000	Dec. 31	Balance	10 680
	Preference Share Dividend	1 400		Net Profit	11 865
	Ordinary Share Dividend	8 000			
		14 400			22 545
	Balance	8 145			
		£22 545			£22 545
			19..		£
			Dec. 31	Balance	8 145

Balance Sheet (as at December 31st 19..)

Fixed Assets				*Ordinary Shareholders' Interest in the Co.*		Authorized	Issued
Freehold Property			95 200	Ordinary Shares of £1			
Motor Vans		14 460		fully paid		80 000	80 000
Less Depreciation		10 142					
			4 318	Reserves			
				Capital:			
			99 518	Premium on Preference			
Current Assets				Shares		2 000	
Stock		17 754		Revenue:			
Debtors	28 325			General			
Less Provision	400			Reserves	10 000		
		27 925		Additions	5 000		
Bank		14 170					
Rates in Advance		272				15 000	
				Balance on Appro-			
		60 121		priation A/c	8 145		
Current Liabilities						23 145	
Ordinary							25 145
Dividend	8 000						
Preference							105 145
Dividend	1 400			Preference Shareholders' Interest in the Co.			
Creditors	24 150			7% Preference Shares of £1 fully paid			20 000
Wages Due	944			(Authorized £20 000)			
		34 494					
Net Working Capital			25 627				
	Net Assets		£125 145				£125 145

(3) Books of Andrew Ltd. (*SPA page 358*)

Trading and Profit and Loss A/c (for year ending December 31st 19..)

19..		£	£	19..		£
Dec. 31	Stock in Trade		18 930	Dec. 31	Sales	240 000
	Purchases		164 740			
			183 670			
	Less Closing Stock		20 470			
			163 200			
	Gross Profit		76 800			
			£240 000			£240 000

19..		£	£	19..		£
Dec. 31	Debenture Interest	1 200		Dec. 31	Gross Profit	76 800
	Interest Due	1 200				
			2 400			
	Wages and Salaries	23 360				
	Wages Due	240				
			23 600			
	Rent and Rates	1 650				
	Less Rates in Advance	75				
			1 575			
	General Expenses		5 120			
	Bad Debts		1 510			
	Provision for Bad Debts		50			
	Depreciation—Fixtures		600			
			34 855			
	Net Profit		41 945			
			£76 800			£76 800

Appropriation A/c (for year ending December 31st 19..)

19..		£	19..		£
Dec. 31	Preliminary Expenses	400	Jan. 1	Balance	14 740
	Dividend Due	24 000	Dec. 31	Profit	41 945
	Balance	32 285			
		£56 685			£56 685
			19..		£
			Jan. 1	Balance	32 285

Balance Sheet (as at December 31st 19..)

Fixed Assets	At Cost	Less Depreciation	Value	Ordinary Shareholders' Interest in the Co.	Authorized	Issued
Freehold Property	265 000	—	265 000	Ordinary Shares of £1 fully paid	200 000	200 000
Fixtures and Fittings	12 000	6 600	5 400	Reserves Revenue:		
	277 000	6 600	270 400	Balance on Appropriation A/c		32 285
Current Assets						232 285
Stock		20 470		Less Preliminary Expenses	2 000	
Debtors	18 950			Deduct Amount		
Less Provisions for Bad Debts	350			Written Off	400	
		18 600				1 600
Rates in Advance		75				
		39 145				230 685
Less Current Liabilities				6% Debentures		40 000
Dividend Due	24 000					
Creditors	12 930					
Debenture Interest Due	1 200					
Bank Overdraft	490					
Wages Due	240					
		38 860				
Net Working Capital			285			
			£270 685			£270 685

(4) Books of Toleymore Ltd. (*SPA page 359*)

Trial Balance (as at February 28th 19..)

	Dr. £	Cr. £
Share Capital		120 000
Premium on Shares		20 000
6% Debentures		40 000
Freehold Buildings at Cost	75 000	
Plant and Machinery at Cost	82 620	
Provision for Depreciation on Plant and Machinery		41 380
Furniture and Equipment at Cost	25 840	
Provision for Depreciation on Furniture and Equipment		13 270
Stock in Trade	42 140	
Profit and Loss A/c (undistributed profit)		21 146
General Reserve		35 000
Provision for Dividend Payable		12 000
Creditors		21 794
Debtors	45 341	
Bank	23 649	
Investments	30 000	
	£324 590	324 590

Balance Sheet (as at February 28th 19..)

Fixed Assets	At Cost	Less Depreciation	Value	Ordinary Shareholders' Interest in the Co.	Authorized	Issued
Freehold				Ordinary Shares of £1		
Buildings	75 000	—	75 000	Fully Paid	120 000	120 000
Plant and						
Machinery	82 620	41 380	41 240	Reserves		
Furniture and				Capital:		
Equipment	25 840	13 270	12 570	Premium on Shares	20 000	
				Revenue:		
			128 810	General Reserves	35 000	
Current Assets				Balance on Profit and		
Stock	42 140			Loss A/c	21 146	
Investments	30 000 (Market Value					76 146
	= £30 080)					
Debtors	45 341					196 146
Bank	23 649			6% Debentures		
		141 130		(redeemable in 1986)		40 000
Less Current Liabilities						
Provision for						
Dividend	12 000					
Creditors	21 794					
		33 794				
			107 336			
			£236 146			£236 146

(5) Books of Box Ltd. (*SPA page 360*)

Trading and Profit and Loss A/c (for year ending December 31st 19..)

19..		£	19..			£
Dec. 31	Opening Stock	13 428	Dec. 31	Sales		121 498
	Purchases	90 620				
		104 048				
	Less Closing Stock	16 426				
		87 622				
	Gross Profit	33 876				
		£121 498				£121 498

19..		£	£	19..			£
Dec. 31	Bad Debts		601	Dec. 31	Gross Profit		33 876
	Wages and Salaries	9 820			Rent Received	390	
	Less Amount				Add Amount		
	Capitalized	796			Due	130	
			9 024				520
	Insurance	693					34 396
	Less Amount in Advance	86					
			607				
	Office Expenses		1 142				
	Debenture Interest	800					
	Add Amount Due	800					
			1 600				
	Rates		210				
	Directors Salaries		6 000				
	General Expenses		1 246				
	Provision for Bad Debts		50				
	Depreciation—Furniture and						
	Equipment		150				
			20 630				
	Net Profit		13 766				
			£34 396				£34 396

Appropriation A/c (for year ending December 31st 19..)

19..		£	19..			£
Dec. 31	General Reserve	7 000	Jan. 1	Balance		2 900
	Dividend	4 000	Dec. 31	Net Profit		13 766
	Balance	5 666				
		£16 666				£16 666
			19..			£
			Jan. 1	Balance		5 666

Balance Sheet (as at December 31st 19..)

Ordinary Shareholders' Interest in the Co.

		Authorized	Issued
Ordinary Shares of £1 fully paid		40 000	40 000

Reserves

Capital:			
Share Premium		10 000	
Revenue:			
General Reserve (addition)	7 000		
Balance on Appropriation A/c	5 666		
		12 666	
			22 666
Ordinary Shareholders' Equity			62 666
8% Debentures			20 000
			£82 666

Represented by:

Fixed Assets	At Cost	*Less* Depreciation to date	Value £
Freehold Property	50 000		
Add Amount Capitalized	796		
	50 796	—	50 796
Furniture and Fittings	3 000	900	2 100
			52 896

Current Assets			
Closing Stock		16 426	
Debtors	16 923		
Less Provision for Bad Debts	300		
		16 623	
Bank		14 294	
Rent Receivable Due		130	
Insurance in Advance		86	
		47 559	
Less Current Liabilities			
Dividend Due	4 000·00		
Creditors	12 989·00		
Debenture Interest Due	800·00		
		17 789	
Net Working Capital			29 770
			£82 666

(6) Books of Green and Brown Ltd. (*SPA page 361*)

Trial Balance (as at March 31st 19..)

	Dr. £	Cr. £
Share Capital A/c (Authorized £200 000)		100 000
Freehold Land and Buildings	40 000	
Share Premiums		10 000
Machinery at Cost	60 000	
Stock	37 040	
Creditors		19 743
Debtors	43 221	
Provision for Bad Debts		524
Bank	22 028	
General Reserve A/c		25 000
Investments at Cost	25 000	
Loan Secured on Land and Buildings		20 000
Dividend Payable		10 000
Provision for Depreciation on Machinery		32 000
Furniture and Fittings at Cost	22 506	
Provision for Depreciation of Furniture and Fittings		10 006
Profit and Loss A/c Balance		22 522
	£249 795	249 795

Balance Sheet (as at March 31st 19..)

Fixed Assets				*Ordinary Shareholders' Interest in the Co.*			
						Authorized	Issued
Freehold Land and Buildings at Cost			40 000	Ordinary Shares of £1 fully paid		200 000	100 000
Machinery at Cost	60 000						
Less Depreciation	32 000						
			28 000	Reserves			
Furniture and Fittings	22 506			Capital:			
Less Depreciation	10 006			Share Premium		10 000	
			12 500	Revenue:			
				General			
			80 500	Reserve	25 000		
Current Assets				Balance on Appropriation			
Stock		37 040		A/c	22 522		
Investments at Cost		25 000				47 522	
(Market Value = £28 050)							57 522
Debtors	43 221						
Less Provision	524			Ordinary Shareholders' Equity			157 522
		42 697		Long-term Liability			
Bank		22 028		Loan Secured on Land and			
		126 765		Buildings			20 000
Current Liabilities							
Dividend	10 000						
Creditors	19 743						
		29 743					
			97 022				
			£177 522				£177 522

(7) Books of Ham Ltd. *(SPA page 361)*

Trial Balance (as at December 31st 19..)

	Dr. £	Cr. £
Share Capital (Authorized £50 000)		40 000
6% Debentures		9 000
Premises at Cost	22 000	
Machinery at Cost *less* Depreciation	24 000	
Creditors		7 430
Debtors	16 150	
Stock in Trade	12 920	
Share Premium		4 000
Profit and Loss A/c (Balance)		3 420
General Reserve		8 000
Fixtures at Cost (*Less* Depreciation)	1 200	
Provision for Bad Debts		250
Bank	15 030	
Profit for Year		19 200
	£91 300	91 300

Appropriation A/c (for year ending December 31st 19..)

19..			£	19..			£ ..
Dec. 31	General Reserve		10 000	Dec. 31	Profit and Loss A/c		3 420
	Dividend		4 000		Profit		19 200
	Balance	c/d	8 620				
			£22 620				£22 620
				19..			£
				Dec. 31	Balance	B/d	8 620

Balance Sheet (as at December 31st 19..)

Fixed Assets				Ordinary Shareholders' Interest in the Co.		Authorized	Issued
Premises			22 000	Ordinary Shares of £1			
Machinery at Cost		29 000		fully paid		50 000	40 000
Less Depreciation		5 000					
			24 000	Reserves			
Fixtures at Cost		2 200		Capital:			
Less Depreciation		1 000		Share Premium		4 000	
			1 200	Revenue:			
			47 200	General			
				Reserve	8 000		
Current Assets				Additions	10 000		
Stock in Trade		12 920				18 000	
Debtors	16 150			Balance on			
Less Provision	250			Appropriation	8 620		
		15 900				26 620	
Bank		15 030					30 620
		43 850					
Less Current Liabilities				Ordinary Shareholders' Equity			70 620
Dividend Due	4 000			6% Debentures			9 000
Creditors	7 430						
		11 430					
Net Working Capital			32 420				
			£79 620				£79 620

(8) Books of Excel Traders Ltd. (*SPA page 362*)

Appropriation A/c (for year ending December 31st 19..)

19..		£	19..		£
Dec. 31	General Reserve	3 000	Jan. 1	Balance	1 460
	Dividend	9 000	Dec. 31	Net Profit	14 670
	Balance	4 130			
		£16 130			£16 130
			19..		£
			Jan. 1	Balance	4 130

Balance Sheet (as at December 31st 19..)

	£			*Ordinary Shareholders' Interest in the Co.*		
					Authorized	Issued
Fixed Assets						
Freehold Premises		48 000		Ordinary Shares of £1		
Machinery at Cost	37 000			fully paid	100 000	60 000
Less Depreciation	14 500					
		22 500		Reserves		
Fixtures and Fittings				Revenue:		
at Cost	4 800			General Reserve	10 000	
Less Depreciation	1 600			Additions	3 000	
		3 200				
					13 000	
		73 700		Balance on		
Current Assets				Appropriation A/c	4 130	
Stock	8 850					17 130
Debtors	9 250					
Less Provision	370			Ordinary Shareholders' Equity		77 130
		8 880				
		17 730				
Less Current Liabilities						
Dividend Due	9 000					
Creditors	3 440					
Bank Overdraft	1 860					
		14 300				
Net Working Capital		3 430				
		£77 130				£77 130

(9) Books of Solarheaters Ltd. (*SPA page 363*)

Appropriation A/c (for year ending December 31st 19..)

19..		£	19..		£
Dec. 31	General Reserve	6 000	Jan. 1	Balance	1 260
	Dividend	5 000	Dec. 31	Net Profit	15 270
	Balance	5 530			
		£16 530			£16 530
			19..		£
			Jan. 1		5 530

Balance Sheet (as at December 31st 19..)

				Ordinary Shareholders' Interest in the Co.		Authorized	Issued
Fixed Assets							
Freehold Premises			38 400	Ordinary Shares of 50p			
Machinery at Cost		35 800		fully paid		80 000	50 000
Less Depreciation		4 900					
			30 900	Reserves			
Fixtures and Fittings				Revenue:			
at Cost		6 000		General Reserves		20 000	
Less Depreciation		1 200		Additions		6 000	
			4 800			26 000	
			74 100	Appropriation A/c		5 530	
							31 530
Current Assets							
Stock		9 900					
Debtors	8 200			Ordinary Shareholders' Equity			81 530
Less Provision	550						
		7 650					
			17 550				
Less Current Liabilities							
Dividend Due	5 000						
Creditors	3 260						
Bank	1 860						
		10 120					
			7 430				
			£81 530				£81 530

(10) Books of Turnip Tops Ltd. (*SPA page 364*)

Trading and Profit and Loss A/c (for year ending December 31st 19..)

19..		£	19..		£
Dec. 31	Opening Stock	23 846	Dec. 31	Sales	134 720
	Purchases 97 468			*Less* Returns in Wards	621
	Less Returns Out 417				
		97 051		Net Turnover	134 099
		120 897			
	Less Closing Stock	32 779			
	Cost of Stock Sold	88 118			
	Gross Profit	45 981			
		£134 099			£134 099

19..		£	19..		£
Dec. 31	Bad Debts	427	Dec. 31	Gross Profit	45 981
	Motor Expenses	1 127		Discount Received	907
	Rent and Rates 1 850				46 888
	Add Rent Due 550				
		2 400			
	Insurance 160				
	Less Amount in				
	Advance 40				
		120			
	Salaries	11 206			
	General Administration				
	Expenses	10 426			
	Directors' Fees	5 000			
	Discount Allowed	1 461			
	Provision for Bad Debts	64			
	Debenture Interest Due	600			
	Depreciation:				
	Plant 4 000				
	Motor Vehicles 1 000				
		5 000			
		37 831			
	Gross Profit	9 057			
		£46 888			£46 888

Appropriation A/c (for year ending December 31st 19..)

19..		£	19..		£
Dec. 31	General Reserve	5 000	Dec. 31	Balance	11 469
	Dividend	8 000		Net Profit	9 057
	Balance c/d	7 526			
		£20 526			£20 526
			19..		£
			Jan. 1	Balance B/d	7 526

Balance Sheet (as at December 31st 19..)

Ordinary Shareholders' Interest in the Co.		Authorized	Issued
Ordinary Shares of £1 fully paid		80 000	80 000
Reserves			
Capital:			
Premium on Shares		25 000	
Revenue:			
General Reserve	5 000		
Balance on Appropriation A/c	7 526		
		12 526	
			37 526
Ordinary Shareholders' Equity			117 526
6% Debentures			10 000
			£127 526

	At Cost	*Less* Depreciation to date	Value
Represented by			
Fixed Assets			
Freehold Buildings	70 000	—	70 000
Plant	40 000	22 000	18 000
Motor Vehicles	4 000	2 500	1 500
	114 000	24 500	89 500

Current Assets			
Stock		32 779	
Debtors	13 099		
Less Provision	685		
		12 414	
Bank		10 641	
Insurance in Advance		40	
			55 874
Less Current Liabilities			
Dividend	8 000		
Creditors	8 698		
Rent Due	550		
Debenture Interest Due	600		
		17 848	
Net Working Capital			38 026
			£127 526

(11) Books of Dark Shadows Ltd. (*SPA page 365*)

Trading and Profit and Loss A/c (for year ending December 31st 19..)

19..		£	19..		£
Dec. 31	Opening Stock	18 260	Dec. 31	Sales	142 620
	Purchases 116 940			*Less* Returns In	227
	Less Returns 359				
		116 581		Net Turnover	142 393
		.134 841			
	Less Closing Stock	19 621			
		115 220			
	Gross Profit	27 173			
		£142 393			£142 393

19..			£	19..		£
Dec. 31	Bad Debts		348	Dec. 31	Gross Profit	27 173
	Rent and Rates	1 050			Bad Debts Provision	
	Less Amount in Advance	50			Recovered	20
			1 000			
	Light and Heat	420				27 193
	Add Amount Due	71				
			491			
	Salaries		12 240			
	General Expenses		2 661			
	Debenture Interest	600				
	Add Amount Due	600				
			1 200			
	Depreciation		2 000			
			19 940			
	Net Profit		7 253			
			£27 193			£27 193

Appropriation A/c (for year ending December 31st 19..)

19..		£	19..			£
Dec. 31	Dividend	4 000	Jan. 1		Balance	2 142
	Balance	5 395	Dec. 31		Net Profit	7 253
		£9 395				£9 395
			19..			£
			Jan. 1		Balance	5 395

Balance Sheet (as at December 31st 19..)

Ordinary Shareholders' Interest in the Co.			Authorized	Issued
				£
Ordinary Shares of £1 fully paid			40 000	40 000
Reserves				
Capital:				
Share Premium		10 000		
Revenue:				
Balance on Appropriation A/c		5 395		
				15 395
Ordinary Shareholders' Equity				55 395
6% Debentures				20 000
				£75 395

Represented by		At Cost	*Less* Depreciation	Value
Fixed Assets				
Freehold Premises		40 000	—	40 000
Furniture and Equipment		20 000	9 400	10 600
		60 000	9 400	50 600
Current Assets				
Stock		19 621		
Debtors	16 260			
Less Provision	240			
		16 020		
Bank		2 955		
Rates in Advance		50		
			38 646	
Less Current Liabilities				
Dividend Payable	4 000			
Creditors	9 180			
Light and Heat Due	71			
Debenture Interest Due	600			
			13 851	
Net Working Capital				24 795
				£75 395

(12) Books of Green Swan Ltd. (*SPA page 366*)

Trading and Profit and Loss A/c (for year ending December 31st 19..)

19..			£	19..		£
Dec. 31	Opening Stock		24 269	Dec. 31	Sales	134 689
	Purchases		88 792			
			113 061			
	Less Closing Stock		26 922			
	Cost of Stock Sold		86 139			
	Gross Profit		48 550			
			£134 689			£134 689

19..			£	19..		£
Dec. 31	Rent and Rates	3 000		Dec. 31	Gross Profit	48 550
	Less Rates in Advance	400				
			2 600			
	Salaries	12 294				
	Add Salaries Due	121				
			12 415			
	General Expenses		9 946			
	Bad Debts		349			
	Debenture Interest	500				
	Add Amount Due	500				
			1 000			
	Bank Charges Due		24			
	Depreciation					
	Plant	3 560				
	Motor Vehicles	1 700				
			5 260			
	Provision for Bad Debts		34			
			31 628			
	Net Profit		16 922			
			£48 550			£48 550

Appropriation A/c (for year ending December 31st 19..)

19..		£	19..			£
Dec. 31	Interim Dividend	4 000	Jan. 1	Balance		3 296
	Final Dividend	8 000	Dec. 31	Net Profit		16 922
	Balance	8 218				
		£20 218				£20 218
			19..			£
			Jan. 1	Balance		8 218

Balance Sheet (as at December 31st 19..)

Ordinary Shareholders' Interest in the Co.		Authorized	Issued
		£	£
Ordinary Shares of £1 fully paid		80 000	80 000
Reserves			
Revenue:			
General Reserve	10 000		
Balance on Appropriation A/c	8 218		
			18 218
Ordinary Shareholders' Equity			98 218
5% Debentures			20 000
			£118 218

Represented by				
Fixed Assets		At Cost	*Less* Depreciation	Value
Freehold Buildings		50 000	—	50 000
Plant		35 600	13 310	22 290
Motor Vehicles		8 500	5 680	2 820
		94 100	18 990	75 110

Current Assets				
Stock		26 922		
Debtors	13 294			
Less Provision	462			
		12 832		
Bank		20 090		
Rates in Advance		400		
			60 244	
Less Current Liabilities				
Dividend Due		8 000		
Creditors		8 491		
Bank Charges Due		24		
Debenture Interest Due		500		
Salaries Due		121		
			17 136	
Net Working Capital				43 108
				£118 218

Interpreting Final Accounts: the Control of a Business

Exercises Set 45: Gross-Profit Percentage

(1) Books of Mr. A. (*SPA page 373*)

$$\text{Gross-Profit percentage} = \frac{\text{Gross profit}}{\text{Turnover}} \times 100$$

$$\text{Year I} = \frac{5\,000}{27\,000} \times 100$$

$$= \frac{500}{27}$$

$$= 18{\cdot}5\%$$

$$\text{Year II} = \frac{6\,000}{35\,000} \times 100$$

$$= \frac{120}{7}$$

$$= 17{\cdot}1\%$$

Comments:

(*a*) Turnover of the business has risen by almost one-third; gross-profit percentage has fallen away by 1·4 per cent. It should stay constant. He should examine the business to make sure there has not been any leakage of profits in theft of cash or stock.

(*b*) If the business is having to operate on tighter profit margins, which means that the extra sales can only be achieved by cutting prices, he should watch the situation carefully and not expand beyond the point where the extra work and worry ceases to be worth while.

(2) Books of R. Dawson (*SPA page 373*)

Gross Profit:

	£		£
Junior Model: Sales	5 800	Senior Model: Sales	25 600
Less Sales Returns	1 800	*Less* Sales Returns	1 600
Net Turnover	4 000	Net Turnover	24 000
Less Cost of Sales	3 800	*Less* Cost of Sales	16 500
Gross Profit	£ 200	Gross Profit	£ 7 500

$$\text{Gross-profit percentage: Junior Model} = \frac{200}{4\,000} \times 100 = 5\%$$

$$\text{Senior Model} = \frac{7\,500}{24\,000} \times 100 = 31\cdot25\%$$

Advice

In view of the very different rates of gross-profit percentage Dawson is advised to: (*a*) raise the selling prices of the Junior model to achieve a more realistic margin of profit; (*b*) reduce the share of space allocated to the production of the Junior model and increase that for the Senior model.

(3) Books of R. Marshall (*SPA page 373*)

(*a*) Yes, embezzlement would reduce the sales figure, and hence lower the gross profit and the gross-profit percentage.

(*b*) Yes, this is known as 'passing out' goods, and reduces the takings figure, i.e. sales, and hence reduces the gross profit and the gross-profit percentage.

(*c*) No, this would not reduce the gross profit, since salaries are a Profit and Loss Account item and only affect the net profit.

(*d*) Yes, competition of this sort lowers the profit, and hence the gross-profit percentage.

(*e*) Yes, this type of drawings in kind reduces the stock and hence raises the cost of stock sold and lowers gross profit and gross-profit percentage.

(*f*) Yes, sale of goods, to clear them at cut prices, lowers the sales figure and reduces the gross profit and the gross-profit percentage.

(4) Books of K. Newing (*SPA page 374*)

(*a*) 'Gross profit' is the overall profit on trading which is found when the 'Cost of Sales' is deducted from the 'Net Sales' figure in the Trading Account.

(*b*) 'Gross-profit percentage' is the percentage found when the gross profit is expressed as a percentage of the net turnover. It is found by the formula

$$\frac{\text{Gross profit}}{\text{Turnover}} \times 100$$

It should be a constant from year to year if the business is being conducted properly.

(c)

Trading A/c of K. Newing (for year ending December 31st 19..)

19..		£		19..		£
Dec. 31	Opening Stock		4 500	Dec. 31	Sales:	
	Purchases				Cash	23 000
	Cash	1 000			Credit	8 000
	Credit	12 500				
						31 000
		13 500			*Less* Returns In	1 000
	Add Carriage In	500				
						30 000
		14 000				
	Less Returns Out	1 000				
			13 000			
			17 500			
	Less Closing Stock		5 500			
			12 000			
	Gross Profit		18 000			
			£30 000			£30 000

$$\therefore \text{Gross profit} = 18\,000$$

$$\text{Gross-profit percentage} = \frac{18\,000}{30\,000} \times 100$$

$$= 60\%$$

(5) Books of E. Randall (*SPA page 374*)

Trading A/c (for year ending December 31st 19..)

19..		£		19..		£
Dec. 31	Opening Stock		2 785	Dec. 31	Sales	7 642
	Purchases	6 908			*Less* Returns In	262
	Add Import Charges	126				
						7 380
		7 034				
	Less Returns Out	195				
			6 839			
			9 624			
	Less Closing Stock		4 440			
	Cost of Stock Sold		5 184			
	Add Wages	700				
	And Wages Due	20				
			720			
	Cost of Sales		5 904			
	Gross Profit		1 476			
			£7 380			£7 380

$$\text{Gross-profit percentage} = \frac{1\,476}{7\,380} \times 100$$

$$= 20\%$$

Exercises Set 46: The Rate of Stock Turnover

(1) Books of L. Perry (*SPA page 375*)

Calculation of Rate of Stockturn:

		£
Sales at Selling Price	=	78 750
Less Profit Margin	=	15 750
Cost of Stock Sold	=	63 000

$$\therefore \text{ Rate of Stock Turnover} = \frac{63\ 000}{5\ 250}$$

$$= \text{12 times}$$

(2) Books of A. Reddington (*SPA page 375*)

Calculation of Rate of Stockturn:

		£
Sales at Selling Price	=	159 375
Less Profit Margin	=	31 875
Cost of Stock Sold	=	127 500

$$\therefore \text{ Rate of Stock Turnover} = \frac{127\ 500}{8\ 500}$$

$$= \text{15 times}$$

(3) Books of A. Trader (*SPA page 375*)

(a) Average stock $= \dfrac{\text{Opening stock } + \text{ Closing stock}}{2} = \dfrac{£2\ 100 + £1\ 560}{2} = \dfrac{£3\ 660}{2}$

$$= £1\ 830$$

(b) Rate of stockturn $= \dfrac{\text{Cost of stock soid}}{\text{Average stock}} = \dfrac{£5\ 490}{£1\ 830} = \text{3 times}$

(c) Average time an item of stock was in stock $= \dfrac{\text{I year}}{\text{Rate of stockturn}} = \dfrac{\text{I year}}{3}$

$$= \text{4 months}$$

(4) Books of M. Lewis (*SPA page 376*)

(a) Average stock = $\dfrac{\text{Opening stock} + \text{Closing stock}}{2}$

$= \dfrac{£2\,400 + £1\,920}{2} = \dfrac{£4\,320}{2} = £2\,160$

(b) Rate of stockturn = $\dfrac{\text{Cost of stock sold}}{\text{Average stock}} = \dfrac{£51\,840}{£2\,160} = 24 \text{ times}$

(c) Average length of time an item was in stock = $\dfrac{1 \text{ year}}{\text{Rate of stockturn}} = \dfrac{1 \text{ year}}{24}$

$= 15 \text{ days}$

(5) Books of D. Hancock (*SPA page 376*)

(a) Average stock = $\dfrac{\text{Opening stock} + \text{Closing stock}}{2}$

$= \dfrac{£2\,500 + £2\,560}{2} = \dfrac{£5\,060}{2} = £2\,530$

(b) Rate of stockturn = $\dfrac{\text{Cost of stock sold}}{\text{Average stock}} = \dfrac{£20\,240}{£\,2\,530} = 8 \text{ times}$

(c) Average time an item is in stock = $\dfrac{1 \text{ year}}{\text{Rate of stockturn}}$

$= \dfrac{365 \text{ days}}{8}$

$= 46 \text{ days}$ (1½ months would be an acceptable answer here)

(6) Books of Downtown Do-It-Yourself Stores (*SPA page 377*)

(a)

Trading A/c (for year ending September 30th 19..)

19..		£	£	19..		£
Dec. 31	Opening Stock		2 134	Dec. 31	Sales	16 065
	Purchases	12 909			*Less* Returns In	873
	Less Returns Out	297				
			12 612		Net Turnover	15 192
			14 746			
	Less Closing Stock		2 086			
	Cost of Stock Sold		12 660			
	Gross Profit		2 532			
			£15 192			£15 192

(b) Cost of goods sold (as calculated above) = £12 660

(c) Gross profit/sales percentage = $\dfrac{\text{Gross profit}}{\text{Turnover}} \times 100 = \dfrac{2\,532}{15\,192} \times 100$

$= 16\tfrac{2}{3}\%$

(d) Average time in stock: To find this figure we need to use the formula

$$\frac{1 \text{ year}}{\text{Rate of Stockturn}}$$

$$\text{Rate of Stockturn} = \frac{\text{Cost of stock sold}}{\text{Average stock}}$$

$$\text{Average Stock} = \frac{\text{Opening stock} + \text{Closing stock}}{2} = \frac{\pounds 2\,134 + \pounds 2\,086}{2}$$

$$= \frac{\pounds 4\,220}{2}$$

$$= \pounds 2\,110$$

$$\therefore \text{ Rate of stockturn} = \frac{\pounds 12\,660}{\pounds\,2\,110} = 6 \text{ times}$$

$$\therefore \text{ Average time in stock} = \frac{1 \text{ year}}{6} = 2 \text{ months}$$

(7) Books of J. F. Roe (*SPA page 377*)

(a) (i) Rate of Stock Turnover $= \dfrac{910}{70} = 13 \text{ times}$

(ii) Gross Profit Calculation:

Trading A/c (for year ending December 31st 19..)

19.. Dec. 31		£	19.. Dec. 31		£
	Cost of Manufactured Goods	16 380		Sales	22 750
	Gross Profit	6 370			
		£22 750			£22 750

$$\therefore \text{ Gross Profit} = \pounds 6\,370$$

(b) (i) Turnover for next year $= 70 \times 15$ bicycles at $\dfrac{90}{100} \times \pounds 25$

$$= 1\,050 \times \pounds 22 \cdot 50$$
$$= \pounds 23\,625 \cdot 00$$

(ii) Cost of manufacture of each bicycle:

Turnover	$=$	$\pounds 23\,625 \cdot 00$
Deduct Gross Profit	$=$	$\pounds\,6\,825 \cdot 00$
Total Cost of Manufacture	$=$	$\pounds 16\,800 \cdot 00$

$$\therefore \text{ Cost of each bicycle} = \frac{\pounds 16\,800 \cdot 00}{1\,050} = \pounds 16 \cdot 00$$

(8) Books of M. Regent (*SPA page 378*)

(a) (i) Rate of Turnover of Stock $= \dfrac{1\,200}{80} = 15 \text{ times}$

(ii) Gross Profit Calculation:

$$\begin{array}{lllll}
 & & & & \pounds \\
\text{Sales} & = & 1\,200 \times \pounds 35\cdot 00 & = & 42\,000\cdot 00 \\
\text{Cost of Sales} & = & 1\,200 \times \pounds 20\cdot 00 & = & 24\,000\cdot 00 \\
\\
\text{Gross Profit} & & & & \underline{\underline{\pounds 18\,000\cdot 00}}
\end{array}$$

(b) Next year

(i) Turnover $= 80 \times 20 \times \dfrac{90}{100} \times \pounds 35\cdot 00$

$$= 1\,600 \times \pounds 31\cdot 50$$
$$= \underline{\underline{\pounds 50\,400\cdot 00}}$$

(ii) Cost of manufacture of each cycle:

$$\begin{array}{lll}
\text{Turnover} & = & \pounds 50\,400\cdot 00 \\
\textit{Less} \text{ Gross Profit} & = & \pounds 19\,200\cdot 00 \\
\text{Cost of Total Manufactures} & = & \pounds 31\,200\cdot 00
\end{array}$$

$$\therefore \text{ Cost per cycle} = \frac{\pounds 31\,200\cdot 00}{1\,600}$$

$$= \underline{\underline{\pounds 19\cdot 50}}$$

Exercises Set 47: Net-Profit Percentage

(1) Books of F. Azouqua (SPA page 380)

We will present them to bring out the Gross-Profit Percentages and Net-Profit Percentages of the two years.

	Year 1	Year 2
Gross-profit percentages	$\dfrac{14\,400}{72\,000} \times 100$	$\dfrac{16\,200}{80\,000} \times 100$

i.e $\dfrac{\text{Gross profit}}{\text{Turnover}} \times 100$

$$= \underline{20\%} \qquad = \underline{20\cdot 25\%}$$

Net-profit percentages

i.e $\dfrac{\text{Net profit}}{\text{Turnover}} \times 100 \qquad \dfrac{8\,000}{72\,000} \times 100 \qquad \dfrac{9\,000}{80\,000} \times 100$

$$= \underline{\underline{11\cdot 1\%}} \qquad = \underline{\underline{11\cdot 25\%}}$$

Conclusion:

The results from year to year are consistent and it appears that the increased volume of goods being handled is being handled without either increasing the rate of profit or reducing it. In other words no economies are being achieved by the handling of the extra goods, and no diseconomies are being suffered.

(2) Books of K. Penn (*SPA page 380*)

		January–June	July–December
Gross-profit percentages			

$$\text{i.e. } \frac{\text{Gross profit}}{\text{Turnover}} \times 100 \qquad \frac{18\,400}{46\,000} \times 100 \qquad \frac{22\,400}{80\,000} \times 100$$

$$= 40\% \qquad\qquad = 28\%$$

Net-profit percentages

$$\text{i.e. } \frac{\text{Net profit}}{\text{Turnover}} \times 100 \qquad \frac{5\,520}{46\,000} \times 100 \qquad \frac{7\,520}{80\,000} \times 100$$

$$= 12\% \qquad\qquad = 9{\cdot}4\%$$

Conclusions:

The serious decline in gross-profit percentage, which means that the extra turnover being handled is only being achieved by serious markdowns in prices to customers, poses the question whether the extra work is worth while. If prices have not in fact been cut then some really serious thefts of cash or stock are occurring. A rigorous investigation appears to be called for.

(3) Books of R. Spurling (a manufacturer) (*SPA page 380*)

Note: It is assumed in these answers that Spurling does not extract a separate Manufacturing Profit.

	Effect on Gross Profit	Effect on Net Profit
(i)	+ £20	+ £20
(ii)	No effect	− £650
(iii)	− £250	− £250
(iv)	No effect	− £210
(v)	No effect	No effect
(vi)	− £60	− £60
(vii)	− £300	− £300

(4) Books of R. James (*SPA page 381*)

(*a*) An *expense ratio* is a percentage figure showing the expense incurred on any heading as a percentage of turnover. It enables the item of expense to be studied from year to year, to detect any trend in its behaviour. It is found by the formula:

$$\frac{\text{Expense item}}{\text{Turnover}} \times 100$$

(b) R. James's expenses ratios are as follows:

$$\text{Discount allowed} = \frac{750}{30\ 000} \times 100 = 2\tfrac{1}{2}\%$$

$$\text{Office Light and Heat} = \frac{1\ 200}{30\ 000} \times 100 = 4\%$$

$$\text{Office Salaries} = \frac{3\ 200}{30\ 000} \times 100 = 10\tfrac{2}{3}\%$$

(5) Books of M. Truman (SPA page 381)

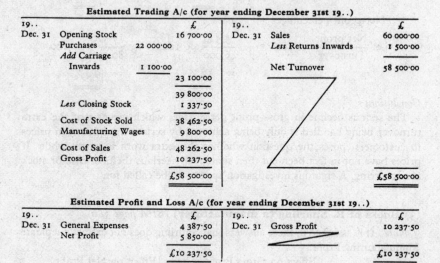

Estimated Trading A/c (for year ending December 31st 19..)

19..		£		19..		£
Dec. 31	Opening Stock	16 700·00		Dec. 31	Sales	60 000·00
	Purchases	22 000·00			Less Returns Inwards	1 500·00
	Add Carriage					
	Inwards	1 100·00			Net Turnover	58 500·00
		23 100·00				
		39 800·00				
	Less Closing Stock	1 337·50				
	Cost of Stock Sold	38 462·50				
	Manufacturing Wages	9 800·00				
	Cost of Sales	48 262·50				
	Gross Profit	10 237·50				
		£58 500·00				£58 500·00

Estimated Profit and Loss A/c (for year ending December 31st 19..)

19..		£		19..		£
Dec. 31	General Expenses	4 387·50		Dec. 31	Gross Profit	10 237·50
	Net Profit	5 850·00				
		£10 237·50				£10 237·50

(6) Books of F. Fraser (SPA page 381)

(a)

Trading A/c (for year ending December 31st 19..)

19..		£		19..		£
Dec. 31	Stock	2 880		Dec. 31	Sales	21 885
	Purchases	16 720			Less Returns	135
		19 600			Net Turnover	21 750
	Less Closing Stock	2 740				
	Cost of Stock Sold	16 860				
	Gross Profit	4 890				
		£21 750				£21 750

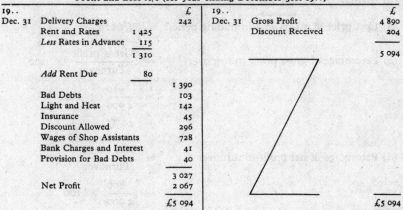

Profit and Loss A/c (for year ending December 31st 19..)

19..		£		19..		£
Dec. 31	Delivery Charges		242	Dec. 31	Gross Profit	4 890
	Rent and Rates	1 425			Discount Received	204
	Less Rates in Advance	115				
		1 310				5 094
	Add Rent Due	80				
			1 390			
	Bad Debts		103			
	Light and Heat		142			
	Insurance		45			
	Discount Allowed		296			
	Wages of Shop Assistants		728			
	Bank Charges and Interest		41			
	Provision for Bad Debts		40			
			3 027			
	Net Profit		2 067			
			£5 094			£5 094

(b) (i) Turnover = £21 750

(ii) Rate of turnover $= \dfrac{\text{Cost of stock sold}}{\text{Average stock at cost price}} = \dfrac{£16\,860}{£2\,810}$

$= 6 \text{ times}$

(iii) It would only affect his profit to the extent that he depreciated it at the end of the year, and of course by the amount of the running expenses

(iv) Net profit percentage $= \dfrac{\text{Net profit}}{\text{Turnover}} \times 100 = \dfrac{2\,067}{21\,750} \times 100$

$= 9.5\%$

(7) Books of M. Tyler *(SPA page 382)*

Trading A/c (for the month ending December 31st 19..)

19..		£		19..		£
Dec. 31	Stock		6 000	Dec. 31	Sales	5 500
	Purchases	3 080			*Less* Returns Inwards	600
	Less Returns Out	80				
			3 000		Net Turnover	4 900
			9 000			
	Less Closing Stock		5 080			
	Cost of Stock Sold		3 920			
	Gross Profit		980			
			£4 900			£4 900

Profit and Loss A/c (for month ending December 31st 19..)

19..		£		19..		£
Dec. 31	General Expenses		180	Dec. 31	Gross Profit	980
	Net Profit		800			
			£980			£980

(a) Turnover = £4 900

(b) Cost price of goods sold in trading period = £3 920

(c) Percentage of gross profit to turnover $= \dfrac{\text{Gross profit}}{\text{Turnover}} \times 100$

$= \dfrac{980}{4\,900} \times 100$

$= 20\%$

(d) Percentage of net profit to turnover $= \dfrac{\text{Net profit}}{\text{Turnover}} \times 100$

$= \dfrac{800}{4\,900} \times 100$

$= 16 \cdot 3\%$

(e) General-expenses ratio to turnover $= \dfrac{\text{General expenses}}{\text{Turnover}} \times 100$

$= \dfrac{180}{4\,900} \times 100$

$= 3 \cdot 67\%$

(8) Books of J. R. Tee (*SPA page 382*)

(a) Preliminary Calculations:

	£
Average stock at cost price =	5 640
Add 25 % to obtain selling price =	1 410
	7 050 Selling price

Turnover = £84 600

∴ Rate of turnover $= \dfrac{£84\,600}{£\,7\,050} = 12$ times

Selling and administration expenses = 11 % of turnover
= £9 306

(i) Gross Profit for year:

Trading A/c—Year 1

	£		£
Purchases	67 680	Sales	84 600
Gross Profit	16 920		
	£84 600		£84 600

A mathematical solution will do equally well:

$$\text{Profit on a single stock turn} \quad = \quad £\ 1\ 410$$
$$\therefore \text{Gross profit} \ = \ 12 \times £1\ 410 \quad = \quad £16\ 920$$

(ii) Rate of turnover: =   12 times

(iii) Net profit for year:

Profit and Loss A/c—Year 1

	£		£
Selling Expenses		Gross Profit	16 920
etc.	9 306		
Net Profit	7 614		
	£16 920		£16 920

			£
(b)	Net profit required next year	=	7 600
	Selling and administration expenses	=	9 448
	Advertising	=	1 000
	Minimum gross profit required		18 048
	Average stock at cost price	=	5 640
	Profit margin 20%	=	1 128
	$\therefore$ Profit per unit of average stock	=	1 128

$$\therefore \text{Stock must turn over} \ \frac{£18\ 048}{£\ 1\ 128} \ \text{times} \ = \ 16 \text{ times}$$

(9) Books of T. Lumley (*SPA page 383*)

(a) Preliminary calculations:

		£
Average stock at cost price	=	8 000
Mark-up at 25%	=	2 000
Selling price of average stock	=	£10 000

Turnover = £100 000

$$\therefore \text{Rate of stockturn} \ = \ \frac{£100\ 000}{10\ 000} \ = \ 10 \text{ times}$$

$$\text{Selling and administration expenses} \ = \ 12\% \text{ of Turnover}$$
$$= \ \frac{12}{100} \times £100\ 000$$
$$= \ £12\ 000$$

(i) Gross profit

Trading A/c

	£		£
Purchases	80 000	Sales	100 000
Gross Profit	20 000		
	£100 000		£100 000

A mathematical calculation will do equally well:

	£
Profit on one volume of average stock =	2 000
× Rate of stockturn =	× 10
Gross profit =	£20 000

(ii) Rate of turnover of stock (see above) = 10 times

(iii) Net profit = £8 000

Profit and Loss A/c

	£		£
Selling etc.		Gross Profit	20 000
Expenses	12 000		
Net Profit	8 000		
	£20 000		£20 000

(b) Second Year:

	£
Net profit required	12 000
Expenses to be covered	10 000
Advertising	2 000
	£24 000

∴ Gross profit needed = £24 000

Gross profit per unit of stockturn = £8 000 $\times \dfrac{20}{100}$ = £1 600

∴ Number of times stock must turnover = $\dfrac{£24\ 000}{£\ 1\ 600}$ = 15 times

Exercises Set 48: The Appraisal of Balance Sheets

(1) Books of A. Brewis (SPA page 390)

(a) Capital owned = £6 550

(b) Capital employed = Total Assets — Debtors
  = £12 250 — £3 000
  = £ 9 250

(c) Fixed capital = Fixed Assets = £5 500

(*d*) Working capital   =   Current assets   — Current liabilities
                  =   £6 750 — £2 700
                  =   £4 050

(2) Books of R. Hemingway (*SPA page 391*)

(*a*) Capital owned   =   £83 550
(*b*) Capital employed   =   Total assets   — Debtors
                    =   £104 250   — £4 800
                    =   £ 99 450
(*c*) Fixed capital   =   Fixed assets   =   £45 500
(*d*) Working capital   =   Current assets   — Current liabilities
                  =   £58 750   — £5 700
                  =   £53 050

(3) Books of Fides Ltd. (*SPA page 391*)

(*a*) Capital employed   =   Total assets   — Debtors
                  =   £49 000   — £9 000
                  =   £40 000

(*b*) Current Assets   £
    Stock   8 500
    Debtors   9 000
    Bank   6 000

    Current assets   £23 500

(*c*) Current liabilities   =   Creditors   £8 000
(*d*) Working capital   =   Current assets   — Current liabilities
                  =   £23 500   — £8 000
                  =   £15 500

(4) Books of Coolbawn Ltd. (*SPA page 391*)

Balance Sheet (as at March 31st 19..)

	£	£		£	£
Fixed Assets			Ordinary Shareholders' Interest in the Co.		
Freehold at Cost		85 000	Ordinary Share Capital		100 000
Plant at Cost	70 600		Reserves		
Less Provision for			Capital:		
Depreciation	25 400		Premium on Shares	25 000	
		45 200	Revenue:		
		130 200	Balance on Appropriation		
			A/c	18 922	
Current Assets					43 922
Stock in Trade	32 147				
Debtors	21 096				
Bank	15 260		Ordinary Shareholders' Interest		143 922
			6% Debentures		30 000
	68 503				
Less Current Liabilities	24 781		Capital Employed		173 922
Net Working Capital		43 722			

Note: The 'Capital Employed' shown here is the total of the Ordinary Shareholders' Interest and the loans from debenture holders. It is a meaning often attributed to the term 'Capital Employed' but strictly speaking it is incorrect (see page 384)

| | £173 922 | | | | £173 922 |

(5) Books of Holder Ltd. (*SPA page 392*)

Balance Sheet (as at March 31st 19..)

	£	£		£	£
Fixed Assets			Ordinary Shareholders' Interest in the Co.		
Freehold at Cost		95 000	Ordinary Share Capital		180 000
Plant at Cost	90 000		Reserves		
Less Provision for			Capital:		
Depreciation	20 700		Premium on Shares	26 000	
		69 300	Revenue:		
		164 300	Balance on Appropriation		
			A/c	28 500	
Current Assets					54 500
Stock	44 155				
Debtors	26 250				
Bank	30 500		Ordinary Shareholders' Interest		234 500
			7% Debentures		20 000
	100 905				
Less Current Liabilities	10 705		Capital Employed		254 500
Net Working Capital		90 200			

Note: The 'Capital Employed' figure shown here is the total of the Ordinary Shareholders' Interest and the loans made by the debenture holders. It is not strictly an accurate term to use since loans cannot be regarded as capital, but it is frequently used by accountants (see page 384)

| | £254 500 | | | | £254 500 |

(6) (*SPA page 392*)

Capital Invested	=	£5 000	Interest at 5 per cent	=	£250
Add Sum Invested in July	=	£400	Interest for half-year	=	£10
			Interest to be claimed from Profits	=	£260

(7) Books of R. T. (*SPA page 393*)

Balance Sheet (as at December 31st 19..)

	£	£		£	£
Fixed Assets			Capital		
Freehold Premises		20 000	At Start		40 000
Fixtures and Fittings		6 500	*Add* Net Profit	8 800	
Motor Vans		2 800	*Less* Drawings	3 500	
					5 300
		29 300			
Current Assets			Net Worth to the Owner		45 300
Stock	6 200				
Debtors	4 200				
Cash in Hand and at Bank	8 100				
	18 500				
Less Current Liabilities					
Creditors	2 400				
Expenses Due	100				
	2 500				
Net Working Capital		16 000			
Net Book Value of Assets		£45 300			£45 300

(8) Books of J. Kay (*SPA page 393*)

Balance Sheet (as at December 31st 19..)

	£	£		£	£
Fixed Assets			Capital		
Freehold Premises		15 000	At Start		26 280
Fixtures and Fittings		1 150	*Add* Net Profit	5 705	
Motor Vehicles		2 340	*Less* Drawings	4 000	
		18 490			1 705
Current Assets			Net Worth to the Owner		27 985
Stock	5 610				
Debtors	3 668				
Cash in Hand and at Bank	2 235				
	11 513				
Less Current Liabilities					
Creditors	1 946				
Expenses Due	72				
	2 018				
Net Working Capital		9 495			
Net Book Value of Assets		£27 985			£27 985

	Effect on Capital	*Effect on Working Capital*
(i)	No effect	− £120
(ii)	No effect	No effect
(iii)	+ £40	+ £40
(iv)	− £76	− £76
(v)	− £300	− £300
(vi)	− £470	No effect

(9) Books of M. Peters (*SPA page 395*)

(*a*) Cash flow statement for current year:

Sources of funds in current year:	£
Net Profit	3 900
Bank Balance from Previous Year	850
Cash Used from Previous Year	100
Bank Overdraft	2 250
Extra Credit taken from Suppliers	300
	£7 400

Application of these funds:	£
Purchase of extra Land and Buildings	3 000
Purchase of extra Fittings	400
Purchase of extra Motor Vans	900
Purchase of extra Stock	1 000
Extra Credit given to Debtors	300
Drawings	1 800
	£7 400

(*b*) To improve the situation Peters could:

(i) Put an embargo on purchases of all capital items running at a high figure in the current year.

(ii) Run down stocks where possible, rather than re-order.

(iii) Tighten up on credit to debtors.

(iv) Reduce drawings in the months ahead.

(v) Watch all expenditure very closely in the months ahead.

(vi) Raise profit margins on items where sales are unlikely to be affected by a price increase.

(10) Books of J. Wooding (*SPA page 396*)

(*a*) As there is no set form for a cash flow statement, it would have to be presented like this.

Extra activities carried on this year:

	£
Purchase of Land and Buildings	8 000
Purchase of Fittings	1 000
Purchase of Motor Vans	2 800
Extra Credit given to Debtors	3 300
Extra Cash in Hand	100
Drawings	5 500
	£20 700

Source of funds to finance these activities:

	£
Net Profit for Year	6 500
Funds released by holding smaller stocks	50
Extra Credit obtained from Suppliers	800
Mortgage arranged	8 000
	15 350
Consequent Increase in Bank Overdraft	5 350
	£20 700

(*b*) To improve the situation Mr Wooding could:
   (i) Reduce his drawings which were considerable in the year just ended.
  (ii) Cut down on capital expenditure (on Fittings and Motor Vans) in the year ahead.
 (iii) Pay particular attention to his debtors. (These increased in number in the year just ended.)
 (iv) Carefully control all outgoings in the months ahead and make any savings he can to reduce his overdraft.

Unit Thirty-Three
Departmental Accounts

Exercises Set 49: Departmental Accounts

(1) Books of R. Rogers (SPA page 399)

Departmental Trading A/c (for year ending December 31st 19..)

	Dept. A £	Dept. A £	Dept. B £	Dept. B £	Total £
Opening Stock		2 800		3 860	6 660
Purchases	15 290		27 420		42 710
Carriage In	144		142		286
	15 434		27 562		42 996
Less Returns Out	460		280		740
Net Purchases		14 974		27 282	42 256
Total Stock Available		17 774		31 142	48 916
Less Closing Stock		1 840		1 540	3 380
Cost of Stock Sold		15 934		29 602	45 536
Wages		2 000		3 040	5 040
Cost of Sales		17 934		32 642	50 576
Gross Profit		12 000		7 998	19 998
		£29 934		40 640	70 574

	Dept. A £	Dept. B £	Total £
Sales	30 234	41 040	71 274
Less Returns In	300	400	700
Net Turnover	29 934	40 640	70 574
	£29 934	40 640	70 574

(2) Books of V. Bartlett (*SPA page 400*)

Departmental Trading A/c and Profit and Loss A/c (for year ending December 31st 19..)

Debit side

	Dept. A £		Dept. B £		Total £
Opening Stock		3 800		3 210	7 010
Purchases	27 000		15 000	42 000	
Less Returns Out	450		230	680	
Net Purchases		26 550		14 770	41 320
Total Stock Available		30 350		17 980	48 330
Less Closing Stock		2 500		2 650	5 150
Cost of Stock Sold		27 850		15 330	43 180
Warehouse Wages		4 850		2 700	7 550
Cost of Sales		32 700		18 030	50 730
Gross Profit		21 350		8 710	30 060
		£54 050		26 740	80 790
Salaries		3 500		2 200	5 700
Rent and Rates		320		180	500
Sundry Expenses		730		530	1 260
Total Expenses		4 550		2 910	7 460
Net Profit		16 800		5 800	22 600
		£21 350		8 710	30 060

Credit side

	Dept. A £	Dept. B £	Total £
Sales	55 000	27 000	82 000
Less Returns In	950	260	1 210
Net Turnover	54 050	26 740	80 790
	£54 050	26 740	80 790
Gross Profit	21 350	8 710	30 060
	£21 350	8 710	30 060

Department A

$$\text{Gross Profit Percentage} = \frac{\text{Gross Profit}}{\text{Turnover}} \times 100 = \frac{21\ 350}{54\ 050} \times 100$$

$$= \frac{42\ 700}{1\ 081}\ \%$$

$$= \underline{\underline{39{\cdot}5\ \%}}$$

$$\text{Net Profit Percentage} = \frac{\text{Net Profit}}{\text{Turnover}} \times 100 = \frac{16\ 800}{54\ 050} \times 100$$

$$= \frac{33\ 600}{1\ 081}\ \%$$

$$= \underline{\underline{31{\cdot}1\ \%}}$$

Department B

$$\text{Gross Profit Percentage} = \frac{8\ 710}{26\ 740} \times 100 = \frac{87\ 100}{2\ 674}\ \% = \underline{\underline{32{\cdot}6\ \%}}$$

$$\text{Net Profit Percentage} = \frac{5\ 800}{26\ 740} \times 100 = \frac{58\ 000}{2\ 674}\ \% = \underline{\underline{21{\cdot}7\ \%}}$$

Firm as a Whole

$$\text{Gross Profit Percentage} = \frac{30\ 060}{80\ 790} \times 100 = \frac{100\ 200}{2\ 693}\ \% = \underline{\underline{37{\cdot}2\ \%}}$$

$$\text{Net Profit Percentage} = \frac{22\ 600}{80\ 790} \times 100 = \frac{226\ 000}{8\ 079}\ \% = \underline{\underline{28{\cdot}0\ \%}}$$

(3) Books of Carlingford Ltd. (SPA page 400)

Departmental Trading A/c (for year ending December 31st 19..)

	Dept. A £	Dept. B £	Dept. C £	Dept. D £	Total £		Dept. A £	Dept. B £	Dept. C £	Dept. D £	Total £
Opening Stock	2 940	3 760	4 100	1 670	12 470	Sales	21 800	33 200	24 800	18 600	98 400
Purchases	16 900	24 700	21 100	15 900	78 600						
	19 840	28 460	25 200	17 570	91 070						
Less Closing Stock	3 490	1 900	2 880	1 760	10 030						
Cost of Stock Sold	16 350	26 560	22 320	15 810	81 040						
Gross Profit	5 450	6 640	2 480	2 790	17 360						
	£21 800	33 200	24 800	18 600	98 400		£21 800	33 200	24 800	18 600	98 400

$$\text{Gross-profit percentage} = \frac{\text{Gross profit}}{\text{Turnover}} \times 100$$

Dept. A
$$\frac{5\ 450}{21\ 800} \times 100 = 25\%$$

Dept. B
$$\frac{6\ 640}{33\ 200} \times 100 = 20\%$$

Dept. C
$$\frac{2\ 480}{24\ 800} \times 100 = 10\%$$

Dept. D
$$\frac{2\ 790}{18\ 600} \times 100 = 15\%$$

(4) Books of Slumbersweet Ltd. (*SPA page 401*)

Departmental Trading A/c (for year ending December 31st 19..)

	Dept. A £	Dept. B £	Dept. C £	Dept. D £	Total £		Dept. A £	Dept. B £	Dept. C £	Dept. D £	Total £
Opening Stock	5 950	7 280	8 640	2 150	24 020	Sales	78 000	65 200	58 000	12 800	214 000
Purchases	41 150	31 000	27 850	11 000	111 000						
	47 100	38 280	36 490	13 150	135 020						
Less Closing Stock	7 120	3 380	7 250	6 540	24 290						
	39 980	34 900	29 240	6 610	110 730						
Gross Profit	38 020	30 300	28 760	6 190	103 270						
	£78 000	65 200	58 000	12 800	214 000		£78 000	65 200	58 000	12 800	214 000

$$\text{Gross Profit Percentage} = \frac{\text{Gross Profit}}{\text{Turnover}} \times 100$$

Dept. A

$$\frac{38\,020}{78\,000} \times 100$$

$$= 48.7\%$$

Dept. B

$$\frac{30\,300}{65\,200} \times 100$$

$$= 46.5\%$$

Dept. C

$$\frac{28\,760}{58\,000} \times 100$$

$$= 49.6\%$$

Dept. D

$$\frac{6\,190}{12\,800} \times 100$$

$$= 48.4\%$$

(5) Books of R. Winter (SPA page 401)

Departmental Trading A/c (for year ending December 31st 19..)

	Dept. A £	Dept. B £	Total £		Dept. A £	Dept. B £	Total £
Opening Stock	7 900	9 560	17 460	Sales	42 620	48 624	91 244
Purchases	30 200	42 382	72 582				
	38 100	51 942	90 042				
Less Closing Stock	8 200	10 656	18 856				
	29 900	41 286	71 186				
Gross Profit	12 720	7 338	20 058				
	£42 620	48 624	91 244		£42 620	48 624	91 244

Profit and Loss A/c ((for year ending December 31st 19..)

	£		£
Rent and Rates	1 776	Gross Profit	20 058
Salaries	7 940		
Bad Debts	560		
General Expenses	2 140		
	12 416		
Net Profit	7 642		
	£20 058		£20 058

Balance Sheet (as at December 31st 19..)

	£	£		£	£
Fixed Assets			Capital		
Furniture, etc.		3 240	At Start		22 438
Motor Vans		2 260	Net Profit	7 642	
		5 500	Less Drawings	3 400	
Current Assets					4 242
Stock A	8 200				26 680
Stock B	10 656				
		18 856	Current Liabilities		
Debtors	8570		Creditors		6 328
Less Provision	538				
		8 032			
Bank		620			
		27 508			
		£33 008			£33 008

Unit Thirty-Four
Control Accounts

Exercises Set 50: Control Accounts

(1) R. Martin's Accounts (*SPA page 408*)

Sales-Ledger Control A/c

19..			£	19..				£
Jan. 1	Balance	B/d	35 850	Jan. 1	Balance	B/d		127
1-31	Sales	SDB 17	38 560	1-31	Cash Received	CB 27		29 726
31	Balance	c/d	36	1-31	Discount			
					Allowed	CB 27		743
				1-31	Returns and			
					Allowances	SRB 5		1 026
				1-31	Bad Debts	J 5		154
				31	Balance	c/d		42 670
			£74 446					£74 446
19..			£	19..				£
Feb. 1	Balance	B/d	42 670	Feb. 1	Balance	B/d		36

(2) Sheering Ltd.'s Accounts (*SPA page 409*)

Sales-Ledger Control A/c

19..			£	19..				£
Jan. 1	Balance	B/d	34 296	Jan. 1	Balance	B/d		26
1-31	Sales	SDB 11	51 264	1-31	Cash Received	CB 27		28 629
31	Balance	c/d	32	1-31	Discount			
					Allowed	CB 27		824
				1-31	Returns and			
				1-31	Allowances	SRB 10		968
				1-31	Bad Debts	J 7		426
				31	Balance	C/d		54 719
			£85 592					£85 592
19..			£	19..				£
Feb. 1	Balance	B/d	54 719	Feb. 1	Balance	B/d		32

(3) L. Renton's Accounts (*SPA page 409*)

Sales-Ledger Control A/c (No. 1)

19..			£	19..				£
Nov. 1	Balance	B/d	2 670	Nov. 30	Cash and			
30	Sales	SDB 19	2 890		Cheques	CB 37		2 405
30	Contra	J 27	120	30	Discount			
					Allowed	CB 27		125
				30	Sales Returns	SRB 15		65
				30	Balance	c/d		3 085
			£5 680					£5 680
19..			£					
Dec. 1	Balance	B/d	3 085					

Purchases-Ledger Control A/c

19..			£	19..			£
Nov. 30	Cash and			Nov. 1	Balance	B/d	4 140
	Cheques	CB 37	3 920	30	Purchases	PDB 15	3 960
30	Discount			30	Contra	J 3	120
	Received	CB 37	95				
30	Purchases						
	Returns	PRB 18	145				
30	Balance	c/d	4 060				
			£8 220				£8 220
				19..			£
				Dec. 1	Balance	B/d	4 060

(4) M. Lucas's Accounts (*SPA page 409*)

Sales-Ledger Control A/c (No. 1)

19..			£	19..			£
Nov. 1	Balance	c/d	3 875	Nov. 30	Cash and		
30	Sales	SDB 1	3 525		Cheques	CB 11	3 650
				30	Discount		
					Allowed	CB 11	91
				30	Sales Returns	SRB 15	127
				30	Contra	J 15	36
				30	Balance	c/d	3 496
			£7 400				£7 400
19..			£				
Dec. 1	Balance		3 496				

Purchases-Ledger Control A/c

19..			£	19..			£
Nov. 30	Cash and			Nov. 1	Balance	c/d	4 182
	Cheques	CB 11	3 973	30	Purchases	PDB 21	4 395
30	Discount						
	Received	CB 11	209				
30	Purchases						
	Returns	PRB 18	382				
30	Contra	J 15	36				
30	Balance	c/d	3 977				
			£8 577				£8 577
				19..			£
				Dec. 1	Balance	B/d	3 977

(5) Books of S. Hardy (*SPA page 410*)

(*a*) Sales Ledger: personal accounts of debtors.
   Purchases Ledger: personal accounts of creditors.
   General Ledger: nominal and real accounts of the business.

(*b*) F. J. Doe's Account: Purchases Ledger
   R. T. Ray's Account: Sales Ledger
   Sales Account: General Ledger
   Stock Account: General Ledger

(c)

R. T. Ray's A/c

19..			£	19..			£
May 1	Balance	B/d	329	May 10	Bank	CB 15	329
10	Sales	SDB 17	189	17	Sales		
					Allowance	SRB 5	17
				31	Balance	c/d	172
			£518				£518
19..			£				
June 1	Balance	B/d	172				

(d)

Sales-Ledger Control A/c

19..			£	19..			£
May 1	Balance	c/d	3 107	May 31	Cash and		
31	Sales	SDB 27	3 406		Cheques	CB 12	2 905
				31	Sales Returns		
					and Allow-	SRB 8	146
					ances		
				31	Discount		
				31	Allowed	CB 21	75
				31	Bad Debts	J 5	36
					Balance	c/d	3 351
			£6 513				£6 513
19..			£				
June 1	Balance	B/d	3 351				

Purchases-Ledger Control A/c

19..			£	19..			£
May 31	Cash and			May 1	Balance	c/d	4 201
	Cheques	CB 12	3 800	31	Purchases	PDB 18	2 803
31	Discount						
	Received	CB 12	210				
31	Balance	c/d	2 994				
			£7 004				£7 004
				19..			£
				June 1	Balance	B/d	2 994

(6) L. Martin's Accounts (*SPA page 411*)

Sales-Ledger Control A/c

19..			£	19..			£
May 1	Balance	B/d	4 206	May 31	Cash and		
31	Sales	SDB 8	3 815		Cheques	CB 5	4 101
				31	Sales Returns		
					and Allow-	SRB 10	386
					ances		
				31	Discount	CB 5	
					Allowed	J 5	105
				31	Bad Debts	c/d	136
				31	Balance		3 293
			£8 021				£8 021
19..			£				
June 1	Balance	B/d	3 293				

Purchases-Ledger Control A/c

19 . May 31	Cash and Cheques	CB 7	£ 4 680	19.. May 1	Balances	B/d	£ 5 107
31	Discount Received	CB 7	120	31	Purchases	PDB 8	6 258
31	Balance	c/d	6 565				
			£11 365				£11 365
				19.. June 1	Balance	B/d	£ 6 565

(7) Bartlow's Books (*SPA page 411*)

Sales-Ledger Control A/c

19.. Jan. 1	Balance	B/d	£ 7 249	19.. Jan. 1	Balance	B/d	£ 62
31	Sales	SDB 28	81 296	31	Cheques Received	CB 5	76 424
31	Dishonoured Cheque	J 5	39	31	Sales Returns and Allow- ances	SRB 17	1 291
31	Balance	c/d	149	31	Discount Allowed	CB 5	3 468
				31	Bad Debts	J 4	421
				31	Balance	c/d	7 067
			£88 733				£88 733
19.. Feb. 1	Balance	B/d	£ 7 067	19.. Feb. 1	Balance	B/d	£ 149

(8) Clover Ltd. Total Accounts (*SPA page 411*)

Purchases-Ledger Total A/c

19.. Jan. 31	Discount Received	CB 19	£ 8 289	19.. Jan. 1	Balances	B/d	£ 40 921
31	Purchases Returns	PRB 7	825	31	Purchases	PDB 25	498 216
31	Cash and Cheques	CB 19	456 227				
31	Balance	c/d	73 796				
			£539 137				£539 137
				19.. Feb. 1	Balance	B/d	£ 73 796

Sales-Ledger Total A/c

19.. Jan. 1	Balance	B/d	£ 50 420	19.. Jan. 31	Discount Allowed	CB 19	£ 10 498
31	Sales	SDB 8	628 421	31	Sales Returns	SRB 8	1 422
				31	Bad Debts	J 5	623
				31	Cash Received	CB 19	582 989
				31	Balance	c/d	83 309
			£678 841				£678 841
19.. Feb. 1	Balance	B/d	£ 83 309				

Conclusion:

The clerk keeping the Purchases Ledger has made an error and it would be best to check that book. Alternatively the Total Account itself could be wrong, so that a check of the total figures extracted from the books of original entry should be made. The Sales-Ledger book-keepers appear to have done their work well.

(9) Accounts of Colvin and Hodge (*SPA page 412*)

Bought-Ledger Control A/c

19..			£	19..				£
Jan. 31	Discount Received	CB 11	210	Jan. 1	Balance	B/d	7 000
31	Returns Out	PRB 7	20	31	Purchases	PDB 19	19 000
31	Cash and Cheques	CB 11	16 000				
31	Balance	c/d	9 770				
			£26 000				£26 000
				19.. Feb. 1	Balance	B/d	£ 9 770

Sales-Ledger Control A/c

19..			£	19..				£
Jan. 1	Balance	B/d	6 000	Jan. 31	Discounts Allowed	CB 15	400
31	Sales	SDB 19	40 000	31	Returns Inwards	SRB 7	300
				31	Cash Received	CB 15	35 000
				31	Bad Debts	J 19	500
				31	Balance	c/d	9 800
			£46 000				£46 000
19.. Feb. 1	Balance	B/d	9 800				

Conclusion:

The error must be in the General Ledger since both the Bought Ledger and the Sales Ledger seem to be correct.

Unit Thirty-Five
Amalgamations

Exercises Set 51: Amalgamations

(1) Amalgamation of A. Young and B. Old (*SPA page 416*)

Balance Sheet of Young and Old (as at January 1st 19..)

	£	£		£	£
Fixed Assets			Capital		
Premises		5 000	Young	1 000	
Fixtures and Fittings		800	Old	7 100	
Motor Vehicles		500			8 100
		6 300			
Current Assets			Current Liabilities		
Stock	2 500		Creditors		2 200
Debtors	1 000				
Cash in Hand	500				
		4 000			
		£10 300			£10 300

(2) Amalgamation of Maker and Seller (*SPA page 416*)

Balance Sheet of Maker and Seller (as at January 1st 19..)

	£	£		£	£
Fixed Assets			Capital		
Premises		10 000	Maker	8 180	
Fixtures and Fittings		2 800	Seller	14 800	
Motor Vehicles		2 000			22 980
		14 800			
Current Assets			Current Liabilities		
Stock		5 350	Creditors		2 300
Debtors	1 850				
Provision	250				
		1 600			
Bank		3 350			
Cash		180			
		10 480			
		£25 280			£25 280

(3) Amalgamation of W. Sandon and M. Sandon (*SPA page 417*)

Balance Sheet of W. and M. Sandon (as at January 1st 19..)

	£	£		£	£
Fixed Assets			Capital		
Goodwill		2 000	W. Sandon	16 195	
Land and Buildings		6 000	M. Sandon	5 785	
Machinery		4 000			21 980
Furniture and Fittings		1 800			
		13 800			
Current Assets			Current Liabilities		
Stocks—Raw Materials	1 400		Creditors	850	
Work in Progress	680		Rents Due	50	
Finished Goods	2 570				900
	4 650				
Debtors	1 500				
Less Provision for Bad Debts	150				
	1 350				
Bank	2 970				
Cash in Hand	110				
		9 080			
		£22 880			£22 880

(4) Amalgamation of A and B (*SPA page 417*)

Balance Sheet of A and B (as at January 1st 19..)

	£	£		£	£
Fixed Assets			Capital		
Goodwill		5 490	A	18 000	
Freehold Premises		18 000	B	14 000	
Furniture and Fittings		1 090			32 000
Motor Vans		3 010	Long-term Liability		
		27 590	7% Loan by A		1 000
Current Assets			Current Liability		
Stock	5 420		Creditors		4 945
Debtors	3 530				
Less Provision for Bad Debts	300				
	3 230				
Insurance Prepaid	35				
Cash at Bank	1 670				
		10 355			
		£37 945			£37 945

Appropriation A/c

	£		£
Interest on Loan	70	Net Profit	6 770
Goodwill	500		
Share of Residue			
A	3 100		
B	3 100		
	6 200		
	£6 770		£6 770

Current A/c (A)

	£		£
Drawings	3 000	Interest on Loan	70
Balance	170	Share of Residue	
			3 100
	£3 170		£3 170
			£
		Balance	170

Current A/c (B)

	£		£
Drawings	3 000	Share of Residue	
Balance	100		3 100
	£3 100		£3 100
			£
		Balance	100

(5) Amalgamation of X and Y (SPA page 418)

Balance Sheet of X and Y (as at January 1st 19..)

	£	£		£	£
Fixed Assets			Capital		
Goodwill		6 000	X	25 000	
Premises		22 000	Y	17 000	
Fixtures and Fittings		1 800			42 000
Motor Vans		4 500	Long-term Liability		
		34 300	Loan from X		2 000
Current Assets			Current Liability		
Stock	7 350		Creditors		3 670
Debtors	2 950				
Less Provision for					
Bad Debts	450				
	2 500				
Bank	3 470				
Insurance Prepaid	50				
		13 370			
		£47 670			£47 670

Appropriation A/c

	£		£
Interest (X)	140	Net Profit	6 320
Goodwill	1 000		
Share of Residue			
X	3 108		
Y	2 072		
	5 180		
	£6 320		£6 320

Current A/c X

	£		£
Drawings	2 500	Interest on Loan	140
Balance	748	Share of Residue	
			3 108
	£3 248		£3 248
		Balance	748

Current A/c Y

	£		£
Drawings	1 500	Share of Residue	
Balance	572		2 072
	£2 072		£2 072
		Balance	572

Purchase of a Business

Exercises Set 52: Purchase of a Business

(1) A. Robertson's Accounts (*SPA page 425*)

Journal Proper

19..						£	£
Jan.	1	Purchase of Business A/c	Dr.	L	1	12 000	
		R. Long (Vendor)		L	2		12 000
		Being agreed purchase price payable on take-over					
	1	Freehold Premises	Dr.	L	3	6 000	
		Furniture and Fittings	Dr.	L	4	2 200	
		Stock	Dr.	L	5	1 500	
		Debtors	Dr.	L 6 etc.		550	
		Goodwill	Dr.	L	20	1 750	
		Purchase of Business A/c		L	1		12 000
		Being assets taken over at this date					
	1	Bank	Dr.	CB	1	15 000	
		Capital (A. Robertson)		L	21		15 000
		Being capital contributed by the proprietor at commencement of business					
	1	R. Long	Dr.	L	2	12 000	
		Bank		CB	1		12 000
		Being payment of agreed purchase price by cheque at this date					

Balance Sheet (A. Robertson) as at January 1st 19..

	£	£		£
Fixed Assets			Capital	
Goodwill		1 750	At Start	15 000
Freehold Property		6 000		
Furniture and Fittings		2 200		
		9 950		
Current Assets				
Stock	1 500			
Debtors	550			
Cash at Bank	3 000			
		5 050		
		£15 000		£15 000

(2) R. Killinchy's Purchase of P. Fitzpatrick's Business (*SPA page 425*)

Journal Proper

19..					£	£
Jan.	1	Purchase of Business A/c	Dr.	L 1	33 350	
		P. Fitzpatrick (Vendor)		L 2		33 350
		Being purchase price agreed to be payable on take-over				
	1	Freehold Property	Dr.	L 3	16 000	
		Plant	Dr.	L 4	8 800	
		Motor Vehicles	Dr.	L 5	3 600	
		Stock	Dr.	L 6	2 950	
		Goodwill	Dr.	L 7	2 000	
		Purchase of Business A/c		L 1		33 350
		Being assets taken over at this date				
	1	Bank A/c	Dr.	CB 1	35 000	
		Capital (R. Killinchy)		L 8		35 000
		Being capital contributed at this date				
	1	P. Fitzpatrick	Dr.	L 2	33 350	
		Bank A/c		CB 1		33 350
		Being payment of agreed price by cheque				

Balance Sheet (as at January 1st 19..)

	£			£
Fixed Assets		Capital		
Goodwill	2 000	At Start		35 000
Freehold Property	16 000			
Plant	8 800			
Motor Vehicles	3 600			
	30 400			
Current Assets				
Stock	2 950			
Cash at Bank	1 650			
	4 600			
	£35 000			£35 000

(3) M. Phillips' Purchase of R. Morgan's Business (*SPA page 426*)

Journal Proper

19..					£	£
Jan.	1	Purchase of Business A/c	Dr.	L 1	36 000	
		R. Morgan (Vendor)		L 2		36 000
		Being agreed purchase price on take-over				
	1	Freehold Property	Dr.	L 3	20 000	
		Plant	Dr.	L 4	7 500	
		Motor Vehicles	Dr.	L 5	3 000	
		Stock	Dr.	L 6	1 800	
		Goodwill	Dr.	L 7	5 200	
		Purchase of Business A/c		L 1		37 500
		Being assets taken over at this date				
	1	Purchase of Business A/c	Dr.	L 1	1 500	
		Sundry Creditors		L 8–15		1 500
		Being liabilities taken over at this date				
	1	Bank A/c	Dr.	CB 1	25 000	
		Capital		L 16		25 000
		Being capital contributed by proprietor on commencement of business				
	1	Bank A/c	Dr.	CB 1	12 000	
		Mortgage on Property		L 17		12 000
		Being loan secured on property				
	2	R. Morgan	Dr.	L 2	36 000	
		Bank		CB 1		36 000
		Being payment of agreed price by cheque				

Balance Sheet of M. Phillips (as at January 1st 19..)

	£			£
Fixed Assets			Capital	
Goodwill	5 200		At Start	25 000
Freehold Property	20 000			
Plant	7 500		Long-term Liability	
Motor Vehicles	3 000		Mortgage (secured on property)	12 000
	35 700			
Current Assets			Current Liabilities	
Stock	1 800		Creditors	1 500
Cash at Bank	1 000			
	2 800			
	£38 500			£38 500

(4) R. Lyons' Purchase of J. Kelleher's Business (*SPA page 426*)

Journal Proper

19..					£	£
Oct.	1	Purchase of Business A/c	Dr.	L 1	10 000·00	
		J. Kelleher (Vendor)		L 2		10 000·00
		Being agreed purchase price to be paid on take-over				
	1	Fixtures and Fittings	Dr.	L 3	1 850·00	
		Stock	Dr.	L 4	6 250·00	
		Motor Vehicles	Dr.	L 5	850·00	
		Electrical Installation Deposit	Dr.	L 6	25·00	
		Rent	Dr.	L 7	50·00	
		Rates	Dr.	L 8	30·00	
		Goodwill	Dr.	L 9	1 777·00	
		Purchase of Business A/c		L 1		10 832·00
		Being assets taken over at this date				
	1	Purchase of Business A/c	Dr.	L 1	832·00	
		Creditors (Sundry)		L 10–15		785·00
		Telephone Expenses A/c		L 16		9·55
		Electricity		L 17		37·45
		Being liabilities taken over				
	1	Bank A/c	Dr.	CB 1	11 900·00	
		Cash A/c	Dr.	CB 1	100·00	
		Capital		L 18		12 000·00
		Being capital subscribed by the new proprietor at this date				
	1	J. Kelleher	Dr.	L 2	10 000·00	
		Bank A/c		CB 1		10 000·00
		Being payment of purchase price				

Balance Sheet of R. Lyons (as at October 1st 19..)

	£	£		£	£
Fixed Assets			Capital		
Goodwill		1 777	At Start		12 000
Fixtures and Fittings		1 850			
Motor Vehicles		850			
		4 477			
Current Assets			Current Liabilities		
Stock	6 250		Creditors	785·00	
Cash in Bank	1 900		Telephone Expenses Due	9·55	
Cash in Hand	100		Electricity Bill Due	37·45	
Electrical Installation					832
Deposit	25				
Rent in Advance	50				
Rates in Advance	30				
		8 355			
		£12 832			£12 832

(5) White, Rock and Sandy's Purchase of Ardmillan's Business
(*SPA page 427*)

Calculations:

		£
Price of Ardmillan's assets		50 000

		£	
Net assets = Assets		52 740	
Less External liabilities		8 140	
			44 600
∴ Goodwill valuation (excess paid over value of net assets)			5 400

		£
Capital contributed by	(i) White	30 000
	(ii) Sandy	20 000
		£50 000

		£
∴ New capital positions:	White	80 000
	Rock	40 000
	Sandy	50 000
		£170 000

New asset values:

		£
Freeholds		58 000
Plant	(37 400 + 29 600)	67 000
Transport	(10 500 + 9 600)	20 100
Stock	(15 426 + 8 430)	23 856
Debtors	(11 319 + 5 110)	16 429
Bank	(3 869 − 160)	3 709

Balance Sheet of White, Rock and Sandy (as at January 1st 19..)

	£	£		£	£
Fixed Assets			Capital		
Goodwill		5 400	White		80 000
Freeholds		58 000	Rock		40 000
Plant		67 000	Sandy		50 000
Transport		20 100			
					170 000
		150 500			
Current Assets			Current Accounts		
Stock	23 856		White	1 722	
Debtors	16 429		Rock	—	
Bank	3 709		Sandy	—	
		43 994			1 722
			Current Liabilities		
			Creditors (14 792 + 7 980)		22 772
		£194 494			£194 494

Unit Thirty-Seven

Covering the Syllabus

Exercises Set 53: Specimen Examination Papers
EAST ANGLIAN EXAMINATIONS BOARD
19.. —Paper I

SECTION A

A 1. Books of M. Lucas (*SPA page* 431)

P. B. Lowe

CL 39

19..			£	19..			£
Feb. 2	Bank	CB 1	702·39	Feb. 1	Balance	B/d	720·40
2	Discount	CB 1	18·01	11	Purchases	PDB 5	425·50
14	Returns	PRB 5	25·50	19	Purchases	PDB 8	185·50
27	Motor			20	Carriage	J 4	12·50
	Vehicles	J 5	650·00	28	Balance	c/d	52·00
			£1 395·90				£1 395·90
19..							
Mar. 1	Balance	B/d	52·00				

(a) Lowe was a creditor on February 1st 19...

(b) On February 14th Lucas returned goods to Lowe valued at £25·50.

(c) On February 27th he sold Lowe a motor vehicle, which must have been surplus to his requirements, for £650·00.

(d) On February 28th Lowe was a debtor.

A 2. Books of Pop Musical Co. (*SPA page* 431)

Date	Details	Sheet Music and Records	Record Players	Hi-Fi	Musical Instruments	F	Details	Total
19..		£	£	£	£		£	£
Apr. 1	*NEM Ltd.*							
	6 guitars @ £8·50				51·00	L 1		51·00
11	*W. H. Foster*							
	12 record players @ £15·25		183·00				183·00	
	Sheet music	25·50					25·50	
						L 2		208·50
19	*Gale and Co.*							
	200 L.P. discs @ £1·00	200·00					200·00	
	4 violins @ £3·75				15·00		15·00	
						L 3		215·00
25	*A. Noakes*							
	2 saxophones @ £29·00				58·00	L 4		58·00
30	*R.K. Radios*							
	10 Hi-Fi panels @ £5·75			57·50		L 5		57·50
		225·50	183·00	57·50	124·00			£590·00
								L 6

A 3. Books of R. Smart (*SPA page* 432)

Light and Heat A/c

19..			£	19..			£
Jan. 1	Stock of Fuel Oil	B/d	42·50	Jan. 1	Electricity Bill Due	B/d	62·50
16	Eastern Electricity Board		62·50	Dec. 31	Stock of Fuel Oil	c/d	51·40
Mar. 31	Morgan Ltd.		96·50	31	Profit and Loss A/c		422·80
Apr. 20	Eastern Electricity Board		55·75				
July 18	Eastern Electricity Board		45·25				
Sept. 30	Morgan Ltd.		100·20				
Oct. 16	Eastern Electricity Board		0·90				
17	Eastern Electricity Board		52·50				
Dec. 31	Electricity Bill Due	c/d	80·60				
			£536·70				£536·70
19..				19..			
Jan. 1	Stock of Fuel Oil	B/d	51·40	Jan. 1	Electricity Bill Due	B/d	80·60

SECTION B

B 4. (*SPA page* 432)
  (1) Debtor.
  (2) Creditor.
  (3) Debit.
  (4) Credit.
  (5) Invoice.
  (6) Credit note.
  (7) Voucher.
  (8) Depreciation.
  (9) Reconciliation.
  (10) Gross profit.

B 5. Books of M. Rooselar (*SPA page* 433)

Trading A/c (for year ending December 31st 19..)

19..		£	£	19..		£
Dec. 31	Opening Stock		1 950	Dec. 31	Sales	34 000
	Purchases	25 000			*Less* Returns In	86
	Less Returns Out	36				33 914
			24 964			
			26 914			
	Less Closing Stock		3 000			
	Cost of Stock Sold		23 914			
	Gross Profit		10 000			
			£33 914			£33 914

Profit and Loss A/c (for year ending December 31st 19..)

19..		£	£	19..		£
Dec. 31	Carriage Out		26	Dec. 31	Gross Profit	10 000
	Sundry Expenses		300		Discount Received	125
	Salaries		2 350			10 125
	Discount Allowed		26			
	Light and Heat		190			
	Commission Paid		760			
	Rent and Rates	242				
	Rent Due	18				
			260			
	Bad Debts		50			
			3 962			
	Net Profit		6 163			
			£10 125			£10 125

Balance Sheet (as at December 31st 19..)

	£	£		£	£
Fixed Assets			Capital		
Land and Buildings		3 500	At Start		6 377
Plant and Machinery		1 500	Net Profit		6 163
Office Furniture		1 850			12 540
		6 850			
Current Assets			Current Liabilities		
Stock	3 000		Creditors	3 676	
Debtors	3 484		Rent Due	18	
Bank	2 875				3 694
Cash	25				
		9 384			
		£16 234			£16 234

19 . . —Paper II

1. Books of R. Peters (*SPA page* 434)

Balance Sheet (as at March 31st 19..)

	£		£
Current Assets		Current Liabilities	
Cash (£25 + 125)	150	Creditors (£1 650 — 500 + 75)	1 225
Bank (£200 + 100)	300		
Debtors (£530 — 125 + 190)	595	Long-term Liabilities	
Stock (£2 000 + 75 — 140)	1 935	Loan	1 000
	2 980	Capital (R. Peters)	
Fixed Assets		(£2 450 — 150 + 50)	2 350
Machinery (£1 545 + 300 — 250)	1 595		
	£4 575		£4 575

2. Books of F. Jones (*SPA page* 434)

Trial Balance (as at March 31st 19..)

	Dr. £	Cr. £
Capital (at April 1st 19..)		8 951
Drawings	1 050	
Stock (at April 1st 19..)	3 725	
Purchases	23 100	
Sales		39 426
Motor Vehicles	1 475	
Cash in Hand	110	
Sundry Creditors		4 925
Sundry Debtors	13 920	
Bank (Overdraft)		975
Wages and Salaries	6 205	
Lighting and Heating	310	
Equipment	3 600	
Carriage Outwards	231	
Returns Inwards	105	
Provision for Bad Debts		350
Returns Outwards		290
Discount Allowed	286	
Discount Received		315
Rent, Rates and Insurance	1 115	
	£55 232	£55 232

3. Books of J. Brown (*SPA page* 435)

(*a*) The basis of stock valuation is 'Cost Price or Current Selling Price, whichever is lower'.

(b) He will value stock as follows:

		£
20 tonnes (damaged stock) at £30		600·00
20 tonnes at cost £42·50 per tonne		850·00
60 tonnes at cost £41·50 per tonne		2 490·00
100 tonnes at cost £39·00 per tonne		3 900·00
		£7 840·00

4. Books of A. Farmer (*SPA page* 435)

Herds and Flocks A/c

Year 1			£	Year 1			£
Jan. 1	Balance	B/d	12 780	Dec. 31	Balance	c/d	15 500
Dec. 31	Profit and Loss A/c L12		2 720				
			£15 500				£15 500

Year 2			£	Year 2			£
Jan. 1	Balance	B/d	15 500	Nov. 30	Bank	CB 27	2 000
				Dec. 31	Profit and Loss A/c L12		7 250
				Dec. 31	31 Balance	c/d	6 250
			£15 500				£15 500

Year 3			£
Jan. 1	Balance	B/d	6 250

5. Books of A. Firm (*SPA page* 436)

Provision for Bad Debts A/c

19..		£	19..		£
July 31	Bad Debts	185	Jan. 1	Provision for Bad Debts	130
Dec. 31	Balance	240	Dec. 31	Profit and Loss A/c	295
		£425			£425
			19..		£
			Jan. 1	Balance	240

EAST ANGLIAN EXAMINATIONS BOARD

19 . . —Paper I

SECTION A

A 1. (*SPA page* 436)

(a) Double-entry book-keeping is a system by which every debit entry is balanced by an equal credit entry.

(b) (i) Debit R. Brown £50, credit Sales Account £50.

(ii) Debit R. Douglas £5, credit Bank Account £5.

(iii) Debit Motor Vehicles £600, Sale of Motor Vehicles A/c £50, credit Bank £650.

(iv) Debit Bank £18, Bad Debts Account £18, credit T. Harper £36.

A 2. Books of D. Cann (*SPA page* 436)

Dr.	19..	Details	Total	Petty Cash Voucher	Postage	Travelling expenses	Refreshments	Sundry expenses	F	Ledger A/cs Cr.
20·00	Mar. 6	Imprest		CB 1						
	6	Stamps	0·15	1	0·15					
	6	Teas	0·32	2			0·32			
	6	Travelling expenses	0·10	3		0·10				
	7	Teas	0·26	4			0·26			
	7	Registered parcel	0·40	5	0·40					
	7	R. Morton	2·78	6					L 21	2·78
	8	Repairs	1·65	7				1·65		
	8	Travelling expenses	0·36	8		0·36				
	8	Window cleaner	0·25	9				0·25		
	8	Teas	0·32	10			0·32			
	9	Teas	0·16	11			0·16			
0·20	9	Telephone call		L 7						
	10	Teas	0·38	12			0·38			
	10	Balance	7·13	c/d						
£20·20			13·07		0·55	0·46	1·44	1·90		2·78
			£20·20		L 5	L 6	L 7	L 8		2·78
13·07	19.. Mar. 13	Balance		B/d						

A 3. Books of M. Luckhurst (*SPA page* 437)

Cash Book (Bank Columns only)

19..			£	19..			£
Feb.	1	Balance	278·50	Feb.	1	Charges	5·50
						Dishonoured Cheque	55·00
						Balance	218·00
			£278·50				£278·50
19..							
Feb.	1	Balance	218·00				

Bank Reconciliation Statement (as at February 1st 19..)

	£
Balance as per Cash Book	218·00
Add Cheque not yet presented	37·50
	£255·50

SECTION B

B 4. Books of A. Long (*SPA page* 437)

19..		—				
Jan. 11	Machinery A/c		Dr	L 27	£350	
	New Machines Ltd.			L 54		£350
	Being purchase of new machine Ref.					
	68754/22E for £400 in part exchange					
	old machine Ref. 13824/5E at its					
	book value £50					

B 5. Books of B. Burley (*SPA page* 438)

Trial Balance (as at December 31st 19..)

	Dr.	Cr.
	£	£
Purchases and Sales	8 525	12 954
Sales Returns and Purchases Returns	54	125
Opening Stock	1 500	
Land and Buildings	6 000	
Furniture and Fittings	1 800	
Carriage on Sales	250	
Office Salaries	2 830	
Office Expenses	659	
Commission Received		1 610
Capital		6 600
Drawings	850	
Mortgage on Premises		4 000
Cash in Hand	56	
Cash at Bank	1 955	
Debtors and Creditors	2 860	2 050
	£27 339	£27 339

Trading A/c (for year ending December 31st 19..)

19..		£	£	19..		£
Dec. 31	Opening Stock		1 500	Dec. 31	Sales	12 954
	Purchases	8 525			Less Returns	54
	Less Returns	125				
			8 400			12 900
			9 900			
	Less Closing Stock		1 800			
			8 100			
	Gross Profit		4 800			
			£12 900			£12 900

Profit and Loss A/c (for year ending December 31st 19..)

19..		£	19..		£
Dec. 31	Carriage on Sales	250	Dec. 31	Gross Profit	4 800
	Office Salaries	2 830		Commission Received	1 610
	Office Expenses	659			6 410
		3 739			
	Net Profit	2 671			
		£6 410			£6 410

Balance Sheet (as at December 31st 19..)

	£	£		£	£	£
Fixed Assets			Capital			
Land and Buildings		6 000	At Start		6 600	
Fixtures and Fittings		1 800	Add Profit	2 671		
		7 800	Less Drawings	850		
					1 821	
						8 421
Current Assets			Long-Term Liability			
Stock	1 800		Mortgage			4 000
Debtors	2 860					
Bank	1 955		Current Liability			
Cash	56		Creditors			2 050
		6 671				
		£14 471				£14 471

19 . . —Paper II

1. Books of Keats and Shelley (*SPA page* 438)

In order to make the answer clear it is necessary to show the Appropriation Account for the partnership, although not actually asked for in the question.

Appropriation A/c (for year ending December 31st 19..)

19..		£		19..		£
Dec. 31	Salary (Shelley)		1 000	Dec. 31	Net Profit	5 800
	Interest on Capital					
	Keats	480				
	Shelley	240				
			720			
	Share of Residue					
	Keats	2 720				
	Shelley	1 360				
			4 080			
			£5 800			£5 800

Capital A/c (Shelley)

				19..		£
				Jan. 1	Balance	4 000

Current A/c (Shelley)

19..		£	19..		£
Jan. 1	Balance	60	Dec. 31	Salary	1 000
Dec. 31	Drawings	1 200	31	Interest on Capital	240
31	Balance	1 340	31	Share of Residue	1 360
		£2 600			£2 600
			19..		£
			Jan. 1	Balance	1 340

Drawings A/c (Shelley)

19..		£	19..		£
Jan.-Dec.	Bank	1 200	Dec. 31	Transfer to Current Account	1 200
		£1 200			£1 200

2. Books of Happy Roadsters' Club (*SPA page* 439)

Income and Expenditure A/c (for season ending September 30th 19..)

19..		£	19..		£
Sept. 30	Fête Expenses	35·00	Sept. 30	Subscriptions	160·00
	Refreshments for Guests	43·00	30	Proceeds from Rallies	38·00
	Secretarial Expenses	15·50	30	Donations	42·00
		93·50			
	Surplus for Year	146·50			
		£240·00			£240·00

3. Books of R. Lewis (*SPA page* 439)

(a) This Balance Sheet is arranged in the order of liquidity.

(b) The fixed capital of this firm is £10 700.

(c) The circulating capital of this firm is £4 000.

(d) The working capital of this firm is £1 400 (current assets — current liabilities).

(e) The drawings were excessive, since they exceeded the profits earned, thus causing Lewis to 'live on his capital' to the tune of £1 900.

4. Books of R. Joy (*SPA page* 440)

Machinery A/c

19..			£	19..			£
Jan. 1	Bank		4 800	Dec. 31	Depreciation		960
				31	Balance	c/d	3 840
			£4 800				£4 800
19..	Year 2		£	19..			£
Jan. 1	Balance	B/d	3 840	Dec. 31	Depreciation		768
				31	Balance	c/d	3 072
			£3 840				£3 840
19..	Year 3		£	19..			£
Jan. 1	Balance	B/d	3 072	Dec. 31	Depreciation		614
				31	Balance	c/d	2 458
			£3 072				£3 072
19..	Year 4		£				
Jan. 1	Balance	B/d	2 458				

5. Books of R. Taylor (*SPA page* 440)

(a) Gross-profit percentage on turnover:

$$= \frac{\text{Gross Profit}}{\text{Turnover}} \times 100$$

$$= \frac{3\ 600}{24\ 000} \times 100$$

$$= 15\%$$

(*b*) Comments:

   (i) It is too low a gross-profit percentage.

   (ii) Since the expenses deductible are £3 000 the net profit will be only £600.

   (iii) The owner and his wife work full time in the business. It seems likely that they would each earn much more than £600 a year in employment, quite apart from their capital which, even in the safest of investments, would earn about £240 per annum.

   (iv) They should therefore raise their prices to increase the gross-profit percentage. If this is impossible because of competition they should sell the business and cease trading unless the non-monetary satisfactions they enjoy are more important to them than the financial rewards.

ASSOCIATED EXAMINING BOARD.

19 . . —Principles of Accounts

SECTION A

1. Books of C. R. Wood (*SPA page* 442)

		£
Net Profit before Adjustment		2 000
	£	
Add Sales of Spare Parts	28	
Rates Pre-paid	40	
Stock Omitted	42	
		110
		2 110
Less Water Rate Due		6
Corrected Profit Figure		£2 104

2. Books of A. Trader (*SPA page* 442)

Sundry Debtors' Control A/c

19..			£	19..			£
May 1	Balances		820	May 1–31	Bank		1 076
1–31	Sales on Credit		876	1–31	Discount Allowed		20
				1–31	Returns		40
				31	Balances	c/d	560
			£1 696				£1 696
19..			£				
June 1	Balances	B/d	560				

Trading A/c (for month ending May 31st 19..)

19..		£		19..			£
May 1	Opening Stock		1 000	May 31	Cash Sales		1 700
	Purchases	1 900			Credit Sales		876
	Cash Purchases	80					2 576
			1 980		*Less* Returns		40
			2 980		Net Turnover		2 536
	Less Closing Stock		1 240				
			1 740				
	Gross Profit		796				
			£2 536				£2 536

Profit and Loss A/c (for month ending May 31st 19..)

19..			£	19..			£
May 31	Expenses		250	May 31	Gross Profit		796
	Discount Allowed		20				
	Net Profit	c/d	526				
			£796				£796
				19..			£
				June 1	Balance	B/d	526

3. Books of A. Fitners (*SPA page* 443)

(i) Estimate of stock in hand

	£
Cash Sales	1 500
Debtors	220
Total Sales	1 720
Profit Margin 30%	516
Cost of Sales	1 204
	£
Purchases:	
Paid For	1 180
Due	270
	1 450
Less Stock Sold (Cost of Sales)	1 204
Value of Stock in Hand	246

(ii) To prepare a Balance Sheet at the end of the month it is helpful to prepare the Trading Account and Profit and Loss Account, although, strictly speaking, these were not asked for in the question. An opening Balance Sheet is also helpful.

Opening Balance Sheet (as at July 1st 19..)

	£		£
Fixed Assets		Capital	
Furniture and Fittings	60	At Start	3 710
Motor Vehicle	650		
	710		
Current Assets			
Bank	3 000		
	£3 710		£3 710

Trading and Profit and Loss A/c (month ending July 31st 19..)

19..		£	19..		£
July 31	Purchases (cash)	1 180	July 31	Cash Sales	1 500
	Purchases (due)	270		Sales on Credit	220
		1 450			1 720
	Less Closing Stock	246			
		1 204			
	Gross Profit	516			
		£1 720			£1 720

		£			£
Wages		75	Gross Profit		516
Sundry Expenses	25				
Amount due	15				
		40			
Rent		50			
		165			
Net Profit		351			
		£516			£516

Balance Sheet (as at July 31st 19..)

	£	£		£	£
Fixed Assets			Capital		
Furniture and Fittings		910	At Start		3 710
Motor Vehicles		650	Net Profit	351	
		1 560	*Less* Drawings	100	
					251
					3 961
Current Assets			Current Liabilities		
Stock	246		Trade Creditors	270	
Debtors	220		Expense Creditors	15	
Bank	2 770		Asset Creditors	650	
Rent in Advance	100				935
		3 336			
		£4 896			£4 896

4. Books of L. Parkinson (*SPA page* 444)

Comparison of use of funds over 2 years

Use of funds:

	£
Extra Expenditure on Fixed Assets	1 120
Extra Expenditure on Stock	200
Extra Credit Given to Debtors	630
Extra Drawings by Proprietor	450
	£2 400

Source of funds to finance above expenditure:

Extra Profits	300
Extra Credit Taken from Creditors	400
Extra Capital Ploughed in from Previous Year	750
Extra Overdraft Rendered Necessary	950
	£2 400

SECTION B

5A. Books of A. Wheeler Ltd. (*SPA page* 444)

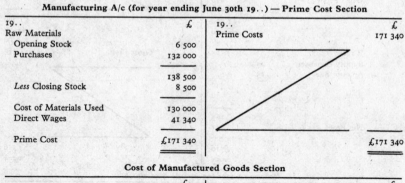

Manufacturing A/c (for year ending June 30th 19. .) — Prime Cost Section

19..		£	19..		£
Raw Materials			Prime Costs		171 340
Opening Stock		6 500			
Purchases		132 000			
		138 500			
Less Closing Stock		8 500			
Cost of Materials Used		130 000			
Direct Wages		41 340			
Prime Cost		£171 340			£171 340

Cost of Manufactured Goods Section

		£		£
Prime Costs		171 340	Factory Cost of Goods Completed	199 055
Overheads				
Other Factory Materials	3 900			
Fuel and Power	4 100			
Heat and Light	1 200			
Fire Insurance 1 215				
Less Amount				
in Advance 200				
	1 015			
Rent and Rates	4 500			
Factory Salaries	7 000			
Depreciation on Machinery	6 000			
		27 715		
		£199 055		£199 055

Trading A/c (for year ending June 30th 19..)

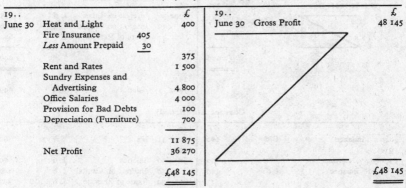

19.. June 30		£	19.. June 30	Sales	£ 247 000
	Opening Stock of Finished Goods	5 700			
	Cost of Manufactured Goods	199 055			
		204 755			
	Less Closing Stock	5 900			
	Cost of Sales	198 855			
	Gross Profit	48 145			
		£247 000			£247 000

Profit and Loss A/c (for year ending June 30th 19..)

19.. June 30			£	19.. June 30	Gross Profit	£ 48 145
	Heat and Light		400			
	Fire Insurance	405				
	Less Amount Prepaid	30				
			375			
	Rent and Rates		1 500			
	Sundry Expenses and Advertising		4 800			
	Office Salaries		4 000			
	Provision for Bad Debts		100			
	Depreciation (Furniture)		700			
			11 875			
	Net Profit		36 270			
			£48 145			£48 145

5 B. (i) Books of Stevens and Platt (*SPA page* 445)

Advice to Stevens and Platt:

(i) Platt is wrong about his contention that the profits should be shared equally as laid down in the Partnership Act of 1890. The Act says that in the absence of agreement between the partners profits should be shared equally. Agreement between the parties can be proved:

(*a*) By proving an oral agreement, i.e. by witnesses.

(*b*) By proving a written agreement, i.e. by producing the written agreement.

(*c*) By proving a course of conduct by the parties. In this case Stevens has been taking a two thirds share with the knowledge of Platt. The courts would take this to imply agreement at an earlier date.

If Platt is so disgruntled about the present arrangements he is of course free to disband the partnership by giving notice. This might induce his partner to concede a more equal division for the future.

(ii) Books of Wide and Broad (*SPA page 445*)

Capital A/c (Wide)   L 1

			£
	19..		
	July 1 Balance	B/d	6 000
	19..		
	June 30 Loan A/c	L 5	1 500

Capital A/c (Broad)   L 2

			£
	19..		
	July 1 Balance	B/d	5 000

Current A/c (Wide)   L 3

19..			£	19..			£
June 30	Drawings		1 800	July 1	Balance	B/d	800
30	Balance	c/d	249	19..			
				June 30	Interest on Loan	L 6	75
				30	Interest on Capital	L 6	480
				30	Share of Residue	L 6	694
			£2 049				£2 049
				19..			£
				July 1	Balance	B/d	249

Current A/c (Broad)   L 4

19..			£	19..			£
July 1	Balance	B/d	100	Aug. 31	Bank	CB 17	100
19..				19..			
June 30	Drawings		1 600	June 30	Salaries	L 6	1 000
30	Balance	c/d	147	30	Interest on Capital	L 6	400
				30	Share of Residue	L 6	347
			£1 847				£1 847
				19..			£
				July 1	Balance	B/d	147

Loan A/c (Wide)   L 5

19..			£	19..			£
June 30	Capital A/c	L 1	1 500	July 1	Balance	B/d	1 500

Appropriation A/c   L 6

19..			£	19..		£
June 30	Interest on Loan (Wide)		75	June 30	Net Profit	2 996
	Salary (Broad)		1 000			
	Interest on Capital					
	W	480				
	B	400				
			880			
	Share of Residue					
	W	694				
	B	347				
			1 041			
			£2 996			£2 996

6A. Books of a Trader (*SPA page 446*)

(i) *Depreciation*

(a) *Wear and Tear.* An asset which is constantly in use, such as a motor vehicle or a machine, will gradually decline in efficiency due to wear and tear. This decline must be recognized by reducing the value of the asset on the books, and charging this loss to the Profit and Loss Account as depreciation. The calculation may be made on one of a number of alternative bases, of which the 'straight-line' method and the 'diminishing balance' method are the best known.

(b) *Lapse of Time.* An asset with a known life, such as a lease on property, wastes away with the passage of time. Its value on the books must be reduced accordingly, and is said to be 'amortized' (from the French mort = dead). This depreciation in value is written off the profits in the Profit and Loss Account.

(c) *Obsolescence.* An asset which is overtaken by the pace of technological advance may be rendered obsolete before its useful life is ended. Thus a computer may still be in good working order but because it operates at slower speeds than more modern machines or is unable to give the same variety of services it is cheaper to invest in a new machine. The resulting depreciation, while heavy, may not be as great a loss as the loss that will follow if the business is left behind by its competitors using more advanced models.

(ii)

Motor Cars A/c   L 1

	£			£
Year 1		Year 1		
Oct. 1 Balance	900	Dec. 31 Depreciation		25
Year 2		Sale of Machine		420
June 30 Central Garage Ltd.	880	Loss on Sale of Vehicle		55
		Year 2		
		Sept. 30 Depreciation		62
		Balance c/d		1 218
	£1 780			£1 780
Year 2	£			
Oct. 1 Balance B/d	1 218			

6 B.

(i) Books of A. Vickers (*SPA page 447*)

19..May	15	Machinery A/c	Dr.	L 17	£2 000	
		Purchases A/c		L 21		£2 000
		Being correction of error whereby machinery purchased was incorrectly debited to Purchases A/c				
	15	Wyatt and Co. A/c	Dr.	L 51	18	
		Sales A/c		L 38		18
		Being correction of error whereby goods sold to Wyatt and Co. for £364 were incorrectly entered as £346				
	15	Discount Received A/c	Dr.	L 27	8	
		R. Mead A/c		L 56		8
		Being discount deducted when paying Mead's account, which Mead now refuses to allow				
	15		Dr.	L 22		3
		Purchases Returns A/c				
		Being a single-sided Journal entry made necessary because an allowance agreed by A. Creditor and entered in his account had not been credited to Purchases Returns A/c				

(ii) (*SPA page 447*)

Value of Stock at June 30th

		£
Value of Stock at June 28th		2 890
Add Stock Received		326
		3 216
Add Goods Returned at Cost Price		
Selling Price = £30		
Less Margin = ⅙ = 5		
		25
		3 241
Less Sales at Cost Price		
Selling Price = £684		
Less Margin = ⅙ = 114		
		570
		£2 671

ASSOCIATED EXAMINING BOARD

19 . . —Principles of Accounts
SECTION A

1. Books of R. Hargreaves (*SPA page 447*)

Statement of Affairs (as at June 1st 19..)

	£		£
Fixed Assets		Capital or Net Worth	
Freehold Premises	3 000	At Start	6 120
Shop Fittings	900		
Equipment	300		
	4 200		
Current Assets		Current Liabilities	
Stock	1 400	Creditors	150
Debtors	320		
Bank	350		
	2 070		
	£6 270		£6 270

Statement of Affairs (as at June 1st 19..)

		£		£
Fixed Assets			Capital or Net Worth	
Freehold Premises		3 000	At Close of Year	6 880
Shop Fittings	1 100			
Less Depreciation	100			
		1 000		
Equipment	450			
Less Depreciation	30			
		420		
		4 420		
Current Assets			Current Liabilities	
Stock		1 600	Creditors	90
Debtors	640			
Less Bad Debts	80			
		560		
Bank		390		
		2 550		
		£6 970		£6 970

Statement of Profit

		£
Increase in Net Worth = £6 880 − 6 120 =		760
Add Drawings:		
In Cash	1 000	
In Kind	140	
		1 140
		1 900
Deduct Legacy		700
True Profit for Year		£1 200

2. Books of E. Taylor (*SPA page 448*)

(i) Working Capital = Current Assets — Current Liabilities

Current Assets	Year 1	Year 2	Year 3	Year 4
Cash in Hand	40	60	80	20
Bank	400	240	720	—
Debtors	740	700	620	720
Stock	800	1 040	1 180	1 100
Total	1 980	2 040	2 600	1 840
Less Current Liabilities				
Creditors	1 280	1 120	800	120
Bank Overdraft	—	—	—	400
				520
Net Working Capital	£ 700	920	1 800	1 320

(ii) Current Ratio = $\dfrac{\text{Current Assets}}{\text{Current Liabilities}}$ =

$\dfrac{1\,980}{1\,280}$	$\dfrac{2\,040}{1\,120}$	$\dfrac{2\,600}{800}$	$\dfrac{1\,840}{520}$
= 1·5	1·8	3·3	3·5

(iii) The information available is not sufficient to enable us to give a perfectly satisfactory answer here. The following points are worth making.

(*a*) The extra premises cost £2 000, which was financed almost entirely by a long-term loan of £1 600 and a bank overdraft of £400. *Prima facie* there does not seem to be much wrong with that.

(*b*) The working capital has been increasing over the years and is, by Year 4, more than adequate, so there does not seem much wrong with that either. However, the liquid capital ratio is much more significant in this case. (What a pity the examiner did not ask us to calculate it.)

Liquid Capital = Current Assets — Stock = £740

Liquid Capital Ratio = Liquid Capital ÷ Current Liabilities = $\dfrac{740}{520}$ = 1·4

This is on the low side. Even so it does not make the purchase of the extra premises wrong.

(*c*) What we cannot really tell from these figures is how the profits are going. One suspects they are not going too well since capital was consumed last year. Stocks are rising so what is he wanting the extra premises for? He does not seem to be doing all that well.

Conclusion: Nothing really wrong with purchasing the extra premises. More information needed about last year's business before a sound judgment can be made.

3. Books of L. Stoke (*SPA page 448*)

(i) When a Trial Balance fails to agree the procedure is as follows:

(*a*) Add the Trial Balance up again to see if the addition was correct.

(*b*) If this does not reveal the error take one side from the other to discover the amount of the difference. Does this amount strike a chord?

(*c*) If not, halve the difference. Is there an item for this amount on the wrong side of the Trial Balance?

(*d*) If not, take out Control Accounts on the Purchases and Sales Ledgers if that is possible.

(*e*) If this does not prove useful check all entries for the month.

(*f*) Finally, if this does not reveal the error, open a Suspense Account for the difference on the books.

(ii)

Trading and Profit and Loss A/c (for year ending December 31st 19..)

19.. Dec. 31		£	£	19.. Dec. 31		£	£
	Opening Stock		1 500		Sales		6 500
	Purchases	3 820			*Less* Returns		190
	Add Carriage In	20					
					Net Turnover		6 310
		3 840					
	Less Returns	100					
			3 740				
			5 240				
	Less Closing Stock		1 200				
			4 040				
	Wages		500				
			4 540				
	Gross Profit		1 770				
			£6 310				£6 310
			£				£
	Carriage Out		10		Gross Profit		1 770
	Rent and Rates		300		Appreciation on Motor		
	Insurance		60		Vehicle		50
	Sundry Expenses		140				
							1 820
			510				
	Net Profit		1 310				
			£1 820				£1 820

Items omitted:

(*a*) Purchase of van — a capital expense.

(*b*) Drawings — an appropriation of profit.

(*c*) Balance £60 — there is no such thing as a balance of this sort, which only arose because of Stoke's ignorance of accounting procedures.

4. (*SPA page 449*)

Why has the net profit not changed?

(*a*) The increased sales could only be achieved by cutting the price of all units, so that the increased revenue was only £4 500, against which had to be set the cost of the extra units = £3 750. This meant only a small profit of £750.

(*b*) The whole of this £750 was used up in extra administrative expenses. The extra sales therefore yielded no extra profit.

SECTION B

5A. Books of Anglo Engineering Co. (*SPA page 449*)

Appropriation A/c (for year ending March 31st 19..)

19..			£	19..			£
Mar. 31	General Reserve		4 000	Apr. 1	Balance	B/d	6 000
31	Ordinary Dividend		9 000	19..			
31	Balance	c/d	7 960	Mar. 31	Net Profit		14 960
			£20 960				£20 960
				19..			£
				Apr. 1	Balance	B/d	7 960

Balance Sheet (as at March 31st 19..)

	At Cost	Less Depreciation	Value	Ordinary Shareholders' Interest in the Co.		Authorized	Issued
Fixed Assets				Ordinary Shares of £1			
Machinery	62 500	19 000	43 500	Fully Paid		100 000	60 000
Motor Vehicles	4 200	1 000	3 200				
Furniture and							
Fittings	7 780	1 600	6 180				
	74 480	21 600	52 880				
Current Assets				Reserves			
Stock		15 800		General Reserves	10 000		
Debtors		10 560		Additions in Year	4 000		
Cash		16 400			14 000		
		42 760		Balance on			
Less Current Liabilities				Appropriation A/c	7 960		
Dividend	9 000						21 960
Creditors	4 680						
		13 680		Ordinary Shareholders' Equity			81 960
Net working capital			29 080				
Net assets			£81 960				£81 960

5B. Books of the South West Town Football Club (*SPA page 450*)

Receipts and Payments A/c (for year ending April 30th 19..)

19..		£	19..		£
Donations		100	Land and Pavilion		1 740
Gate Money Received		1 045	Equipment		120
Collections at Matches		160	Catering Expenses		426
Receipts from Catering		672	Rates		30
Loan		1 200	Wages of Groundsman		400
			Match Expenses		63
			Printing etc.		89
			General Expenses		45
			Balance in Hand	c/d	264
		£3 177			£3 177
19..		£			
May 1 Balance in Hand	B/d	264			

Catering Trading A/c (for year ending April 30th 19..)

19..	£	19..	£
Purchases	426	Sales	672
Add Amount Due	7		
	433		
Less Closing Stock	16		
	417		
Profit on Catering	255		
	£672		£672

Income and Expenditure A/c (for year ending April 30th 19..)

19..		£	19..	£
Rates	30		Gate Money Received	1 045
Less Amounts in Advance	5		Collections at Matches	160
		25	Profits from Catering	255
Wages of Groundsman		400		1 460
Match Expenses		63		
Printing etc.		89		
General Expenses		45		
Interest on Loan		48		
Depreciation		24		
		694		
Surplus for Year		766		
		£1 460		£1 460

Balance Sheet (as at April 30th 19..)

	£	£		£	£
Fixed Assets			Accumulated Fund		
Land and Pavilion		1 740	Donations		100
Equipment	120		Surplus for Year		766
Less Depreciation	24				
		96			866
		1 836	Long-Term Liability		
Current Assets			Loan (secured on land)		1 200
Stock of Refreshments	16				
Rates in Advance	5		Current Liabilities		
Cash in Hand	264		Creditors	7	
		285	Interest Accrued	48	
					55
		£2 121			£2 121

6A. Books of R. Lucas (*SPA page 451*)

A. Marshall A/c

19..			£	19..			£
Apr.	7	Bank	78	Apr.	4	Balance	80
	7	Discount	2		12	Purchases	19
	18	Returns	4		19	Purchases	27
	21	Balance	c/d	45		21	Undercharge	3
			£129				£129
				19..			£
				Apr.	22	Balance	B/d	45

(a) Balance = £45.

(b) It is a credit balance, and means that Lucas owes A. Marshall £45.

(c) Lucas deducted 2½% discount.

(d) Lucas deducted discount because he was paying promptly.

(e) Traders allow cash discount as an inducement to debtors to settle accounts promptly. Until accounts are settled the debtor is making use of the supplier's capital, and preventing the supplier from turning his funds over by a further series of transactions.

(f) A. Marshall would have sent a debit note for the undercharge.

6B. (*SPA page 451*)

Uses of analysis books.

(a) They enable the businessman to follow the conduct of his affairs in particular fields rather than in general. Thus analytical Sales Day Books enable him to follow sales of particular items or particular departments.

(b) They simplify postings to ledger accounts, for example in the Petty Cash Book they collect together many small items under a particular heading which enables them to be posted in a single entry.

(c) They assist control procedures, for example in analytical Cash Books they provide the control account figures for sectional balancing of ledgers. This simplifies the discovery of errors on the Trial Balance.

(d) They clarify particular expenditures to assist in the understanding of accounting activities, for example in the payment of wages they enumerate wages earned under various headings, they tabulate deductions and result in net totals payable to employees.

Examples:

Analytical Day Books.
Analytical Cash Books.
Petty Cash Books.
Wages Books.
Bill Books.
Cost Sheets.
Departmental Accounts.

Unit Thirty-Eight
Value Added Tax Accounting

38.6 Exercises Set 54: Value Added Tax

1. Check the facts of your answer with the text (*SPA page 452*).
2. Compare your answer with *Fig 38.1*.
3. **Books of R. Jones** (*SPA page 459*).

	HM Customs and Excise Department VAT Account		L294
19..		£	
Feb. 28	Purchases (Input Tax)	4 274·94	
28	Other inputs VAT	371·50	
Mar. 31	Purchases (Input Tax)	3 887·67	
31	Other inputs VAT	298·65	
Apr. 30	Purchases (Input Tax)	2 995·55	
30	Other inputs VAT	725·35	
30	Balance c/d	38 384·76	
		£50 938·42	
19..		£	
May 25	Bank CB17	38 384·76	

	HM Customs and Excise Department VAT Account	
19..		£
Feb. 28	Sales (Output Tax)	17 284·24
Mar. 31	Sales (Output Tax)	19 327·62
Apr. 30	Sales (Output Tax)	14 326·56
		£50 938·42
19..		£
May 1	Balance B/d	38 384·76

4. Books of N. Bennett (*SPA page 460*).

HM Customs and Excise Department   L297
VAT Account

19..			£	19..			£
Jan.	1	Balance	B/d	131·75	Jan.	16	Bank	CB37	131·75
	31	Input Tax (goods)	181·75		31	Balance	c/d	267·99
	31	Input Tax (services)	86·24					
			£399·74					£399·74

19..			£
Feb.	1	Balance	267·99

A Note on Answers to Questions

In the first edition of *Success in Principles of Accounting* the answer to Question 1 on page 15 was as follows, and not as shown on page 1 of this *Answer Book*.

Total of the Trial Balance, £1 615·00. M. Thomas's accounts were as follows: Capital A/c £1 000·00; Bank A/c £890·00; Purchases A/c £500·00; Spare Parts A/c £10·00; Cash A/c £95·00; A. Debtor £120·00; Sales A/c £615·00.